"Jeff Lasseigne has always been a clear and ready Bible expositor with years of experience to buttress his love for the Scriptures. *Unlocking the Last Days* will help the reader unlock God's plan for the future and make the book of Revelation not only understandable but exciting. Jeff will help you see that this last book of the Bible is compelling and practical. I highly recommend his book."

—**Skip Heitzig**, author, Bible teacher, pastor, Calvary of Albuquerque

"In a warm conversational style, the author expounds the great truths of the book of the Revelation and applies them practically to the individual believer and the local church. If you have never studied Revelation, or if you need a refresher course in the light of current events, this is an excellent text to use. You need not agree with the author on every detail, but you will agree with his emphasis that we love the Lord, look for his appearing, and live like it may be today."

—**Warren W. Wiersbe**, bestselling author of over a hundred books, including *50 People Every Christian Should Know*

"Jeff Lasseigne is a faithful pastor and excellent communicator of God's Word. *Unlocking the Last Days* is an urgent biblical message that must be heard and heeded!"

—**Dr. James MacDonald**, senior pastor, Harvest Bible Chapel

"Being a student of Bible prophecy for many years and now a teacher of current and coming prophecy, I have found Jeff's book to be outstanding and informative. His book is engaging and humorous when necessary. This is perhaps the best book on Revelation I have ever read. I am certain you will agree, it is a must for your library!"

—**Tom Hughes**, senior pastor, Calvary Chapel San Jacinto

"A lot of people are asking some serious questions these days: 'Why is the world coming apart at the seams? Where is it all headed? Should I be worried about my future or is there hope?' Whether you're asking those questions yourself or wanting to share the answers with those who are, *Unlocking the Last Days* is a resource you can't afford to be without. By going straight to the source of God's Word, Jeff Lasseigne thoroughly and authoritatively explains what's happening and what's to come. But beyond that, he provides the hope that is so desperately needed and exclusively found in Jesus Christ."

—**Bob Coy**, senior pastor, Calvary Chapel Ft. Lauderdale

"Martin Luther once said, 'There are two days in my calendar, this day and that Day.' We would be wise to follow his lead, living in light of the imminent return of Jesus Christ. Jeff Lasseigne's epic book, *Unlocking the Last Days*, will help you do just that. As a result of reading this book, you won't be combing through news stories trying to figure out who the Antichrist is—you'll be motivated to reach out to lost and hurting people before time runs out."

—**Levi Lusko**, pastor, Fresh Life Church

UNLOCKING
^{THE} LAST
DAYS

A Guide to the Book
of Revelation & the End Times

Jeff Lasseigne

BakerBooks
a division of Baker Publishing Group
Grand Rapids, Michigan

© 2011 by Jeff Lasseigne

Published by Baker Books
a division of Baker Publishing Group
P.O. Box 6287, Grand Rapids, MI 49516-6287
www.bakerbooks.com

Printed in the United States of America

Library of Congress Cataloging-in-Publication Data
Lasseigne, Jeff, 1955–
    Unlocking the last days : a guide to the book of Revelation & the end times / Jeff Lasseigne.
        p.   cm.
    Includes bibliographical references (p.   ).
    ISBN 978-0-8010-1353-9 (pbk. : alk. paper)
    1. Bible. N.T. Revelation—Commentaries. I. Title.
BS2825.53.L38 2011
228'.077—dc22   2010044973

11   12   13   14   15   16   17   7   6   5   4   3   2   1

To Pastor Mike Brazeal, whom the Spirit used to bring me to Christ in 1980 and who patiently answered my many questions about the last days during that process.

Contents

Foreword by Greg Laurie   9

Acknowledgments   11

Introduction   13

1. Pulling Back the Curtain   15

2. What Does Jesus Look Like?   22

3. What Christ Thinks of the Church—Part 1   33

4. What Christ Thinks of the Church—Part 2   42

5. What Christ Thinks of the Church—Part 3   52

6. What Christ Thinks of the Church—Part 4   63

7. Casting Crowns   74

8. The Lion and the Lamb   84

9. The Four Horsemen of the Apocalypse   92

10. Heavenly and Earthly Responses   102

11. Who Is Able to Stand?   110

12. The Terrible Trumpets   119

13. Something Wicked This Way Comes   129

Contents

14. A Message from God   139

15. The Temple and the Two Witnesses   146

16. A History of Hatred   160

17. The Blasphemous Beast   172

18. Satan's Worship Leader   182

19. The Certainties of God   190

20. The Beginning of the End   202

21. God's Righteous Judgments   212

22. Judgment of the Harlot   221

23. Babylon Is Fallen!   232

24. A Marriage Made in Heaven   242

25. Return of the King   253

26. The Millennial Kingdom   262

27. The Great White Throne Judgment   272

28. The Best Is Yet to Come   283

29. Home Sweet Home   294

30. Great Expectations   305

31. Responding to Revelation   316

Notes   327

Foreword

There's an old saying that timing is everything, and that certainly applies to Jeff Lasseigne's new book, *Unlocking the Last Days*. The world *revelation* means "unveiling," and in his new book, Jeff does just that. He helps us, in his down-to-earth yet thoroughly biblical way, to understand what is happening in our world today, and what is yet to come. The world is rapidly drawing closer to the Lord's return, and a study of the Bible's final book is essential for the times in which we're living. In fact, Revelation promises a blessing to the person who reads, hears, and keeps the words of that book. In his verse-by-verse guide to the Book of Revelation and the end times, Jeff breaks down each chapter in an easy to understand manner, which will benefit both the new believer as well as the seasoned saint. It's a valuable resource, for both teachers and students of God's Word. I'm very pleased to recommend Jeff's book. Jesus said, "Behold I come quickly," and after you read this book, you'll find yourself saying, "Even so, come quickly, Lord Jesus!"

Greg Laurie, pastor, Harvest Christian Fellowship;
evangelist, Harvest Crusades

Acknowledgments

With sincere apologies to anyone I'll fail to acknowledge, I would like to thank the following people for their roles in helping to bring about this book:

Thanks to Pastor Greg Laurie for his leadership, encouragement, and support.

Thanks to the Wednesday night congregation at Harvest Christian Fellowship for their love of God's Word and for their continuous encouragement and support of me—even to the point of laughing at my jokes.

Thanks to Pat Mazza for introducing me to Baker Books, and to Chad Allen and the staff at Baker Books for their professional and friendly assistance.

Thanks to Brian Jackson for his patient and skilled editing.

Thanks to those who helped with the development of this book in various ways, including Diane Jackson, Karen Zapico, Paul Eaton, and Buddy Williams.

Thanks to all my faithful friends who prayed with me through the process.

Thanks to my fellow pastors at Harvest—I love serving God with you.

A special thanks to my wife, Lorraine, for her endless support and encouragement.

And most of all, to God be the glory (Luke 1:49)!

Introduction

Can we really understand the book of Revelation? According to some, Revelation is too difficult to comprehend. But is that really true? The very name *Revelation* means "unveiling," and therefore God's desire is to reveal the truths, warnings, and promises contained in this final book of the Bible.

God promises a special blessing for the person who reads, hears, and keeps the words of this book (Rev. 1:3). In fact, Revelation is the only book of the Bible that pronounces this specific blessing. It was Vance Havner who said, "I do not understand all the details of the book of Revelation, but there is a special blessing promised to all who read, hear, and keep its message, and I don't want to miss that blessing."[1]

I believe that we're living in the last days before the return of Jesus and that many of the details and descriptions contained in Revelation are now coming to light. Some of the information, which would have been confusing and perplexing just fifty or sixty years ago, is now making much more sense in the light of current events and modern technology. Therefore, the time is ripe for studying and applying the truths of Revelation, especially as we are living in the days when these events may very well come to pass.

On the sixtieth anniversary of Israel's rebirth as a nation, I was standing on the Temple Mount area in Jerusalem with some believers. We were enjoying a discussion about Israel's history, and it was then that the Lord impressed on my heart that I should begin a series of studies in Revelation. This book is the result of thirty-two verse-by-verse Bible studies from Revelation, taught during the midweek service at Harvest Christian Fellowship in Riverside, California. My desire and prayer are that God would use this book to encourage and help prepare believers for His return soon.

1

Pulling Back the Curtain

Revelation 1:1–3

Within sixty days of the writing of these words, world headlines included a high-magnitude earthquake, a devastating cyclone, fighting and air strikes in the Gaza Strip, heightened conflict and preemptive maneuvers between Israel and her neighbors, floods, droughts, wildfires, and increased recognition of homosexual marriages. A steady stream of shocking news that once might have spanned decades now unravels in just months.

So while there have always been wars and rumors of war, earthquakes, disasters, and rampant immorality, we are now seeing these things escalate. The downward slide is picking up speed, and the labor pains and birth pangs of the last days appear to be coming closer together. All this makes our study of the book of Revelation both relevant and timely.

"Revelation" comes from the Greek word *apokalupsis*, which gives us our English word *apocalypse*. People hear that word, and they undoubtedly think of chaos and calamity. But Revelation literally means in its infinitive verb form "to unveil, to uncover, and to reveal."[1] God's desire in Revelation is not to conceal but to reveal. In Revelation, God is pulling back the curtain and allowing us to see into the future. In the climactic scene from the classic movie *The Wizard of Oz*, the curtain is finally pulled back and the Wizard is revealed. That's what Revelation does for us as believers: it pulls back the curtain and reveals the King of kings and Lord of lords.

Let's remove some of the misconceptions commonly associated with the book of Revelation. I disagree with those who contend that Revelation is too difficult and confusing to understand. Revelation is the only book of the Bible that begins and ends with a special promise of blessing for the person who reads, hears, and keeps the words of the book:

> The Revelation of Jesus Christ, which God gave Him to show His servants—things which must shortly take place. And He sent and signified it by His angel to His servant John, who bore witness to the word of God, and to the testimony of Jesus Christ, to all things that he saw. Blessed is he who reads and those who hear the words of this prophecy, and keep those things which are written in it; for the time is near.
>
> Revelation 1:1–3

The promise of special blessing in 1:3 is repeated in Revelation 22:7: "Blessed is he who keeps the words of the prophecy of this book." If this book were too difficult to understand, why would God twice promise a special blessing for every believer who reads, hears, and keeps these words?

This is one of the few books in the Bible that contains its own title: "The Revelation of Jesus Christ." Additionally, in verse 19 of chapter 1, the Lord instructs John to "write the things that you have seen, and the things which are, and the things which will take place after this." So Revelation gives its own natural outline, which is as follows:

- "The things that you have seen" (chap. 1): the glorified Lord Jesus. The apostle John had seen the risen Lord Jesus after His resurrection, about sixty years earlier. Here, John has seen the Lord Jesus Christ once again, in this vision.

- "The things which are" (chaps. 2–3): the messages of Jesus to the seven churches. These churches existed at that time, and as we will see in subsequent chapters, they also represent various stages of church history, including the church of the last days. We should keep in mind that John was writing at the end of the first century to fellow believers who were being persecuted for their faith. The messages in chapters 2–3 were written specifically for the congregations of those seven churches.

- "The things which will take place after this" (chaps. 4–22): the rapture of the church, the emergence of the Antichrist, the seven-year tribulation period, the second coming of Jesus Christ, the thousand-year millennial kingdom, the judgment of the unsaved, and the eternal kingdom of heaven. This book applies to us, as last-days believers, who may very well be the generation alive when these events begin to come to pass.

Much of Revelation has become clearer for us in these last days. In the early stages of assembling a jigsaw puzzle, the picture is a muddled mess. But as more pieces are put into place, the picture becomes clearer. Revelation has become much clearer, as the pieces have fallen into place, and we can now understand how certain things might transpire. Listen to what Cyrus Scofield, writing a hundred years ago in the notes of his Scofield Reference Bible, said about Revelation: "Much of what is now obscure will become clear to those for whom it was written, as the time approaches."[2] Those prophetic words are exactly right. Now, in the twenty-first century, what was once difficult to understand is becoming easier to understand and more relevant.

The reason many people become confused with Revelation is that they focus on the obscure rather than the obvious. If you want to know what this final book of the Bible is all about, you need look no farther than the first five words here in verse 1: "The Revelation of Jesus Christ." Our focus in studying this book should not be the symbolism as much as the Savior. It's not about the signs and wonders; it's about the second coming. And it's not the mystery of "666"; it's the marvel of "Holy, holy, holy." Revelation was not intended to be a symbolic mystery but a spiritual preview for the church.

The theme of Revelation is our Lord Jesus, and a strong emphasis is placed on His second coming. More than 300 Old Testament prophecies and promises refer to His second coming, and 330 verses in the New Testament (one in every twenty-five) directly refer to His second coming. For every reference to His first coming in the Bible, there are eight references to His Second Coming. No subject except faith is spoken of more in Scripture.

One technical, but important, detail we should mention is that this is not the book of Revelations, as we sometimes hear people mispronounce it. It's not several different revelations about Jesus but rather *the* revelation of Jesus Christ in the last days. So it's the book of Revelation.

Revelation has been studied with various means of interpretation, so it is no wonder that people find it confusing. Unlike those who take a historical, spiritual, or allegorical approach to Revelation, I approach it from a literal viewpoint and meaning, which treats Revelation like the other sixty-five books of the Bible—taking the literal meaning unless something is clearly symbolic and intended to give us a figurative meaning. This perspective sees all the events recorded in this book as literally coming to pass at some point. Everything after chapter 3 is yet to take place. Together we will conduct our study of Revelation from this literal viewpoint.

This leads to some discussion about the symbolism in Revelation. Even with our literal interpretation, we recognize that there is a lot of symbolic language in this book. However, much of the symbolic language is interpreted for us right here in Revelation. For example, in verse 1:12, John speaks of seeing seven lampstands, and then in verse 1:16, of seeing seven stars. The symbolism in those verses is explained in verse 1:20, where John is told that the seven stars are angels (literally "messengers") and the seven lampstands are seven churches.

At the same time, we can interpret much of the remaining symbolism in Revelation by the rest of Scripture. For example, in Revelation 19:15, regarding the second coming of Jesus, we read that "a sharp sword goes out of His mouth." Jesus doesn't have a literal sword coming out of His mouth, although some preachers have presented it that way. It is no wonder so many people are turned off by such bizarre interpretations.

Genesis records that in the beginning God simply spoke the words, "Let there be light," and there was light. This speaks of the power of God's words. In Ephesians, Paul writes that the sword of the Spirit is the Word of God (Eph. 6:17). So when we read of that sword coming forth from His mouth at His second coming, it speaks of Christ defeating His enemies with the power of His Word. We must always remember that the best commentary on the Bible is the Bible.

Let's look at verse 1, which contains the title and the theme of this book: "The Revelation of Jesus Christ." It continues, "which God gave Him [Jesus] to show to His servants [us]—things which must shortly take place." So this book is about the near future and events that are going to take place on the earth and in heaven.

Other books of both the Old Testament and the New Testament make references to the future, but no other book comes close to describing the future in such detail as does Revelation. We learn things about Jesus and future events that are recorded only in this book. Just as God explains in Genesis how things began, He describes in Revelation how things will end.

Now, some people have taken issue with the statement in verse 1, "the things which must shortly [or swiftly] take place." Also, in verse 3, we read, "For the time is near." But for the past two thousand years, New Testament believers have had an expectation of these events taking place. The meaning here is that these events are imminent, or can take place at any time. When they do begin to take place, they will do so in rapid succession. The entire sequence of last-days events will take place rapidly, like a series of dominos falling over, and the first domino in line is the rapture of the church. The rapture is the next event on God's prophetic calendar, and it coincides with the beginning of the tribulation period. There is no other event that must come to pass between the present time and the rapture of the church. Let's talk for a moment about the rapture.

While all believers agree that Jesus will return, not all believers agree on the timing of His return. The rapture of the church by Jesus and then the return of Jesus at His second coming are two separate events. In fact, that is one of the problems with the last-days theology of some believers. They combine the rapture and the second coming, and they make no distinction between them. A Bible student needs only to read the biblical descriptions of the rapture and the second coming to see that separate events are being described. We will examine these events more fully when we get to the appropriate passages, but it's important to note our pretribulation rapture position, as well as our literal approach to interpretation, as we make our way through this book.

We should also acknowledge that the apostle John was the human writer of this book. The sequence given to us in these first verses is that this revelation of the last days was given to Jesus the Son by God the Father. Jesus then gave this revelation of Himself and of last-days events to His servants, referring to all His followers. At the end of verse 1, we read that this revelation was brought by an angel to the apostle John, who recorded it as Scripture.

John, you will remember, was one of the twelve original disciples who became apostles, with the exception, of course, of Judas Iscariot, who was never saved and who betrayed our Lord. It is believed that John was the youngest of the twelve. John always had a close relationship with Jesus here on earth. Peter was the recognized leader and the most outspoken, but John appears to have been closest to our Lord.

John was the one who rested his head on the chest of Jesus at the Last Supper and in the upper room. John is the one who stood by the cross when all the other male disciples had fled. At the cross, he was the one whom Jesus entrusted with the care of His mother, Mary. John was one of the first two men to arrive at the tomb on Easter morning and the only one of the twelve disciples to believe in the resurrection without seeing the resurrected Lord. According to *Foxe's Book of Martyrs*, John outlived all the other original disciples. The others were martyred for preaching the gospel, but God preserved John's life to write this book.[3]

This is the same John who wrote the fourth Gospel and the three Epistles that bear his name. In about AD 95, when he was a very old man and a prisoner on the island of Patmos, John recorded his vision and revelation of the Lord Jesus Christ. The words that John received and recorded are the very same that we have the privilege of studying together.

We should remember that the primary reason Jesus hasn't already come back is that He is patient and long-suffering, according to the apostle Peter. Peter tells us three key facts about the last days that increase our understanding of these first three verses in Revelation. They are recorded in 2 Peter 3:1–9.

20

1. Scoffers will ridicule His return (see 2 Peter 3:3). We hear unsaved people dismissing the idea of the Lord's return. If He hasn't come back in two thousand years, they argue, why should we look for Him now? But the very fact that people do scoff at the thought of His return gives us one more piece of biblical evidence for Christ's return soon, since Peter said this was exactly what would happen. Please be sure to thank those scoffers for helping to fulfill Scripture! Peter reminds us that in the days of Noah, the judgment of a global flood did come, just as God said it would. And the world is now being prepared for a second global judgment, by the same sure Word of the Lord.

2. God sees time differently than we do (see 2 Peter 3:8). We read in Revelation 1 that these things "will take place shortly" and that "the time is near," but it has been two thousand years. From our viewpoint, it seems like His return has been a long time coming. However, from God's perspective, it has been like a couple days. God's delays are not His denials, and what He has promised He will accomplish, in His timing.

3. The Lord is not late—He is long-suffering (see 2 Peter 3:9). Not wanting people to die in their sins, He is holding back His judgment, allowing time for more people to be saved. If we believe that—and it's certainly what Peter teaches here—then it should affect us in two main ways:

   First, we should be making every effort to allow God to use us in reaching the lost, through our own personal witness and through evangelistic outreach opportunities. Jesus plainly stated that the fields are great for the harvest, but the laborers are few (Luke 10:2). There are plenty of souls to be won for the kingdom of heaven, but the Lord is calling for more of us to plant, water, and harvest the seed.

   Second, if we look farther in 2 Peter 3, we read in verses 11 and 14 that we should be moved to live holy lives. If we truly believe Jesus is coming soon, how could we be willfully, habitually practicing sin? May God help us, as believers living in the last days, to shine our lights and live as holy vessels. May He "keep [us] strong to the end so that [we] will be blameless on the day of our Lord Jesus Christ" (1 Cor. 1:8 NIV).

2

What Does Jesus Look Like?

Revelation 1:4–20

I don't go to the movie theater often—maybe a couple times a year. The main reason is that I'm so easily distracted by noise. I wish that I had better concentration, so I could block out noise. At the theater, someone is either talking on a cell phone, or it takes him six minutes to pull the wrapper off the licorice he bought from the snack bar. By the way, anything that costs seventeen dollars is not a snack—it's more like a time-share!

Despite this aversion to movie theaters, my wife and I recently went to see a fairly popular movie. We went to an early afternoon showing on a weekday to avoid the crowds. Sure enough, there were only ten people in the entire theater. About five minutes after the movie started, a young couple walked in and sat a few rows behind us. Immediately, they started to have a full-blown conversation during the movie. I'll never understand why people go to movie theaters to have conversations. Going to the movies to talk is like going to a restaurant to cook—it just doesn't make any sense. I tried the look-back stare, but that didn't work. I considered moving to another area of the theater but kept hoping they would stop talking. Finally, I think the noise from the action sequences in the movie became louder than their talking.

Whether in the theater, or watching a DVD at home, movies always begin with the trailers (or previews). Whenever I see a movie trailer, I give it my instant, on-the-spot evaluation. More often than not, after watching the preview, I will either make a buzzer sound or say to my wife, "Remind me not to see that movie." Sometimes, the trailer looks good, so we see the movie, only to discover that we basically saw everything that was worth seeing when we watched the trailer.

Some sixty to sixty-five years before the apostle John wrote Revelation, he and two other disciples were given a preview of coming attractions. Jesus had taken Peter, James, and John up a mountain, and our Lord was transfigured in their presence. In other words, He allowed them to see His divine glory, which had been veiled by His humanity. It has been rightly said that the real miracle was not that Jesus revealed His divine glory but rather that He didn't shine all the time. In Revelation 1, the same apostle John, writing many years later as an elderly man, describes for us a glorious vision of Jesus. What John had experienced on the Mount of Transfiguration was like a preview of coming attractions, and he was not disappointed with the later revelation.

This brings us to a commonly asked question: what did Jesus look like? In the Gospels, we have no physical description of our Lord. Earlier, Isaiah had foretold that the Messiah would have no special features to cause Him to stand out (see Isa. 53:2). In His humanity, the divine nature of Jesus was veiled. But in Revelation 1, we have a description of what Jesus looks like as the glorified Lord in heaven.

> John, to the seven churches which are in Asia: Grace to you and peace from Him who is and who was and who is to come, and from the seven Spirits who are before His throne, and from Jesus Christ, the faithful witness, the firstborn from the dead, and the ruler over the kings of the earth. To Him who loved us and washed us from our sins in His own blood, and has made us kings and priests to His God and Father, to Him be glory and dominion forever and ever. Amen. Behold, He is coming with clouds, and every eye will see Him, even they who pierced Him. And all the tribes of the earth will mourn because of Him. Even so, Amen. "I am the Alpha and the Omega, the Begin-

ning and the End," says the Lord, "who is and who was and who is
to come, the Almighty."

Revelation 1:4–8

In the passage above, John describes the Jesus he knew. In verse 4,
we see that this revelation of Jesus Christ was given to John, who
wrote it down and sent it to seven churches in Asia (modern-day
Turkey). We will look at those seven churches much more in later
chapters. This letter from John has been passed down to all the other
churches throughout history, and now to us.

To those believers, John sends blessings of grace and peace. We're
not surprised by this greeting of "grace and peace," since Paul used
it so frequently in his New Testament Epistles. But what is a bit
surprising is that this final book, which deals primarily with God's
wrath and judgment, actually begins with God's grace. As sinners
we deserve God's judgment, but as saints we receive God's grace.

This greeting of grace and peace to believers comes from the
Trinity: Father, Son, and Holy Spirit. "Him who is and who was
and who is to come" (v. 4) describes the Father. This describes His
eternal nature—that He exists past, present, and future. Only the
eternal God in heaven knows the future, and that is exactly why we
are studying His Holy Word.

"The seven Spirits who are before His throne" (v. 4) describes the
person of the Holy Spirit. As mentioned before, we will interpret
much of the symbolism in Revelation by the information given to
us in the rest of Scripture. The description here of the Holy Spirit
as "the seven Spirits who are before His throne" is interpreted for us
in Old Testament passages such as Isaiah 11 and Zechariah 4, where
the number seven signifies the fullness of the Holy Spirit. Isaiah 11
gives us the sevenfold description of the Spirit, while in Zechariah 4
we find the seven-stemmed menorah, symbolizing the presence of
the Holy Spirit in the temple. At the same time, we remember that
Revelation was written to seven churches, so this may also refer to
the Holy Spirit's presence with each church.

In verse 5, we read of Jesus Christ, and John gives us a wonderful threefold description of Him. First he calls Jesus "the faithful
witness." This simply reminds us that everything Jesus says is truth;
as God, He's incapable of lies or falsehoods. Remember that Jesus

24

stood before Pontius Pilate and told him, "You say rightly that I am a king. For this cause I was born, and for this cause I have come into the world, that I should bear witness to the truth" (John 18:37).

Next, John describes Jesus as "the firstborn from the dead." This has caused some misunderstanding on the part of confused believers and some misinterpretation on the part of cults. The Greek word that John uses here for "firstborn" is *prototokos*, which speaks of priority and preeminence. In the White House, the wife of the president is referred to as the First Lady. But obviously, there have been dozens of presidents' wives before her. First Lady refers to her position and prominence, not to her being the first woman who was ever a president's wife.

Jesus is not the first to rise from the dead; others, such as the widow's son raised by Elijah and the son of the widow of Nain, were raised from death to life before Jesus. So this description means that of all those ever raised from the dead, past and future, Jesus is the first and foremost in position and prominence. He is the greatest of them all. Only Jesus is eternal God. At the same time, the others who were raised from death to life prior to Jesus all eventually died again. Jesus was the first to rise from the dead and remain alive forever.

Then John describes Jesus in verse 5 as "the ruler over the kings of the earth." Or as John describes Him in Revelation 19, "He is King of kings, and Lord of lords." There are kings on the earth who rule over their domains, but Jesus is King over all the earth and over all the kings and kingdoms.

The end of verse 5 says that this same Jesus "loved us and washed us from our sins in His own blood." When we visited Jordan, the guides were quick to tell us how much the people love their leader, King Abdullah II. Abdullah is very down-to-earth with his people and has done many things to help improve life for them, including projects financed by his own wealth. But as well regarded as King Abdullah might be, no earthly king has ever provided forgiveness of sins for his people! Only the King of kings, Jesus Christ, has "loved us and washed us from our sins in His own blood."

In doing so, we find in verse 6, He "has made us kings and priests to God." Later on, in Revelation 5:10, we will again read that Jesus has made us kings and priests to our God, and there John adds, "And we shall reign on the earth." So this refers to our future opportunities in the millennial kingdom of Jesus. All of this causes John to break forth in praise, saying, "To Him be the glory and dominion forever and ever. Amen!" When Paul wrote Philippians from a Roman prison, his theme was rejoicing in all circumstances. Here, John is a prisoner of Rome on Patmos, and we find him praising God in his circumstances.

In verse 7, we are given a glimpse of what this whole book is about: "Behold, He is coming with clouds, and every eye will see Him, even they who pierced Him. And all the tribes of the earth will mourn because of Him. Even so, Amen." The prevailing theme of Revelation is the return of Jesus Christ to defeat His enemies and to establish His kingdom on earth. This is the first instance of John using the word *Behold* in this book, something he does nearly thirty times. This word essentially means "look for yourself."

Up to this point, we have been briefly reminded that Jesus was crucified, He was crowned, and now, John says, "He's coming back!" This message is so important that John begins and ends Revelation with references to the Second Coming. John MacArthur points out that the wording used here means that not only is Jesus's coming imminent but He is already on the way.[1] His coming is so certain, it's as good as done!

Jesus is coming with the clouds, and clouds in Scripture are symbolic of God's divine presence. It was a pillar of cloud that led Israel through the wilderness by day (Exod. 13:21–22), and "the cloud of the LORD was above the tabernacle" (Exod. 40:38). Jesus ascended from the Mount of Olives and was taken up into the clouds (Acts 1:9–11). The two angels standing there proceeded to remind His followers that Jesus would return in the clouds, just as He had gone up.

Now we know that John is describing the second coming of Jesus and not the rapture of the church, because he states that "every eye will see Him" (v. 7). At the rapture, Jesus comes secretly in the clouds above the earth, and His church is raptured, or caught up to Him in the clouds. But here at the second coming, "every eye will see Him." That includes those who pierced Him (v. 7), referring to the Jewish people. It was the Roman soldiers who literally pierced Jesus at the crucifixion, but it was the Jewish leaders who handed Jesus over to the Romans for execution. In Peter's sermon on the day of Pentecost, when three thousand Jewish people repented and responded to the gospel for salvation, Peter said, "Therefore let all the house of Israel know assuredly that God has made this Jesus, whom *you* crucified, both Lord and Christ [or Messiah]" (Acts 2:36). Zechariah prophesied about the Jewish people seeing Jesus at His return. In Zechariah 12:10, we're told, "I will pour on the House of David and on the inhabitants of Jerusalem the Spirit of grace and supplication; then they will look on Me whom they pierced. Yes, they will mourn for Him."

In Revelation 1, John goes on to say that "all the tribes of the earth will mourn because of Him" (v. 7). This refers to the Gentiles and to their mourning when they see Jesus. Their rejection of Him will suddenly hit them like a ton of bricks. I cannot begin to imagine how those Jews and Gentiles will feel at that moment. The instantaneous realization that Jesus Christ is exactly whom the Bible declares Him to be—the Son of God, the Messiah, and God eternal—will bring mourning.

In verse 8, God identifies Himself as "the Alpha and the Omega, the Beginning and the End." He is the eternal God. Alpha is the first letter of the Greek alphabet, while omega is the final letter. From the twenty-six letters in our English alphabet, we can communicate all knowledge. In the same way, God is the beginning and the end, and in Him is all knowledge and truth. In John 1:1, Jesus is the *Logos*, or the Word of God.

At the end of verse 8, we have another reference to Jesus as the One "who is to come." The return of Jesus is emphasized in this book, and the message for us is to be ready. There are at least fifty references in the New Testament for us as believers to be ready. It has been rightly said that John wrote his Gospel that we might *believe*; he wrote his Epistles that we might be *sure*; and he wrote Revelation that we might be *ready*![2]

I, John, both your brother and companion in the tribulation and kingdom and patience of Jesus Christ, was on the island that is called Patmos for the word of God and for the testimony of Jesus Christ. I was in the Spirit on the Lord's Day, and I heard behind me a loud voice, as of a trumpet, saying, "I am the Alpha and the Omega, the First and the Last," and, "What you see, write in a book and send it to the seven churches which are in Asia: to Ephesus, to Smyrna, to Pergamos, to Thyatira, to Sardis, to Philadelphia, and to Laodicea."

Revelation 1:9–11

In these verses, John describes the Jesus he heard. In his Gospel and in his Epistles, John had never identified himself by name. But here in verse 9, John identifies himself by name for the third time in this book, and he will do so again a fourth time at the end. Why would he identify himself now but never before?

As John wrote this final book, the scene was extremely bleak for the church. As the Jewish community continued to persecute Christianity, hostility was eventually embraced by the Roman government. The official persecution of the church by the Romans began with Emperor Nero. A fire broke out in Rome in AD 64, and some historians report that Nero himself ordered the fire started to see what Troy would look like in flames. To make matters worse, reports began to circulate that while Rome was burning, Nero was singing and dancing. Hence the expression, "Nero fiddled while Rome burned." To divert attention, Nero blamed the Christians for setting the fire. This brought increased hostility against the believers, and it was during this time that Paul and Peter were executed.

The persecution and hostility continued and even grew worse for the next several years. In the meantime, the original disciples were all dying as martyrs. In AD 81, Domitian became emperor, and, like Nero, he hated the Christians. Domitian wanted people to call him "Lord and God," which, of course, most Christians refused to do.

Toward the end of his reign, in the mid-90s, Domitian banished the apostle John to Patmos. All the other original apostles were dead. The church was discouraged and dispersed. Jerusalem had been devastated. The Lord had been gone for more than sixty years, and the only living apostle of Jesus was an old man in his nineties—banished to a barren island. To make matters worse, the church was losing its first love for Jesus (Rev. 2:4).

But out of the bleak darkness came the light of God's Holy Word to John on Patmos. The message was this: be courageous and be ready, because Jesus is still ruling from heaven, and He's coming back again! To make sure the church knew the validity of this vision, John identified himself three times in the first nine verses. "Hey, fellow

28

believers, hang in there—it's me, John, your brother and companion in tribulation."

According to Tertullian (an early church leader writing about a hundred years after John), the Romans had plunged John into a cauldron of boiling oil, but he emerged unhurt.[3] His writings also tell us that John was pastoring in Ephesus when he was arrested for teaching and preaching about Jesus. So Domitian had John banished and exiled to Patmos. The island is only ten miles long and six miles wide and sits about twenty-five miles south of Ephesus. I have not been there, but a Christian sister who was there showed me pictures from her visit. It is indeed a rocky, barren, and desolate island, with the exception of a small Catholic chapel. John was banished to a seemingly God-forsaken island in the Mediterranean, but God had not forsaken John, nor His church.

Just to finish the story of John before proceeding, Domitian was succeeded in AD 96 by the Emperor Nerva. Nerva did not recognize Christianity as a legitimate religion, but he was much more humane and just than his predecessors. He also refused to recognize any confession of Christ as being a political crime. So he gave the order for John's release from Patmos, and church tradition states that John returned to Ephesus, where he passed away a few years later.[4]

John's circumstances remind us of this truth: the most difficult times in our lives can also be the most fruitful. John Bunyan wrote the great book *The Pilgrim's Progress* while serving a twelve-year jail sentence for the crime of preaching the gospel without a license. Horatio Spafford lost all four of his daughters at one time in a shipwreck. When Spafford visited the area in the sea where his daughters had perished, he wrote the words to the beloved hymn "It Is Well with My Soul." His words include, "When sorrows like sea billows roll, whatever my lot, thou hast taught me to say, 'It is well, it is well, with my soul.'"[5] Some of David's most inspired psalms came out of his difficult wilderness experience, when King Saul was trying to kill him without cause. And on the barren island of Patmos, an old man at the end of his life received the greatest vision ever recorded in the pages of Scripture. It almost makes one want to go through a trial. I said *almost*!

In verse 10, John says, "I was in the Spirit on the Lord's Day." This refers to Sunday. Ever since the church began in Acts 2, historical and biblical records show that the church met on Sunday, in recognition of Jesus rising from the dead on that day. And how fitting it is that the resurrected Lord in heaven would reveal Himself to John on the day believers gather to worship Him—the Lord's Day.

By the way, since John had no calendar or newspaper to tell him what day it was, and after spending so much time on Patmos, how did he know it was Sunday? I suggest to you that John kept track of the days, and every Sunday he worshiped God on the Lord's Day. John couldn't go to church, so the Lord brought church to John. On that Lord's Day, John heard a loud voice that sounded like a trumpet.

The voice of God in verse 11 identified Him a second time as the First and the Last. We have to wonder whether John recognized this voice. It had been more than sixty years since John had heard Jesus speak, but John had always been quick to recognize the voice of Jesus. Jesus instructs John to write down the vision he is receiving and then to send it to the seven churches in Asia.

This brings us to verses 12–20.

> Then I turned to see the voice that spoke with me. And having turned I saw seven golden lampstands, and in the midst of the seven lampstands One like the Son of Man, clothed with a garment down to the feet and girded about the chest with a golden band. His head and hair were white like wool, as white as snow, and His eyes like a flame of fire; His feet were like fine brass, as if refined in a furnace, and His voice as the sound of many waters; He had in His right hand seven stars, out of His mouth went a sharp two-edged sword, and His countenance was like the sun shining in its strength. And when I saw Him, I fell at His feet as dead. But He laid His right hand on me, saying to me, "Do not be afraid; I am the First and the Last. I am He who lives, and was dead, and behold, I am alive forevermore. Amen. And I have the keys of Hades and of Death. Write the things which you have seen, and the things which are, and the things which will take place after this. The mystery of the seven stars which you saw in My right hand, and the seven golden lampstands: The seven stars are the angels of the seven churches, and the seven lampstands which you saw are the seven churches."
>
> Revelation 1:12–20

In this passage, John describes the Jesus he saw. Because this vision of Jesus is indescribable, John resorts to symbolic and comparative language as he struggles to put into words what he was actually seeing. The first thing John saw was seven lampstands, which represent the seven churches from verse 11. More importantly, John sees Jesus walking among the lampstands. Just as Jesus walked with Shadrach, Meshach, and Abed-Nego in the furnace of fire (see Dan. 3:25), so too Jesus is walking with believers today in the fires of affliction and persecution.

In verse 13, Jesus is clothed with a full garment and a gold band across His chest. This describes the garment worn by the high priest, and certainly, as Hebrews reminds us, Jesus has become our High Priest in heaven (Heb. 4:14). As our High Priest, Jesus prays for us and invites us to approach His throne of grace by prayer at any time. Interestingly, John was the only male disciple who stood at the cross and witnessed the crucifixion firsthand. John saw the four Roman soldiers gambling in the shadow of the cross for the seamless garment of Jesus. Now John sees the same Jesus, the glorified Lord in heaven, wearing the full-length garment of the high priest.

In verse 14, His head and hair were white like wool, which represents His holiness. Isaiah reminds us that our sins, which were crimson, have been made white as snow through God's forgiveness (Isa. 1:18). His eyes were like fire. Since this letter was intended for the believers in the seven churches, and for us as believers today, the fire represents how the Lord evaluates our works and our lives. In 1 Corinthians 3, Paul spoke of the Lord evaluating our lives as believers by the fire of judgment. This is not judgment for our sins, because Jesus already took that judgment upon Himself at Calvary. It is rather judgment of our lives as Christians—burning up the hay, wood, and stubble while purifying and preserving the gold, silver, and precious stones of our faith.

Jesus's feet were like fine brass, and brass speaks of judgment in Scripture—like the brazen altar at the temple. His voice, sounding like many waters, reflects His authority. The first time I went to Yellowstone National Park and stood close to the main waterfall, I was impressed by how loud it was. Later I visited Niagara Falls, and it was like Yellowstone on steroids! The roar of Niagara Falls is unbelievably loud, perhaps like the voice of Jesus here in verse 15.

In His right hand were seven stars, which are identified in verse 20 as the angels or, literally, messengers of the seven churches. We will examine these more in the next chapter. Out of His mouth went a two-edged sword, which represents the power of His Holy Word: able to divide soul and spirit, joints and marrow, and a discerner of the thoughts and intents of the human heart (Heb. 4:12). In addition to all that, the brightness of His countenance was so overwhelming that John collapsed on the ground at His feet, as though he were dead.

Let me share something important about John's response to what he saw. As I mentioned, John had known Jesus personally on the earth. Of all the disciples, none was closer to Jesus than John. This is the same John who rested his head on the chest of Jesus at the Last Supper. But we certainly don't see John high-fiving the Lord or calling Him "Bro." Some believers act as if Jesus is their buddy. But if we learn anything from this passage, we learn of the holiness of God. If this vision of Jesus caused John, who knew Him so well, to collapse to the ground, what should be our response? We need not fear Him in terror, but we must reverence Him in holiness.

Take notice that Jesus lovingly put His hand on John and then said to him, "Do not be afraid." Then Jesus tells John that He has "the keys of Hades and Death." It is a reminder to John, and to us, that Jesus is in control of everything. He conquered death and the grave. He lives forevermore. He gives us eternal life. So we need not fear anything.

It was this same John who wrote in his first Epistle, "There is no fear in love; but perfect love casts out fear" (1 John 4:18). So whatever might be bringing fear into our lives—issues from the past, problems in the present, concerns about the future—we can cast all our cares on Him, for He cares for us (1 Peter 5:7). As with John, Jesus places His hand on you and says, "Do not be afraid."

3

What Christ Thinks
of the Church—Part 1

Revelation 2:1-7

A little old lady was amazed at how nice the young man was who lived next door. He would often help her carry things in from her car or assist in her yard. One day the elderly woman finally asked the young man, "Son, how did you grow up to become such a fine young man?" He replied, "Well, all during my childhood, I had an ongoing drug problem." The elderly lady was shocked. "I can't believe that," she said. The young man smiled. "Yes, ma'am, it's true. My parents drug me to church on Sunday morning, they drug me to church on Sunday night, and they drug me to church on Wednesday night!"

We hear a lot these days about what people think of the church. The church may have many critics, but it has no rivals. Much is said and written about the purpose of the church, how it should look, the way it should conduct itself, and so forth. If you want to know what other people think about the church, there is no shortage of materials or opinions on the subject. But here's the far more important question: what does Jesus think of the church? When we come to church, we worship God, we receive instruction from His Word, and we have fellowship with one another. But how often do we stop to consider what the Lord thinks about the church?

In my years as a pastor, I've heard many compliments from people in the congregation about the church, as well as some criticisms and complaints. Interestingly, the compliments usually have to do with the fruit of the ministry. For example, "Our son made a commitment to Christ at this church," "Our marriage was strengthened by the counseling that we received," "Someone from the hospital ministry came and prayed for me during my surgery," and so forth. On the other hand, the complaints and criticisms usually have to do with the method or manner of the church: "You won't allow our two-year-old to sit in the main sanctuary," "You won't allow our junior-high-aged daughter to attend the high school ministry," "You won't let me attend the singles ministry because I'm going through a divorce," etc.

What things would cause Jesus to commend or criticize the church? The answer is given to us in Revelation chapters 2 and 3—in the seven messages that Jesus spoke to seven churches. Back in verse 19 of chapter 1, we read the natural outline for this book: "The things which you have seen, the things which are, and the things which will take place after this." In chapter 1, John described the things that he had seen—primarily his vision of the Lord Jesus. Here in chapters 2 and 3, John describes the things which are—referring to the spiritual state of the church.

Some professing Christians claim they do not need to go to church. Simply put, you cannot say yes to Jesus and say no to the church. It was Jesus Himself who established the church and who gave us the Acts 2 model for ministry. How you treat the church is how you treat Jesus, because Jesus is the Head of the church (Col. 1:18). And if your faith doesn't take you to church, you need to seriously consider whether it will take you to heaven.

Let's examine the seven churches themselves. First and foremost, these were seven actual churches that existed in John's day. Jesus told John to write everything down and send it to the seven churches in Asia, in the cities of Ephesus, Smyrna, Pergamos, Thyatira, Sardis, Philadelphia, and Laodicea.

Second, these churches represent various phases and periods in church history over the past two thousand years. Numbers carry a lot of significance in Revelation—such as the number seven. Seven is the number of fullness, perfection, and completion. Jesus spoke to seven churches, which together give us a full picture of the New Testament church in history. For example, Ephesus, the first church, represents the first-century church; it had started out on fire for the Lord but was slowly losing its zeal. The seventh and final church, Laodicea, represents the church of the last days—lukewarm and wishy-washy, struggling with compromise and carnality.

Third, and most important, every believer belongs to one of these seven churches, spiritually speaking. There is personal application for each one of us, and we must allow the Holy Spirit to examine our hearts as we examine these letters. Most of us are interested in what Revelation has to say about the future, but first, God wants to speak to us about our current relationship with Him.

There is a format by which our Lord evaluates each of these churches:

1. church—Jesus always starts out by identifying the city where the church resides.
2. commendation—Jesus is able to commend most of the churches, and He encourages them to persevere in what they are doing correctly.
3. complaint—Jesus has some words of complaint and criticism for most of the churches, and He warns them about what they are doing wrong. Before Christ judges the world, as we will read about in Revelation 6–20, He must judge the church and His own people. We read in 1 Peter 4:17, "Judgment [must] begin at the house of God."
4. command—Jesus tells the churches what they must do to get right and how to stay right spiritually.
5. comfort—Jesus offers the genuine believers in each church words of comfort and blessing for the future.

John was on Patmos, one of several islands in the Aegean Sea south of Ephesus, the closest city on the mainland. From there, the message would travel north to Smyrna and Pergamos, east to Thyatira, then south to Sardis, southeast to Philadelphia, and finally to Laodicea. This was the Roman postal circuit of that day, the normal route for messengers. These churches were all within fifty miles of each other.

The primary challenges for these churches were the same ones that all churches have faced down through the years. Nearly every challenge, difficulty, and problem facing the church today is addressed in these letters to the seven churches.

Each of these churches has its own spiritual characteristic, and Ephesus is *the careless church*. Let's read about the Ephesian church:

> To the angel of the church of Ephesus write, "These things says He who holds the seven stars in His right hand, who walks in the midst of the seven golden lampstands: 'I know your works, your labor, your patience, and that you cannot bear those who are evil. And you have tested those who say they are apostles and are not, and have found them liars; and you have persevered and have patience, and have labored for My name's sake and have not become weary. Nevertheless I have this against you, that you have left your first love. Remember therefore from where you have fallen; repent and do the first works, or else I will come to you quickly and remove your lampstand from its place—unless you repent. But this you have, that you hate the deeds of the Nicolaitans, which I also hate. He who has an ear, let him hear what the Spirit says to the churches. To him who overcomes I will give to eat from the tree of life, which is in the midst of the paradise of God.'"
>
> Revelation 2:1–7

At the end of chapter 1, we read about "seven stars" that were the "seven angels of the seven churches." We will see that each of the seven letters is addressed to the angel of that church. The word for "angel" is an ordinary Greek word that is more commonly translated as "messenger." So there are two schools of thought concerning those to whom these letters were addressed.

Some Bible students believe that the letters were addressed to actual angels, who were helping to guard and guide the churches. The argument for this is that the book of Revelation came to the apostle John by means of an angel, as Revelation 1:1 tells us. Therefore, this may be following the same pattern, with Jesus communicating His messages for the churches through John and by means of an angel.

Other Bible students prefer to take the more common meaning of the word as messenger and to interpret this as referring to the pastor over each of those churches. They would argue that angels are not the actual leaders in the church and the pastors are. Either way, it is not an overly critical issue, and there can be allowance for differing opinions.

If these letters *were* written to the pastors, imagine yourself as a pastor getting a letter from Jesus about your church. Even though you have tried to do everything biblically, holding a letter in your hand from Jesus—a letter that evaluates the church you pastor—would be intimidating, to say the least. It is like getting an audit letter from the IRS; even though you are very honest and careful with your taxes, it's still intimidating. I have been audited, so I know how it feels!

The church at Ephesus is the only church in the New Testament to receive letters from two apostles. Paul wrote to this church during his imprisonment in Rome, and that Epistle is known as Ephesians. Here in Revelation 2, John writes to the same church from his Roman imprisonment on Patmos, about thirty to thirty-five years after Paul.

We don't know who was the pastor or leader at the church in Ephesus when John's letter arrived. During his second missionary journey, Paul went to Corinth, where he met the faithful couple Priscilla and Aquila, Jewish believers who had fled from Rome and landed in Corinth. Paul stayed with them, since they shared the same faith as Christians and the same trade as tentmakers.

After ministering in Corinth, Paul went to Ephesus, taking the couple with him. Priscilla and Aquila had established a small church in Ephesus some time earlier. Paul immediately preached the gospel there, and a number of people were saved. Paul was obligated to return to Jerusalem, so he left Priscilla and Aquila in Ephesus to disciple and encourage the believers.

All that is recorded in Acts 18, and Acts 19 describes Paul's return to Ephesus on his third missionary journey. This time, Paul stayed for three years, preaching the gospel and pastoring the church. When Paul left Ephesus after those three years, he placed Timothy over the church. So when Paul wrote 1 and 2 Timothy, he was writing to Timothy as the pastor to help Timothy fight against false doctrines that were springing up in various churches. So Acts 18 and 19, Ephesians, 1 and 2 Timothy, and Revelation 2 are all connected to the church in Ephesus, over a period of about forty years. Church tradition tells us that John replaced Timothy as the pastor in Ephesus in the late first century. It was in Ephesus that John was arrested and then exiled to Patmos by the Roman emperor Domitian.

Another good reason for sending the first of these seven letters to the church in Ephesus is that it was the main church in that region of Asia. The Ephesian church had given birth to the other six churches. Ephesus was situated next to the main harbor and was known as "the gateway to Asia." Ephesus was also the location for the great temple of Diana, one of the seven wonders of the ancient world. So false doctrines and cult worship were part of the culture of Ephesus.

In verse 1, Jesus identifies Himself as "He who holds the seven stars in His right hand, who walks in the midst of the seven golden lampstands." This tells those believers, and us, two important things. For one, this is the same description of Jesus from chapter 1, so there is no mistaking the fact that this is the same glorified Lord in heaven speaking to them now.

Second, it reminds them, and us, that Jesus walks in the midst of His churches. Again, for people claiming to be Christians and telling us that they are not "into going to church," we need to remind them that Jesus *is* "into going to church," and He walks in the midst of His churches. By the time we get to the seventh church, Jesus is standing outside, knocking on the door and asking them to invite Him back in (Rev. 3:20).

To each of the seven churches, Jesus begins by saying, "I know." Our Lord always knows what is going on in His churches. Back in chapter 1 we read that the eyes of Jesus are like "a flame of fire," reminding us that the Lord sees and evaluates everything that goes on in the church. Jesus says, "I know what's going on inside My church."

Jesus begins by commending this congregation for many things. The church at Ephesus was a:

- serving church—"I know your works."
- sacrificing church—"I know your exhaustive labors."
- steadfast church—"I know your patience or endurance."
- separated church—"I know that you have kept evil and false teachers out."

In Acts 20, Paul met with the Ephesian elders, near the harbor leading into Ephesus, to give them some final words before his departure. Paul warned them that after his departure, ravenous wolves in sheep's clothing would try to come in. Those church leaders took Paul's warning seriously, and more than thirty years later, Jesus commended them for keeping those false teachers out.

In verse 6, Jesus also commends this church for recognizing the dangerous practices of a group known as the Nicolaitans. Who were the Nicolaitans, and what were their dangerous doctrines and deeds? We don't have complete information, but one early church father named Irenaeus wrote that this church sect followed Nicolas, one of the seven men who had been selected to serve in the church as deacons in Acts 6.[1] Irenaeus wrote that Nicolas was a pseudobeliever who later became an apostate. But since he had been a recognized helper in the church, he was able to lead others astray. This same group also caused a problem in the church at Pergamos, as we'll see later.

The word *Nicolaitan* means "to conquer the people."[2] So their dangerous deeds would have included trying to strong-arm people, perhaps by misusing and misapplying Scripture. They may have done this through legalism or with liberalism. Either way, they were not shepherds with a heart to help the people but rather wolves, wanting to devour the people.

In verses 2–3, Jesus spoke seven words of commendation, but then in verse 4, a key word of complaint: "Nevertheless, I have this against you, that you have left your first love." Loose paraphrase: "You no longer love Me like you did in the beginning." If you and I had visited this church on some Sunday morning, we would have been very impressed. This was a hard-working and active church. The motion was there, but Jesus sees the heart, and what He saw was a problem with the motives. This church was not operating out of love. As Vance Havner pointed out, "The church has no greater need today than to fall in love with Jesus all over again."[3]

A few years ago, I was busy serving the Lord when I began experiencing pain in my chest. This happened sporadically throughout a Memorial Day weekend, so on the following Tuesday, I went to the hospital. My cardiologist was a brother from the church, and he strongly suggested performing an angiogram to pinpoint the problem. During the procedure, he found the culprit. The main artery was 90 percent blocked with cholesterol. He placed a stent into the artery, and by noon on Thursday, I was on my way home.

The church at Ephesus was sailing along smoothly—serving, sacrificing, steadfast, and separated—but little did they know that they had a serious heart problem. It was not a physical heart problem like I had but a spiritual heart problem, which for believers is far more serious. They were doing the right things but with the wrong motives. Their devotion had turned into duty, and they were guilty of substituting work for worship, and labor for love. As Charlie Shedd put it, "The problem is not that churches are filled with empty pews, but that the pews are filled with empty people."[4]

One important question we must continually ask ourselves is, "Why do I do what I do?" Why do I serve, or sing, or share? If the motive is not love for God, then something is seriously wrong. Paul talks about this in 1 Corinthians 13:1–3 when he says, "Though I speak with the tongues of men and of angels . . . and though I have the gift of prophecy and understand all mysteries and all knowledge, and though I have all faith, so that I could remove mountains . . . and though I bestow all my goods to feed the poor, and [even] give my body over to be burned . . . [if] I have not love, it profits me nothing."

Notice in verse 4 that they had not *lost* their first love but rather, Jesus says, "You have *left* your first love." This was no accident; it was a case of neglect. Neglect probably creates more problems in our lives than any other single failure. If I had neglected my chest pains, the problem could have eventually killed me. Jesus was able to look right into the heart and detect the problem at Ephesus. The furnace was still there, but the fire had gone out. So let me ask you this: are you nurturing or neglecting your relationship with God?

Having identified the problem, Jesus then prescribes the solution in verse 5: remember from where you have fallen, repent, and return to doing the first works with the right motive and a heart of love. All of our labor must be a labor of love. Jacob could labor seven years for the hand of Rachel in marriage, because he loved her so much. Those seven years seemed as but a few days to him, because of his love for her (see Gen. 29:20).

The first step is to *remember*. Remember how excited you were when you first were saved? If you were like me, you shared your faith; you read your Bible inside and out, underlining everything;

you went to church several times a week; and you just couldn't get enough of the Lord.

The second step is to *repent*, or to change directions. If we've been backsliding, or growing cold spiritually, we must confess it to the Lord and then seek His forgiveness. Some backsliders are out in the world and away from the church, so they are obvious to us. But there are also backsliders within the church, just like those in Ephesus. Their outward works are there, but their inward passion is dying.

The third step, then, is to *return* to the first works. Get back to the way things were with the Lord, before it's too late. After the cardiologist placed that stent in my main artery, the blood flowed as it had before, and the pain was gone. So get back in the flow of doing the right things, in the right way, and for the right reason. After Peter denied the Lord, and Jesus restored him, He asked Peter just one question, but He asked it three times: "Do you love Me?" (John 21:15–17).

In verse 5, we see the last part of the command from Jesus. "Remember, repent, and return, or else I will *remove* your lampstand." Jesus gave them two choices: revival or removal. The church that leaves its love will soon lose its light. The church at Ephesus continued for some time, but eventually the entire city went into ruin and remains that way to this day.

We read in verse 7, "He who has an ear to hear, let him hear what the Spirit is saying." That applies to you and to me. Just because a person has ears doesn't mean that he is listening. Case in point: when your children are outside playing and you call them in for dinner. Good luck with that! Jesus finishes His letter to Ephesus with a word of comfort: "To him who overcomes, I will give to eat from the tree of life, which is in the midst of the paradise of God." This refers to heaven, and the tree of life symbolizes eternal life. Let us, therefore, examine ourselves and do the works of our first love, that we may overcome.

4

What Christ Thinks
of the Church—Part 2

Revelation 2:8-17

Two cowboys come upon an Indian lying on his stomach with his ear to the ground. One of the cowboys stops and says to the other, "Look, he's listening to the ground. He can hear things for miles in any direction." Just then the Indian looks up and says, "Covered wagon about two miles away. Have two horses. One brown, one white. Man, woman, two children in wagon." "That's incredible!" says the first cowboy to his friend. "Really amazing!" The Indian looks up and says, "Run over me about half hour ago."

In each of His letters to the seven churches, Jesus says, "He who has ears to hear, let him hear what the Spirit is saying." Every church, and every believer, needs to hear the messages of Jesus to His church, and, more importantly, we need to respond. We oftentimes talk about the final words of Jesus to His followers in the Gospels, but actually, our Lord's final words to the church are recorded here in Revelation.

And to the angel of the church in Smyrna write, "These things says the First and the Last, who was dead, and came to life: 'I know your works, tribulation, and poverty (but you are rich); and I know the blasphemy of those who say they are Jews and are not, but are a synagogue of Satan. Do not fear any of those things which you are about to suffer. Indeed, the devil is about to throw some of you into prison, that you may be tested, and you will have tribulation ten days. Be faithful until death, and I will give you the crown of life. He who has an ear, let him hear what the Spirit says to the churches. He who overcomes shall not be hurt by the second death.'"

Revelation 2:8–11

We'll call Smyrna *the courageous church* because of its power and purity, which came from remaining faithful to the Lord in the face of great pain and persecution. The town of Smyrna still exists but is now known as Izmir in Turkey. Smyrna was about thirty-five miles north of Ephesus and was known as "the crown of Asia" for its natural beauty.[1] The New Testament does not record for us how or when this church was established, but it was undoubtedly birthed out of the larger church ministry in Ephesus.

The name *Smyrna* means "bitter" and is related to the word *myrrh*. After the birth of Jesus, the Magi from the East came bearing gifts of gold, frankincense, and myrrh (Matt. 2:11). The gold spoke of the fact that Jesus was born the King of the Jews and, more importantly, that He is the King of kings. Frankincense was an expensive incense that pointed to Jesus as our High Priest and spoke of His deity. The third gift was myrrh, a spice used in the preparation of a body for burial. So the gold represented His royalty, the frankincense His deity, and the myrrh His humanity.

But here's something else worth noting: in Isaiah 60, we read a description of Jesus reigning in the thousand-year millennial kingdom on earth, after the tribulation period. Isaiah speaks of people coming from everywhere, bringing gold and incense and proclaiming the praises of the Lord (Isa. 60:6). They'll bring gold, and they'll bring incense, but they won't bring myrrh, because Jesus will never suffer and die again.

The other interesting thing about myrrh is that the fragrance is produced by crushing the spice. That symbolizes the suffering and

death of Jesus, as well as the suffering and death in the church at
Smyrna. The church has always been the most fragrant when it is
going through times of suffering. It's no wonder that Jesus identifies
Himself to this suffering church as "the First and the Last, who was
dead, and came to life." Being the First and the Last speaks of His
eternal nature. Being the One who was dead and has come back to
life emphasizes the promised resurrection of all true believers.

Jesus then begins to commend this church, and in verse 9, He says,
"I know your works, tribulation, and poverty (but you are rich); and I
know the blasphemy of those who say they are Jews and are not, but
are a synagogue of Satan." Jesus says, "I know your works," as He
does to all seven churches, and it's a reminder that our Lord knows
exactly what is going on in the church, and why. The believers in
Smyrna were *a crushed church*; this faithful church was facing poverty and persecution, and some of them were about to face prison.

The poverty described here refers to being destitute. They had lost
their property and possessions as a result of persecution. They were
very poor in the material sense but very rich in the spiritual sense. It
is good for us to remember that Jesus Himself became poor so that
we might become rich spiritually (2 Cor. 8:9). Jesus owned nothing.
He was born in a borrowed cave, preached from a borrowed boat,
rode into Jerusalem on a borrowed donkey, ate His final supper in
a borrowed room, was crucified on a borrowed cross, and buried in
a borrowed tomb.

But even more than that, Jesus laid aside the robes of His deity
and left His throne in heaven, coming to earth and putting on the
clothes of humanity, so that He could die for our sins. Jesus says to
us, "Do not lay up for yourselves treasures on earth, where moth
and rust destroy and where thieves break in and steal; but lay up for
yourselves treasures in heaven . . . for where your treasure is, there
your heart will be also" (Matt. 6:19–21).

Jesus also commends the believers in Smyrna by stating that He
knows about the persecution against them. They were facing intense
persecution because of their faith in Jesus. Smyrna was the center of
imperial cult worship—the worship of the Roman emperor. So the
Roman authorities were constantly persecuting the believers. At the
same time, there was another group in Smyrna persecuting them as
well, and Jesus calls them "a synagogue of Satan."

This is oftentimes interpreted, because of the word *synagogue*, to mean that there was a group of unsaved Jews who rejected Jesus and were persecuting the believers in Smyrna. But there is no reason not to interpret verse 9 literally when it says, "I know the blasphemy of those who say they are Jews and are not, but are a synagogue of Satan." These troublemakers were claiming to be Jews and were doing the work of Satan by persecuting the believers in Smyrna. It has been said that "persecution is one of the surest signs of the genuineness of our faith."[2]

No doubt some who are reading this book have been facing persecution as a result of their faith. Of course, we recognize that our persecution in America today pales in comparison with the persecution we read about in Smyrna. But you may be among those who are harassed by co-workers or passed over for promotion because you are a Christian. You may have unsaved family members who mistreat you or neighbors who shun you. As He does to the believers in Smyrna, Jesus essentially says to you, "I know your works, and I know the persecution you face, and I am with you." But apart from places such as America, there have been more Christian martyrs in recent years than there were during the first century. According to a study done by Regent University, nearly 164,000 Christians worldwide were martyred for their faith in 1999. In 2000, that number rose to nearly 165,000.[3] With each passing year, the number of Christians who face death for their beliefs increases. It has been estimated that since AD 70, over seventy million Christians have been put to death for refusing to renounce their faith.

As we come to verse 10, we see that Smyrna was also *a committed church*. In spite of their material poverty, they were spiritually rich in their faith. They were genuine believers, unlike those who opposed them. This brings out a couple of unique facts about this letter.

First, Smyrna is one of only two churches that received no complaint or criticism (Philadelphia being the other). Jesus had only commendation and comfort for these committed Christians. Second, because Jesus had no words of complaint, this is the shortest of the letters to the seven churches. The lack of rebuke allowed Jesus to keep His words brief and focused on their faithfulness.

In addition to their poverty and persecution, some of them were going to be thrown into prison. Those who proclaimed Christ as Lord were often persecuted by Roman authorities. This persecution included imprisonment and sometimes death, especially for spiritual leaders who were executed as a deterrent and an example. Jesus says, "Do not fear," and then, "Be faithful unto death." I can't help but wonder what this poverty, persecution, and threat of prison and death would do to the church in America. I guarantee you that the church would shrink, leaving only committed believers. At the same time, the church would become much more pure and powerful, as it was in Smyrna.

Jesus speaks of having "tribulation for ten days," and this statement probably had a double meaning. In the immediate sense, some of these believers would have a brief period of intense persecution, as "ten days" refers to a brief time period. They would be thrown into prison to test and strengthen their faith. But from the perspective of church history, from the time that John sent this letter until the early part of the fourth century, there were ten Roman emperors who persecuted the Christian church. Please make a mental note of that, because that information plays into the circumstances of our next church, at Pergamos.

We also see that Smyrna was *a comforted church*. Jesus promises these faithful believers two special blessings. The first is "a crown of life," mentioned at the end of verse 10. This refers to eternal life in heaven with God.

The second special blessing is promised by Jesus at the end of verse 11: the faithful believer "will not be hurt by the second death." Altogether, there are three types of death described for us in Scripture:

1. spiritual death—this describes the unsaved person who is alive physically but spiritually dead in his sins. Every unsaved person today is described in Scripture as being spiritually dead in trespasses (see Eph. 2:1, 5; Col. 2:13).
2. physical death—this speaks of any person, saved or unsaved, who dies physically.
3. eternal death—this speaks of the unsaved person who is spiritually dead and then dies physically; he experiences eternal death, which is eternal suffering and punishment.

Jesus is speaking here about believers in regard to eternal death. Jesus is simply saying that because of his faith and God's salvation, the believer who dies physically will never experience eternal death or everlasting punishment in the lake of fire.

At no time does Jesus promise that He will deliver these believers from suffering on this side of heaven. Many times God does deliver us, but no such promise is given. In fact, Scripture declares the opposite: "All who desire to live godly lives in Christ Jesus will suffer persecution" (2 Tim. 3:12). God certainly promises strength for the trials, a crown of life, and deliverance from eternal judgment but not necessarily deliverance here and now.

This is an American way of thinking in some segments of the church today—that if you have enough faith, and if you pray hard enough, you can escape hardship in life. God's Word does not teach that, although many popular preachers teach that from their pulpits. Let us never forget that the only way God could provide forgiveness for our sins, and eternal life in heaven, was by sending His Son Jesus to suffer and die. So let us be like myrrh—the more we are crushed, the more the fragrance of Christ will come forth in our lives.

Now we come to the third of the seven churches—the church at Pergamos.

> And to the angel of the church in Pergamos write, "These things says He who has the sharp two-edged sword: 'I know your works, and where you dwell, where Satan's throne is. And you hold fast to My name, and did not deny My faith even in the days in which Antipas was My faithful martyr, who was killed among you, where Satan dwells. But I have a few things against you, because you have there those who hold the doctrine of Balaam, who taught Balak to put a stumbling block before the children of Israel, to eat things sacrificed to idols, and to commit sexual immorality. Thus you also have those who hold the doctrine of the Nicolaitans, which thing I hate. Repent, or else I will come to you quickly and will fight against them with the sword of My mouth. He who has an ear, let him hear what the Spirit says to the churches. To him who overcomes I will give some of the hidden manna to eat. And I will give him a white stone, and on the stone a new name written which no one knows except him who receives it.'"
>
> Revelation 2:12–17

I believe it was Baptist minister Adrian Rogers who said it well: "It is better to be divided by truth than to be united in error. It is better to be hated for telling the truth than to be loved for telling a lie." Our Lord's letter to the church at Pergamos brings us to the very relevant and hot-button topic of tolerance. It is a double-edged sword in the American church today, that those churches that are tolerant of sin and false doctrines are spiritually weak but applauded by society, while those churches that are intolerant of sin or false doctrines are accused of being judgmental and narrow-minded. But given the choice of receiving the world's disapproval or the Lord's disapproval, I can live with the world's disapproval.

Just a few days ago, a letter from a subscriber was printed in the opinion section of the local newspaper. This person started out by saying, "I believe in God." She went on to describe how loving Jesus was in the Gospels. Then she proceeded to urge the churches to be tolerant of homosexual unions in the church because, in her opinion, that's how Jesus would have responded.

This is a very typical perspective of God: that He is all-loving, as well as tolerant and understanding, and therefore the church should be the same. If we truly believe in God, we must also believe and practice His Word, and not just the parts that appeal to our way of thinking. Jesus clearly said, "If you love Me, then keep [or obey] My commandments" (John 14:15).

The Jesus who died on the cross for our sins is the same Jesus who gave us the Bible. And God's Holy Word does not condone sin but condemns it. Scripture condemns all sexual immorality, which is sex outside of heterosexual marriage—including premarital sex, extramarital sex, and homosexuality. One sin is no worse than another—it's all sin. To the woman caught in adultery and who called Jesus "Lord," indicating her repentance, Jesus said, "Neither do I condemn you; now go and sin no more!" (John 8:11). True saving faith in God produces repentance and change.

Earlier, I asked you to make a mental note of how the reference to "ten days" corresponds with ten Roman emperors between the first and fourth centuries who persecuted the church. The next Roman emperor after those ten was Constantine, who allegedly had a vision of a cross in the sky and heard a voice from heaven telling him to conquer in that sign. Constantine then is reported to have become a born-again believer and to have embraced Christianity as the government-sponsored religion. There was a marriage between the church and the government. The persecution against the church ceased, for the most part. Roman babies were soon required to be baptized in the Christian faith. But instead of encountering more blessing, the church spiraled downward. It went from being powerful and pure in the days of persecution to worldly and compromising in the days of prosperity.

The church became very tolerant, as pagan priests were recognized as Christian priests and pagan temples were considered Christian places of worship. This is what has been happening to certain segments of the church in America today. Some churches ordain homosexuals in spite of the clear New Testament teaching that such a lifestyle is condemned by God.

The name *Pergamos* means "marriage." So from the perspective of church history, Pergamos represents the period when the church was worldly and full of compromise. Pergamos was *the compromising church*. To be fair, Pergamos had many faithful believers living in the midst of difficult circumstances. In verse 13, Jesus evaluates this church and says He recognizes how they were living in the area of "Satan's throne." In Pergamos, there was heavy Roman emperor cult worship. There were also a temple and an altar erected to Zeus, the supreme god of the Greeks.

Another deity that was worshiped was Aesculapius, the Greek god of healing. The word *scalpel* comes from this name. This false god was symbolized by a serpent wrapped around a pole, the symbol still used to represent the medical community. At this temple, nonpoisonous snakes roamed freely. (I'm suddenly picturing the first Indiana Jones movie—that scene when Harrison Ford is in a chamber filled with snakes.) But in Pergamos, visitors seeking to be healed would come to this temple and lie on the floor, hoping that one of the snakes would touch them or crawl over them. The belief was that the Greek god would bring healing. It's no coincidence that Satan himself is symbolized in Scripture by the serpent and that Jesus said that Satan's throne was in Pergamos.

Jesus commends the faithful believers in Pergamos because they refused to deny the name of Jesus. Verse 13 mentions a faithful man named Antipas, who was put to death as a martyr for his refusal to renounce his faith. It is believed that Antipas was the pastor, and he was put to death by being roasted inside a brass bull. This took place in the late first century under the hand of the wicked Roman emperor Domitian, the same emperor who banished John to Patmos.

In verse 14, Jesus brings His complaint against this church, and it was for its tolerance and compromise. To be clear, the majority of people in this church were faithful, but some had allowed false doctrines to enter under the banner of tolerance. It's a shocking fact to many people that Jesus Christ hates this kind of tolerance. Two similar false doctrines had been allowed to creep into the church: the doctrine of Balaam and the doctrine of the Nicolaitans.

We've already looked at the Nicolaitans in the last chapter, so let's consider the doctrine of Balaam. The doctrine of Balaam is used as an example of wickedness by three New Testament writers: Peter, Jude, and now John, in Revelation. Balaam's story is found in the book of Numbers. The King of Moab, whose name was Balak, became afraid of the Israelites because of what they had done to the Amorites. So Balak summoned Balaam, a prophet for hire, to curse Israel for him. Balak offered him a great sum of money to do so. Balaam tried three times to curse Israel and was unsuccessful each time, as God turned his words of cursing into blessing.

But Balaam really wanted that money from Balak. So he advised the king to have his Moabite women intermingle with Israel's men. Balaam knew that this would bring idolatry into Israel's camp and would bring God's judgment on Israel. Balaam's plan worked to some degree, and twenty-four thousand Israelites were killed before things got turned around. So the doctrine of Balaam in Pergamos was a false doctrine that allowed immorality and idolatry to creep into the church.

In verse 16, Christ's command to this church is to repent and turn away from unbiblical tolerance, or the Lord would come and deal with those matters by the sword of His mouth. Interestingly, Balaam was killed by the sword (Num. 31:8). Notice in verse 16 the change in pronouns: "I will come to *you* quickly, and I will fight against *them*." The Lord knows how to separate the sheep from the goats and the wheat from the tares. The church belongs to God, and the gates of hell shall not prevail against it. Jesus will protect His true church, and He will hold sinners accountable.

Jesus closes with words of comfort in verse 17. He promises the faithful believers two special blessings: some hidden manna to eat and a white stone with a new name written on it. Manna was the heavenly food provided by God for His people Israel as they wandered through the wilderness. Later, God instructed Moses to place a jar of manna in the ark of the covenant. In John chapter 6, Jesus is described as the bread that comes down from heaven to feed His people spiritually. Just as the jar of manna was hidden in the ark, Jesus has ascended back into heaven, where we cannot see Him. But one day, when we arrive in heaven, we will see Jesus face-to-face.

The white stone has a couple possible meanings. A white stone and a dark stone were used by judges in court cases, with the darker stone representing a guilty verdict and the lighter stone representing acquittal. As our Savior and supreme Judge, Jesus declares us righteous by His blood and therefore not guilty. A small white stone was also handed out to athletes who competed in the games, and the stone was the ticket, or pass, to enter the feast and celebration after the competition. This reminds us of the great marriage supper and feast in which all believers will participate. Either illustration could apply to the text here.

As we consider the churches of Smyrna and Pergamos, these questions should be in our thoughts:

- Are we remaining faithful and courageous in times of persecution?
- Does persecution cause us to stand firm or to shrink back?
- Are we tolerating some sin or some unbiblical practice in our lives?
- What is the Lord speaking to us in this message?
- How will we respond?

5

What Christ Thinks of the Church—Part 3

Revelation 2:18–3:6

A number of years ago, a gopher moved in to our backyard. At first, I didn't take any action, since there were only a couple dirt mounds on the lawn. But within a couple weeks, our backyard began to look like an excavation site. I tried the old trick of putting the garden hose down the hole and turning on the water full blast. I let the water run for about twenty minutes, but no water came up anywhere in my yard. Then I realized that I might be flooding my neighbor's yard, if the gopher had tunneled next door. I tried a couple other things, but nothing worked. A few days later, while I was out in the yard, I saw the gopher popping his little head out of the hole, almost as if he were taunting me. I felt like I was being mocked by a baked potato with legs! So I got my pellet gun and waited for him to pop his head out of the hole again. In case you are a card-carrying member of PETA, I'll spare you the details, but suffice it to say that my little gopher problem suddenly went away. You may have wondered what pastors do on their days off—so there you go.

My biggest mistake, of course, was tolerating that gopher in the first place and not acting more quickly to get rid of him before he did so much damage to my lawn. When we make that same type of mistake spiritually, the consequences are far more serious. We will see this as we continue to examine what Christ thinks of the church.

Our next church in Revelation was in the city of Thyatira. If the name Thyatira sounds familiar, it is because this city is mentioned in Acts. In Acts 16, we meet a woman named Lydia from Thyatira who was living in Philippi. She was among some women who met along the river outside Philippi for a regular prayer meeting. Like Cornelius, they were God-fearing people but not born-again believers. When Paul shared the gospel with those ladies, Lydia was one who responded. After her conversion, Lydia invited Paul and his companions to lodge at her home. First Lydia opened her heart, and then she opened her home. We're told that Lydia was a seller of purple-dyed garments and that she was from Thyatira. It is entirely possible that Lydia took the gospel to her hometown of Thyatira—and that is perhaps how the church was started there. Or she may have written to her family or friends back home to share the story of her conversion.

The letter to the church at Thyatira is the longest of the seven, even though it was the smallest of the seven cities. Unlike the first three cities we looked at, Thyatira was not an important religious center, although it did have a temple dedicated to Apollo, the sun god of Greek and Roman mythology. Thyatira was a military outpost, as well as a center for producing wool and dyed garments, especially purple cloth. Lydia was a seller of this purple cloth, which was expensive to produce but provided a considerable profit, since purple was the color of clothing most desired by royalty.

Because of the garment trade, there were many trade guilds within the city. Each person in the garment industry needed to belong to one of those guilds, like a local union, and each guild had its patron deity. Many festivals were held in honor of the local deities, and the celebrations would oftentimes include idolatry and immorality. Undoubtedly, many of the local church members were dependent on the guilds for their employment, which put them in a position of peer pressure and potential compromise. Let's read about Thyatira in Revelation 2:18–29.

> And to the angel of the church in Thyatira write, "These things says the Son of God, who has eyes like a flame of fire, and His feet like fine brass: 'I know your works, love, service, faith, and your patience; and as for your works, the last are more than the first. Nevertheless I have a few things against you, because you allow that woman Jezebel, who calls herself a prophetess, to teach and seduce My servants to commit sexual immorality and eat things sacrificed to idols. And I gave her time to repent of her sexual immorality, and she did not repent. Indeed I will cast her into a sickbed, and those who commit adultery with her into great tribulation, unless they repent of their deeds. I will kill her children with death, and all the churches shall know that I am He who searches the minds and hearts. And I will give to each one of you according to your works. Now to you I say, and to the rest in Thyatira, as many as do not have this doctrine, who have not known the depths of Satan, as they say, I will put on you no other burden. But hold fast what you have till I come. And he who overcomes, and keeps My works until the end, to him I will give power over the nations—"HE SHALL RULE THEM WITH A ROD OF IRON; THEY SHALL BE DASHED TO PIECES LIKE THE POTTER'S VESSELS"—as I also have received from My Father; and I will give him the morning star. He who has an ear, let him hear what the Spirit says to the churches.'"
>
> Revelation 2:18–29

Jesus identified Himself to this church as "the Son of God," and it is worth noting that while this title is used of Jesus forty-five times in the New Testament, this is the only occurrence in the book of Revelation. The people of Thyatira were familiar with Apollo, the sun God, but Jesus presented Himself as "the Son of God."

Jesus does commend them for their "works, love, service, faith, and patience." He even states that their latter works were greater than their initial works. When we compare this church with the believers in Ephesus, we find that both congregations were very active spiritually. However, the difference was that in Ephesus, they were doing the right things but lacking the right motive of loving God supremely. In Thyatira, they were doing the right things for the right reasons, but they were also tolerating blatant sin. The problem in Thyatira was not outward persecution but rather inward compromise. Therefore, Thyatira was *the corrupted church.*

The source of that internal compromise and corruption is described for us in verses 20–21. Ironically, while the church may have been founded by the testimony of a woman, it was faltering because of the influence of a woman. She is called Jezebel, although it is doubtful that this was her actual name. Jesus appears to be using that name symbolically, alluding to the infamous Jezebel of the Old Testament. For a woman to be called Jezebel is just as bad as a man being called Judas.

It's great when parents want to give their children biblical names. However, some Bible names should be kept off the list. Jezebel and Judas are ones that come to mind. I hope I'm never asked to do a baby dedication on a Sunday morning when the child's name is Jezebel or Judas. Just imagine: "Lord, we bring little Judas before you now" or "Lord, help this Jezebel to become a woman of God." Another name you would want to avoid is Ichabod, which comes from the book of 1 Samuel. It means "the glory has departed." That's a good name for a cat who likes to run away, but not for a baby!

The first Jezebel in Scripture had been dead for many years, but her wickedness was alive in this first-century woman. In verse 10, she is described as "that woman Jezebel," but in a few translations, it is rendered as "your woman Jezebel." Since these letters were being written and sent to the pastors or spiritual leaders of these congregations, some scholars have suggested that this wicked woman was the wife of the pastor or the spiritual leader of the Thyatiran church. If that was the case, it makes her even more of a New Testament Jezebel, because the Old Testament Jezebel was the wife of King Ahab.

Ahab was Israel's king, but he married Jezebel, who came from Sidon, which was known for idolatry. She turned Jezreel into a city that worshiped Baal. In his efforts to please his wife, Ahab erected a sanctuary for Baal that supported hundreds of pagan prophets. When the prophets of God opposed Jezebel, she had them "massacred" (1 Kings 18). After Elijah defeated Jezebel's false prophets of Baal on Mount Carmel, she swore revenge on him, issuing a warrant for his death (1 Kings 19).

After Ahab was killed in battle, Jezebel reigned for ten years through her sons. These sons were killed by Jehu, who then disposed of Jezebel by having her thrown from the palace window, where she was promptly trampled by horses and eaten by wild dogs (1 Kings 21). We read that as Jezebel realized she was about to be killed, she took time to paint her eyes. Jezebel was, by far, the most wicked woman in Scripture—she was the devil in a blue dress.

This New Testament Jezebel of Thyatira was an influential woman who claimed to be empowered by God. She "called herself a prophetess," indicating that she wasn't, although many accepted her as such. Like her Old Testament counterpart, she used her position to bring in idolatry and immorality. Perhaps she was working with the local trade guilds to persuade Christians to participate in idolatry.

The serious mistake that this church made was twofold: first, they allowed her to have a position of teaching in the congregation, and second, they allowed her to teach false doctrine. Even if she were not immoral, the Scriptures teach that women were not to take the primary role of spiritual leaders and teachers in the church (1 Tim. 2:12). In verse 20, Jesus states that she was "teaching and beguiling Christ's servants," referring to the church members. So this church was reaping the consequences of disobeying the Scriptures.

The patience of Jesus is seen in verse 21, where He gave this woman the opportunity to repent, but she did not. In verse 22, Jesus was giving a final warning to others in the church who were involved in these sinful practices to repent before it was too late. Jesus spoke of the punishment that this woman would suffer—in part to remind the church of His holiness, and in part to persuade others to repent. The Lord always prefers repentance and pardon over punishment. The Lord takes no delight in the death of the wicked.

The punishment for this Jezebel-type woman was being cast into a sickbed. In the original Greek, the word *sick* is not attached to the word *bed*. Combining them was the translators' attempt to clarify the statement, but in doing so, they may have actually clouded the words of Jesus. This punishment was much more than just a sickbed of sexually transmitted disease, as some have assumed. Since Jesus gave her the opportunity to repent, and she did not, then this bed is more likely speaking of death and eternal punishment in hell.

For those genuine believers in the church who also failed to repent, Jesus spoke of tribulation against them, which can include death. The Bible speaks of genuine believers sinning to the point of physical death (1 John 5:16). Sometimes the best of believers can commit the worst of sins, including sexual sin. We must remind ourselves that these messages to the seven churches are messages to all believers, throughout the ages, until His return. Therefore, Jesus is saying to some right now, repent and turn away from whatever sexual sins you are involved in, and do so quickly, before it's too late and the Lord's punishment comes upon you. As Charles Spurgeon said, "God loves us far too much to ever let one of His children sin successfully."[1]

At the end of verse 23, Jesus says, "I will give each one of you according to your works." Please remember this important distinction: salvation is always according to faith, while judgment is always according to works. When Christians are judged in heaven, as we read in 1 Corinthians 3, that judgment will be based on our works as believers. The unsaved will also be judged for their works, including their sins. When we get to Revelation 20, we will read about the great white throne judgment for all the unsaved. So Jesus "will give to each one according to their works."

In verse 24, Jesus extends a special word of encouragement to the faithful believers in Thyatira who were not only genuine believers but also faithful in separating themselves from the sexual immorality taking place within the church. Jesus simply says, "I will put no other burden on you." Those faithful believers were already bearing the burden of having this sin in their church and of watching a false teacher run rampant. Jesus recognizes that this was enough of a burden for them to bear.

At the same time, He commands the faithful, in verse 25, to hold on tight to their faith until His return. That is followed by Christ's promise that the faithful believers will rule and reign with Him, referring to the millennial kingdom. Jesus also promises faithful believers "the morning star"—a reference to Himself. In Revelation 22:16, Jesus describes Himself as the morning star, so this probably refers to our eternal life with Him in heaven.

And to the angel of the church in Sardis write, "These things says He who has the seven Spirits of God and the seven stars: 'I know your works, that you have a name that you are alive, but you are dead. Be watchful, and strengthen the things which remain, that are ready to die, for I have not found your works perfect before God. Remember therefore how you have received and heard; hold fast and repent. Therefore if you will not watch, I will come upon you as a thief, and you will not know what hour I will come upon you. You have a few names even in Sardis who have not defiled their garments; and they shall walk with Me in white, for they are worthy. He who overcomes shall be clothed in white garments, and I will not blot out his name from the Book of Life; but I will confess his name before My Father and before His angels. He who has an ear, let him hear what the Spirit says to the churches.'"

Revelation 3:1–6

One of my fellow pastors on our staff worked at a mortuary several years ago. He told me, with a smile, that a mortician can make deceased persons look better than they did when they were still alive. That would be a good analogy of how things were with the church in Sardis.

The message of Jesus to the church at Sardis is one of the most severe. For the poor and persecuted believers back at Smyrna, Jesus had nothing but praise. For the churches at Ephesus, Pergamos, and Thyatira, Jesus had a mixture of praise and rebuke. But for Sardis, Jesus had nothing commendable to say. This is especially surprising when you consider the fact that this church had such a good reputation. The Lord does not commend this church for anything, He does not mention any false doctrine, and He does not mention any persecution. This church was just comfortable, content, coasting, and living off its good reputation. Sardis was *the cold church*.

The city of Sardis was an important trade center, because it was located at the junction of five main roads. It was a wealthy city—its wealth coming from trade and textile manufacturing. The city was built on a high bluff, with the acropolis of Sardis sitting nearly fifteen hundred feet above the main roads. Because of its great height and almost impossible access, Sardis considered itself to be invincible against outside attacks. However, to their surprise, the people of Sardis were conquered twice during a period of just over three hundred years.

In verse 1, after identifying the church at Sardis, Jesus identifies Himself as "He who has the seven Spirits of God and the seven stars." The "seven Spirits of God" is a reference to the fullness of the Holy Spirit. The church at Sardis was dead, so Jesus came with what the church needed most: the power of the Holy Spirit. If you think you need spiritual revival and renewal in your own life, then pray and ask God to empower you by the Holy Spirit. The church began on Pentecost with the coming of the Holy Spirit, and it is the Spirit that brings life.

The problem at Sardis was that the church had reputation without reality. If ever there was a problem with the church in America today, it would be that so many people profess to being Christians (more than 80 percent of Americans claim to be believers),[2] but the reality is nowhere to be found. As Vance Havner asked, "If there is so much light, then why is America so dark? If there is so much salt, then why are things so corrupt?"[3]

Jesus assesses Sardis and says, "You have a name [which says] that you are alive, but you are dead." Apparently, many of the people in this church professed to being Christians but were unsaved. Jesus, the Great Physician, takes the pulse of this church and, spiritually speaking, He finds no pulse.

Ironically, Sardis had a reputation for being alive. If you had been walking down the streets of Sardis on a Sunday morning, and you had asked someone for directions to this church, that person would have known which church you meant and how to get there. Jesus, however, offers no words of commendation to this church.

In many ways, the situation in Sardis is illustrated by the life and death of Samson. Samson had taken a Nazarite vow, which dedicated him to and separated him for the Lord. His spiritual dedication was blessed by God, who gave him supernatural physical strength, symbolized by his long hair. But Samson allowed a woman named Delilah to toy with him until she succeeded in learning the secret to his strength. She arranged to have his hair cut off by the Philistines, causing Samson to lose both his physical and his spiritual strength. But his hair was only symbolic, and Samson really lost his strength because of his disobedience to the Lord.

When the Philistines pounced on Samson, he thought he could fight them off as before, but the Scriptures tell us, "[Samson] did not know that the LORD had departed from him" (Judg. 16:20). So Samson was captured. His eyes were gouged out, and he became a slave to the Philistines. God allowed Samson one final act of vengeance on the Philistines, but it cost Samson his life. Like Samson, the church members at Sardis thought they were secure and strong, but they didn't know that the Lord had departed.

In verse 2, Jesus exhorts this church to wake up and to strengthen what little remained. In other words, they were in great need of spiritual revival. Revival is oftentimes misunderstood, even by Christians. Revival is often associated with a great response to gospel preaching, whereby many people are saved. But that's not revival; that's evangelism and salvation. Revival can and should lead the revived church into greater evangelism and outreach, but revival itself is something different. You don't revive a person who is dead in sins. Revival is not for the unsaved; it is for the family of God. Revival consists of repentance, humility, prayer, and a recommitment to obeying God's Word—things that the church in Sardis needed desperately.

In verse 3, Jesus exhorts them to remember how they had first heard the gospel message and, therefore, to repent. In addition to repenting, Jesus exhorts them to become watchful; otherwise He would come upon them when they least expected it. When Sardis the city had been conquered on two occasions, it was a result of not watching.

In verse 4, Jesus makes specific reference to the faithful few in Sardis "who have not defiled their garments." The Lord always has His remnant and is gracious to His faithful few, even in places such as Sardis. The promise of comfort to the faithful of Sardis was that Christ would clothe them in the white garments of His own righteousness.

He says about each faithful believer, "And I will not blot out his name from the Book of Life." That statement confuses and concerns some believers, because it seems to imply that a genuine believer can lose his salvation. But not only does this text not say that, but I also believe that the Bible does not teach that. Let's start this discussion by talking about what is meant by the Book of Life. Some people believe the Book of Life is a register in which the names of people are added at the moment they become saved. Others believe it's a record of every person who has been born since the time Christ died, and that their names are removed at the end of their lives, if they die in their sins.

It appears from Scripture that there are two books: the Book of the Living and the Book of Life. The Book of the Living is the record of every person who was born. When a person dies, his or her name is removed from the Book of the Living. In Exodus 32, when Moses was interceding on behalf of Israel because of their sin with the golden calf, Moses essentially said to God, "Please forgive Your people, and if You will not forgive them, then blot me out of Your book which You have written."

Moses, the humble servant-leader, was willing to have his life cut short in order to save the people who had sinned. But God responded, "Whoever has sinned against Me, I will blot him out of My book." God was going to punish the guilty with physical death. In Psalm 69:28, David makes a similar statement about God punishing his enemies by "blotting their names out of the book of the living."

But here, in Revelation 3:5, Jesus is talking about the Book of Life. This is a record of every genuine believer. In Philippians 4:3, while describing genuine believers who were his fellow workers, Paul says that their "names are in the Book of Life." Later on, in Revelation 13:8, this record is described as being the "Book of Life of the Lamb." Then in Revelation 20:15, at the judgment of the unsaved, we read that their names were not found in the Book of Life. Finally, in Revelation 21:27, we read that heaven will be inhabited only by those whose names are written in the "Lamb's Book of Life."

So while some have tried to interpret this verse in Revelation 3:5 as the possibility of losing one's salvation, it actually says the opposite. Genuine believers, like the remnant in Sardis, can never have their names blotted out of the Book of Life, which is the book that records the name of every true believer. In Luke 10:20, Jesus told His disciples to rejoice because their names were "written in heaven." New Testament Greek scholar Kenneth Wuest translates that verse, "Your names have been written in heaven and are on permanent record up there."[4] Or as Warren Wiersbe has said, "Our names are not written in the Book of Life with a pencil."[5]

I believe the Bible clearly teaches that genuine believers cannot and will not lose their salvation, but I must emphasize the word *genuine*.

I believe in *eternal security*, but not *eternal presumption*. Not every person who claims to be a Christian actually is.

Most of the people in the church at Sardis professed to be genuine believers, but in reality they were unsaved. They weren't losing their salvation—they never had it to begin with. In Matthew 7 (author's paraphrase), Jesus warns of those on the day of judgment who will say to Him, "Lord, Lord, didn't we do this and didn't we do that?" And Christ's response will be, "Depart from Me, I never knew you." He doesn't say, "Well, I knew you at one time, but you fell away and lost your salvation, so . . . too bad, so sad!" Instead, He will say to them simply, "I *never* knew you!"

Speaking of real and genuine believers, Jesus also said, "My sheep hear My voice, and I know them, and they follow Me. And I give them eternal life, and they shall never perish" (John 10:27–28). In the Greek, Jesus was saying, "And they shall *never*, no *never*, no *never*, perish." God has never torn up a Christian's spiritual birth certificate.

There are a few other important things in this chapter. No matter how strong our faith and service may be, we must separate ourselves from sin. In addition, we must remain alert in the Lord, watching and waiting for His return. God will not allow us to compromise or to coast in our faith. We want to experience ongoing spiritual revival in our hearts.

At the same time, we've been reminded of some very special promises that are in store for the faithful believer. We will rule and reign with Christ. We will be clothed in His garments of righteousness. And we are eternally secure in Christ, who will never ever remove our names from His Book of Life. As Paul wrote at the end of Romans 8, nothing can ever separate us from the love of God that is in Christ Jesus our Lord.

6

What Christ Thinks
of the Church—Part 4

Revelation 3:7–22

I've never quite understood why some people get so excited about hot sauce. I don't eat hot, spicy foods, so my favorite brand of hot sauce is . . . ketchup! Don't get me wrong; I like flavor. I just don't enjoy setting my tongue on fire . . . or burning a hole through my lungs.

A few years ago, a guest speaker at our church was spending a few days with us, so three of us pastors took him out to lunch. The server mentioned that the special was some sort of sandwich that was quite spicy. Immediately, the other two pastors set their menus down and said, "That's what we want." Our guest and I went with a much milder menu selection. After the food arrived and we started eating, I looked over at the two pastors with the spicy sandwiches, and *both* of them were sweating profusely and had tears running down their faces. Then one of them looked at me and said, "You should have ordered this. This is really good!" I responded, "That's

OK—if I ever want to sweat and cry at the same time, I'll just watch a Richard Simmons exercise video."

When it comes to spicy foods, "to each his own," as they say. But when it comes to the temperature of our spiritual lives, it is a far more serious issue. As we come now to the last two of the seven churches, we find one on fire for the Lord and another that is lukewarm and makes Jesus sick.

We begin with the believers living in the first-century city of Philadelphia in Asia Minor.

> And to the angel of the church in Philadelphia write, "These things says He who is holy, He who is true, 'He who has the key of David, He who opens and no one shuts, and shuts and no one opens': 'I know your works. See, I have set before you an open door, and no one can shut it; for you have a little strength, have kept My word, and have not denied My name. Indeed I will make those of the synagogue of Satan, who say they are Jews and are not, but lie—indeed I will make them come and worship before your feet, and to know that I have loved you. Because you have kept My command to persevere, I also will keep you from the hour of trial which shall come upon the whole world, to test those who dwell on the earth. Behold, I am coming quickly! Hold fast what you have, that no one may take your crown. He who overcomes, I will make him a pillar in the temple of My God, and he shall go out no more. I will write on him the name of My God and the name of the city of My God, the New Jerusalem, which comes down out of heaven from My God. And I will write on him My new name. He who has an ear, let him hear what the Spirit says to the churches.'"
>
> Revelation 3:7–13

Philadelphia was the most recently founded of the seven cities, established about 150 years before the birth of Christ. The man who founded the city was a king named Attalus II, and he had such affection for his brother that the city came to be called Philadelphia, which means "brotherly love." In AD 17, almost eighty years before John sent this letter, Philadelphia was severely damaged by an earthquake and several aftershocks. Philadelphia still exists today but now goes by its modern name of Alashehir.

In verse 7, Jesus identifies Himself as "He who is holy and true." With the first five churches, Jesus introduced Himself in terms that had been used to describe Him in chapter 1. However, for the first time in these seven letters, Jesus identifies Himself with a different term. When Jesus speaks of Himself here as being "holy and true," He is identifying Himself as God. In that culture, there were hundreds of false gods and deities, so Jesus distinguishes Himself as the true and genuine God who is holy.

Jesus also identifies Himself as having the power and authority for opening and closing the doors of heaven. In chapter 1, we read that Jesus has "the keys of Hades and of Death." Jesus has all the keys, for death and judgment as well as salvation and heaven. In verse 8, Jesus commends this church, and, having seen their works, He is pleased with their faithfulness, so Jesus "sets before them an open door."

Philadelphia was *the committed church*. The "open door" that Jesus was speaking of undoubtedly refers to an open door for evangelism. For example, Paul had written to the church at Colosse and said, "Pray . . . for us, that God will open up to us a door for the word" (Col. 4:3). Today, God continues to give us many open doors of opportunity. In these last days, we must continue to make the most of those open doors, before the time comes when God finally shuts them.

Jesus also makes the statement, in verse 8, that they "had a little strength," which is the same as saying, "You're weak." But this was a good type of weakness, and having just "a little strength" is a great source of power because it makes us much more dependent on the Lord. In 2 Corinthians 12:9, God told Paul, "My strength is made perfect in weakness." Of the seven churches, only two did not receive any criticism from the Lord: the suffering church at Smyrna, and the church with just a little strength at Philadelphia. Both churches were small and weak, but both were commended by Jesus. The Lord saw their frailty, but He also saw their faithfulness.

In verse 9, we learn that, just like the church at Smyrna, there was a "synagogue of Satan" in Philadelphia. Wherever the gospel is being preached, we can expect Satan to set up his base camp and for his followers to bring opposition. Spiritual opportunities are always met with opposition and obstacles. Wherever God has His church, Satan has his chapels and his synagogues.

In verse 10, Jesus makes a very special promise: "Because you have kept My command to persevere, I also will keep you from the hour of trial which shall come upon the whole world, to test those who dwell on the earth." This is nothing less than a promise to the church that it will not go through the great tribulation period. We know that this was not referring to some local trial just for the Philadelphian believers, because Jesus is speaking of "the trial which shall come upon the whole world." It is also clear that this trial lasts for a specific period of time, as Jesus calls it "the hour of trial." This does not refer to a literal sixty minutes but to a specific period of time—in this case, the seven-year tribulation period. This is the period of judgment when divine wrath will come upon an unbelieving world that has rejected God and the gospel. But as terrible as this judgment will be, it's still described as a test (or trial), meaning that the unsaved will have the opportunity to repent of their sins and to receive Jesus—though for the majority, it will cost them their lives.

Theologically, there are three primary positions on the rapture, in connection with the tribulation period. The pretribulation position states that the church will be taken up to heaven just before or just as the tribulation begins and that the church will not go through the tribulation.

Some others believe the church will be taken up at the midpoint of the tribulation so this is called the midtribulation position on the rapture. The reasoning behind this comes from the mistaken idea that the first half of the tribulation is somewhat peaceful, and that the severe judgments of God will not begin until after the first three and a half years. But as we will see in Revelation 6, that is not the case.

Then there is the posttribulation position, which teaches that the church will be preserved through the tribulation period, and then taken up to be with Jesus after the full seven years. Those who hold to this position believe that God will keep the church on earth and will protect her from the fallout of God's judgment. There are several troublesome points to this position. For one, Jesus is going to set up His millennial kingdom on the earth immediately after the end of the tribulation. So according to the posttribulation position, the church would be raptured up to Jesus and then make an immediate U-turn right back down, since the church will be with Christ during the millennial kingdom. That makes no sense and serves no purpose.

On the other hand, in the pretribulation position, the church is taken up to heaven and is with Jesus for seven years before returning with Him at His second coming. While we are in heaven during those seven years, God will judge and reward believers for what we have done with our lives since the time of our conversion. This judgment of believers is described for us in 1 Corinthians 3. We will not be judged for our sins, since Jesus took all our sins on Himself on the cross at Calvary. But our works as believers will be judged by fire. The works that have eternal value are represented by gold, silver, and precious stones. The other works, which have no eternal value, are represented by hay, wood, and stubble—items that burn with fire.

After that judgment is completed, He will clothe us in His fine linen garments, which represent our faithful works. Then we will return with Him at His second coming, ready to rule and reign with Him on earth for a thousand years. We will also participate in the marriage supper of the Lamb, which we'll examine when we get to Revelation 19.

Another serious issue with the posttribulation position, scripturally speaking, is that the New Testament does not teach that the church will go through the tribulation but that she will be taken up prior, just as we have read here in verse 10. The Greek word translated as "keep," when Jesus said, "I will *keep* you from that hour of trial," literally means "*keep* from" and "*keep* out of."[1] Jesus is going to *keep* His church from His coming wrath and *out of* the coming tribulation.

Notice that there are two instances of the word *keep* here in verse 10. Because genuine believers have *kept* His Word to persevere, Jesus promises to *keep* us from the time of judgment. In fact, what Jesus was saying to the believers in Philadelphia, and to the New Testament believers who have been faithful in all ages, is that because they have already passed the test of remaining faithful, Jesus will spare them from the ultimate test of the tribulation period.

One final point worth mentioning is this: there are three primary rapture passages in the New Testament, and none of them talks about judgment; rather, each one speaks of the church being taken up to heaven. The first passage is in John 14, where Jesus promised His followers that He would return for them and that He would be preparing a place for them in heaven. The second passage is toward the end of 1 Corinthians 15, where Paul talks about our instantaneous removal from the earth, in the twinkling of an eye, up into the kingdom of heaven. The third main passage is found in Paul's words to the church of Thessalonica, in 1 Thessalonians 4. Here we learn that the bodies of deceased believers will be raised first, and believers who are alive at that moment will be caught up or raptured up to meet the Lord.

I read a story about an older country couple who made their first visit to the big city to visit their son. Their son took them shopping at a large department store. The mom had wandered off to look at some clothes while the father and son were standing near the elevator—something the old man had never seen before. The old man watched as the double doors opened, an elderly woman walked in, and the doors closed behind her. A few minutes later, the doors reopened and out walked a young, beautiful woman. The old man got very excited and told his son, "You wait right here; I'm going to get your mother and run her through this thing!"

At the rapture, we will also be taken up and then transformed. In verse 11, Jesus says, "Behold! I am coming quickly!" The word *quickly* means that when Christ does return, it will happen suddenly. His return to rapture the church is imminent and could take place at any moment.

The reference to the "crown" in verse 11 is speaking of the believer's reward. If we hold fast to our faith and continue to walk through those open doors of opportunities that God gives us, then we won't lose the reward for our service.

Every promise we have in this passage as believers is based on what God is going to do. If any of this sounds too good to be true, just remember this: God always keeps His promises.

- In verse 9, Jesus says, *"I will"* make your enemies bow before you.
- In verse 10, He says, *"I will"* keep you from the coming judgment of the world.
- And in verse 12, the Lord says, *"I will"* make you a pillar in heaven.

The great I AM is also the great "I Will!"

God's promise to make us pillars in His temple is a promise of stability and security. These words would have been of particular comfort to the believers in Philadelphia, seeing that their city sat on top of a major geological fault. They had already suffered a devastating earthquake in AD 17 that had leveled their city and was followed by several years of aftershocks. So Jesus promises them a sturdy, unshakable, unmovable standing in heaven.

Jesus also promises that God's name, as well as Christ's name, will be written on those faithful believers. This identifies us as belonging to God. My father always had an excellent reputation in his community. He spent several years working in the local district attorney's office. As I was growing up, it was not uncommon for someone to hear or read my name and then immediately ask me, "Are you, by chance, Jim Lasseigne's son?" Then, invariably, they would proceed to tell me what a great person my dad was. When people watch us, our desire is that our attitude and actions would cause them to ask, "Are you, by chance, a Christian?"

Now let's examine the seventh and final church in Revelation 3:14–22.

> And to the angel of the church of the Laodiceans write, "These things says the Amen, the Faithful and True Witness, the Beginning of the creation of God: 'I know your works, that you are neither cold nor hot. I could wish you were cold or hot. So then, because you are lukewarm, and neither cold nor hot, I will vomit you out of My mouth. Because you say, "I am rich, have become wealthy, and have need of nothing"—and do not know that you are wretched, miserable, poor, blind, and naked—I counsel you to buy from Me gold refined in the fire, that you may be rich; and white garments, that you may be clothed, that the shame of your nakedness may not be revealed; and anoint your eyes with eye salve, that you may see. As many as I love, I rebuke and chasten. Therefore be zealous and repent. Behold, I stand at the door and knock. If anyone hears My voice and opens the door, I will come in to him and dine with him, and he with Me. To him who overcomes I will grant to sit with Me on My throne, as I also overcame and sat down with My Father on His throne. He who has an ear, let him hear what the Spirit says to the churches.'"
>
> Revelation 3:14–22

Laodicea is the only church of the seven to have its name in the dictionary. A *Laodicean* is defined as "a person who is lukewarm or indifferent in religion."[2] So if you ever call a lukewarm Christian a "Laodicean," you're not only being biblical but also using a legitimate dictionary term as well! (That may come in handy the next time you play Scrabble.)

This last church is *the carnal church*. Laodicea was founded by Antiochus II, a ruler who named the city for his wife, Laodice. Laodicea was situated on a plateau, several hundred feet high, making it fairly insurmountable. But because of the city's elevation, the Laodiceans were required to bring in drinking water via aqueduct. The city was known for three things: it was a wealthy banking center, it produced a special eye salve, and it manufactured beautiful black wool cloth.

Laodicea was located near Hieropolis, which was famous for its hot springs, and Colosse, known for its pure, cold refreshing waters. Hieropolis was about seven miles from Laodicea, while Colosse was a little less than ten miles away. Together, they formed a tri-city area in the Lycus River Valley. This proximity explains why, when Paul wrote his Epistle to the church at Colosse (the book of Colossians), he made the closing statement, "Now when this epistle is read among you, see that it is read also in the church of the Laodiceans" (Col. 4:16).

Along with the letter to Sardis, this letter to Laodicea was the most severe. For most of the other churches, Jesus had both praise and rebuke. But for Laodicea, Jesus does not have a single word of praise for the church or for any of its members. There is an ongoing debate concerning the church at Laodicea. Some believe that this church was apostate, filled with professed believers but without any genuine Christians. It was William Barclay who said, "The very expression, a lukewarm Christian, is a contradiction in terms, for a lukewarm Christian has no claim to being called a Christian at all."[3]

But there are Bible students who believe that while this church was in serious spiritual trouble, many of the people were believers. There are verses in this passage that support both views. Undoubtedly, this church was religious and filled with both types of people—those who professed Christianity and were unsaved, and those who were actually saved but anemic in their faith. The Laodiceans were a little too cold to be hot and a little too hot to be cold, so they were lukewarm.[4]

When we look at the panorama of church history in the last two thousand years, this final church at Laodicea symbolizes the last days—an apostate church filled with unsaved religious people, as well as those who are saved but anemic in their faith. John R. Stott puts it this way: "Perhaps none of the seven letters is more appropriate to the last-days church than this one. It describes vividly the respectable, sentimental, nominal, skin-deep religiosity which is so wide spread among us today."[5]

It's no surprise, then, that Jesus begins by identifying Himself to this church as "the Amen, the Faithful and True Witness." This church was carnal and full of compromise, so Jesus calls Himself "the Amen." This church was indifferent and apathetic, so Jesus calls Himself "Faithful." This church had lost its testimony, so Jesus calls Himself "the True Witness."

Then Jesus describes Himself as the "Beginning of the creation of God," which does not mean Jesus was created, as the cults falsely teach. The word for beginning simply means "source," so it is referring to Jesus as being the Creator, and not as something created. In His humanity, Jesus had a beginning, but in His deity, He is the beginning.

At this point, Jesus leapfrogs over any praise and moves right into His accusation against this church: "You are neither cold nor hot. I wish you were cold or hot, but because you are lukewarm and neither cold nor hot, I will vomit you out of my mouth." Jesus says either hate Me or love Me with all your heart, but don't give Me your lukewarm attitude. Tea is something that tastes really good when it's hot, especially if my throat is hoarse from too much speaking. I also like iced tea, as long as there is plenty of ice, but lukewarm tea is unappealing.

Jesus feels that way about lukewarm churches, and there is no way of dressing up these words. Jesus is saying that this church nauseates Him. In Scripture, we find that there are three spiritual temperatures: hot, cold, and lukewarm. When Jesus opened up the Scriptures to some discouraged disciples on the road to Emmaus, their response was to say, "Did not our heart burn within us . . . while He opened the Scriptures to us?" (Luke 24:32). Their spiritual temperature was hot.

When Paul preached the gospel in Athens, at the Areopagus, we read that some of those who were listening, when Paul spoke of the resurrection, began to mock him. Their spiritual temperature was cold, because they were unsaved and dead in their sins. Then in the Old Testament book of Jonah, we meet a prophet of God, who was trying to run away from his spiritual responsibilities. He confessed to fearing God, yet he acknowledged that he was running away in disobedience and simply didn't care. It took Jonah three days inside a fish (which may have been a whale) to repent. Then God caused the great fish to vomit Jonah onto land.

Like Jonah, these Laodiceans were spiritually lukewarm, prompting Jesus to say, "I will vomit you out of My mouth." It's shocking to hear Jesus say that He would prefer for these Laodiceans to be either cold or hot rather than lukewarm. Dr. G. Campbell Morgan stated that "lukewarmness is the worst form of blasphemy."[6]

Once again, Jesus is using words and expressions that would be easily understood by these people in Laodicea. As already mentioned, Laodicea had the cold and refreshing waters of Colosse close by, as well as the famous hot springs of Hieropolis. But between them was Laodicea with its lukewarm waters. These stunning words of Jesus simply mean that cold persons, who readily acknowledge that they are unsaved, have a better chance of coming to Christ and being saved than the lukewarm and cozy religious person who is also unsaved but doesn't even know it.

In verse 16, Christ's reaction to the lukewarm condition of this church was to say, "I will vomit you out of My mouth!" Sometimes visitors would come through Laodicea, and after tasting the lukewarm drinking water, they would immediately spit it out. The trouble at Laodicea can be summed up with two phrases: "You say" and, "But you do not know."

People who live on farms are aware that when a chicken's head is cut off, its body will oftentimes continue to run around for thirty seconds or so. The body is simply convulsing, which gives the appearance of the body still being alive, even with the head gone. Sometimes the body will run in the direction of someone standing by, and it will freak out that person because he thinks the headless chicken is chasing him. One time, a little boy saw all this happening on his grandfather's farm, so he asked why the chickens were doing this. His grandfather replied, "Because they don't even know they're dead yet."

Unfortunately, for many of the people in the church at Laodicea, they didn't even know they were spiritually dead. Whatever religious activity they had, it gave the false appearance of spiritual life. It wasn't that this church was filled with people who were practicing perverse wickedness and sin; the problem was that they just didn't care. They were apathetic, halfhearted, indifferent, and unconcerned.

In verse 18, Jesus counsels this church to do three things. First, they needed to "buy gold from the Lord," so they might truly become rich, spiritually speaking. Second, they needed to receive the "white garments" of righteousness that Jesus offered. Because they manufactured a special black wool cloth in Laodicea, the church thought that it was nicely clothed. But Jesus calls them spiritually "naked." It reminds us of the children's story *The Emperor's New Clothes*. The emperor paraded himself down the street naked, fooled into thinking that he had been sold beautiful royal clothing. That is a spiritual picture of this church. Third, Jesus counsels them to "anoint their eyes with salve." Laodiceans prided themselves on the eye salve they manufactured, but they were spiritually "blind."

In verse 19, in spite of this stern rebuke from the Lord, we see that His motive was love for His church. He then challenges this church to get on fire—to become "zealous and repent." In verse 20, we have the amazing picture of Jesus standing outside His church and knocking on the door to get in. Philadelphia was the church of the open door, while Laodicea was the church of the closed door.

With the other six churches, Jesus speaks to the church that is "in" Smyrna, or the church that is "in" Philadelphia. But notice in verse 14, Jesus addresses this congregation as "the church of the Laodiceans." This is precisely why we find Jesus standing outside the door of this church and knocking for them to let Him back in. It wasn't His church; it was their church. God help us that the church we attend will always remain God's church.

Notice that if these believers were to open the door, Jesus promised to come inside and "dine with them." To dine with someone in this culture was a sign of fellowship and intimacy. In many of the postresurrection appearances of Jesus, He is eating with His disciples. He ate dinner with the two disciples on the road to Emmaus. He ate some fish and honeycomb in the upper room. He prepared some fish and bread along the shore of the Sea of Galilee for Peter, John, and the other disciples, and so forth. And one day, we will all sit down with Jesus at the great marriage supper of the Lamb.

Jesus finishes His seven letters with the same words of warning that He has repeated over and over again: "He who has an ear, let him hear what the Spirit is saying to the churches." So then, which church do you and I belong to? That's the critical question gleaned from these seven letters, and the answer is of vital spiritual importance.

7

Casting Crowns

Revelation 4:1–11

I read the story of a woman who walked in to a Häagen-Dazs ice-cream store in Kansas City. After she made her selection and received her ice-cream cone, she turned and suddenly found herself standing face-to-face with Paul Newman. He smiled and said hello to her, but she froze up and was unable to speak. The woman finally managed to pay for her ice-cream cone, and she left the store with her heart pounding and feeling embarrassed at being unable to speak.

After she gained her composure, she realized that she didn't have her ice-cream cone, so she went back to the Häagen-Dazs store. As she opened the door, Paul Newman was walking out, and he asked her, "Were you looking for your ice-cream cone?" Still unable to speak, she simply nodded her head yes. He smiled at her and said, "I happened to notice that you put your cone in your purse along with your change." As exciting as it must have been for that woman to meet Paul Newman, all Christians are going to have the incredible experience one day of meeting God face-to-face.

As we continue our studies in the book of Revelation, the scene now shifts from the earth to heaven. This shifting back and forth between earth and heaven takes place frequently in Revelation. This shift brings us to the third and final section of the book. Back in Revelation 1:19, John was told to "write the things which you have seen, and the things which are, and the things which will take place after this." "The things which you have seen" refers to John's vision of Jesus in chapter 1. "The things which are" refers to the seven letters to the churches. "The things which will take place after this" refers to the events of the tribulation period, as well as the things that follow the tribulation. Let's begin our study of these future things.

After these things I looked, and behold, a door standing open in heaven. And the first voice which I heard was like a trumpet speaking with me, saying, "Come up here, and I will show you things which must take place after this." Immediately I was in the Spirit; and behold, a throne set in heaven, and One sat on the throne. And He who sat there was like a jasper and a sardius stone in appearance; and there was a rainbow around the throne, in appearance like an emerald. Around the throne were twenty-four thrones, and on the thrones I saw twenty-four elders sitting, clothed in white robes; and they had crowns of gold on their heads. And from the throne proceeded lightnings, thunderings, and voices. Seven lamps of fire were burning before the throne, which are the seven Spirits of God. Before the throne there was a sea of glass, like crystal. And in the midst of the throne, and around the throne, were four living creatures full of eyes in front and in back. The first living creature was like a lion, the second living creature like a calf, the third living creature had a face like a man, and the fourth living creature was like a flying eagle. The four living creatures, each having six wings, were full of eyes around and within. And they do not rest day or night, saying: "Holy, holy, holy, Lord God Almighty, Who was and is and is to come!" Whenever the living creatures give glory and honor and thanks to Him who sits on the throne, who lives forever and ever, the twenty-four elders fall down before Him who sits on the throne and worship Him who lives forever and ever, and cast their crowns before the throne, saying: "You are worthy, O Lord, to receive glory and honor and power; for You created all things, and by Your will they exist and were created."

Revelation 4:1–11

The first thing we see, in verse 1, is *God's summons*. This is a picture of how the church will be summoned up into heaven. In the previous chapter, Jesus promised the faithful believers in the church at Philadelphia, and in all the ages, that they would be kept out of the trial that is coming upon the whole world—the great tribulation. Just to be clear, in this immediate context, verse 1 refers to the fact that John is on Patmos and is supernaturally transported into heaven to witness and record the events of the last days. But at the same time, there is no denying the symbolic picture of the rapture in these words.

John says, "After these things," and he has just finished the seven letters to the seven churches, which serve as a panorama of church history from the first century to the days of the tribulation. After those things—that is to say, after the church age ends—a door is opened in heaven. In John 10:9, John records the words of Jesus when He says, "I am the door. If anyone enters by Me, he will be saved."

John also likens the voice of God to the sound of a trumpet, and in Paul's description of the rapture in 1 Thessalonians 4:16, he writes that "the Lord Himself will descend from heaven with a shout . . . and with the trumpet of God." Then the voice calls out and says, "Come up here"—yet another allusion to the rapture. In verse 2, John writes, "Immediately, I was in the Spirit," reminding us that at the rapture, we will be caught up immediately—in the twinkling of an eye. We also see that this coming up signals the beginning of God's judgment on the earth.

In chapters 3 and 4 of Revelation, three "doors" are mentioned, and they are all related. The first is in Revelation 3:8, where Jesus says to the faithful believers in Philadelphia, "I have set before you an open door, and no one can shut it." The first door is the door of evangelism and the gospel. Then in Revelation 3:20, to the last-days church of Laodicea, Jesus says, "I stand at the door and knock." To the compromising and carnal congregations of the last days, the second door is the door of repentance and response. Here now in Revelation 4:1, a door is standing open in heaven, the door of heaven's throne room. The door of the gospel leads us to the door of repentance and response, which then opens up to the door into heaven.

All Christians desire to know more about heaven. Heaven is mentioned hundreds of time in the Bible, and yet, while we know many things about heaven, there is so much that we don't know or understand. There is no shortage of people who claim to have gone to heaven and then have allegedly come back to tell us about it. For $24.95, you can buy their book and read all about it. Their accounts are usually bizarre, to say the least.

In contrast, we have two very trustworthy human witnesses in Scripture who have been to heaven and back: Paul and John. In 2 Corinthians 12, Paul wrote briefly of his experience in heaven and then stated that he was not permitted to speak of what he saw and heard. Here in Revelation, John has also gone up into heaven, but he is instructed to record what he sees and hears. John gives us reliable details and descriptions.

In the movie *Field of Dreams*, Kevin Costner's character has a conversation with his deceased father on a baseball field in the cornfields of Iowa. His father asks him, "Is this heaven?" Costner's character replies, "No, it's Iowa." The father responds, "Iowa? I could have sworn this was heaven." That was an entertaining movie, but believe me when I tell you that none of us will be confusing the throne room in heaven with a cornfield in Iowa!

In verse 1, John looks up and sees a door opened into heaven, and hears the voice of God summoning him. Let me just say a word about the various "heavens" mentioned in the New Testament. When Paul described his heavenly experience in 2 Corinthians 12, he specifically stated that he was caught up into the third heaven. This raises the question: what are the first and second heavens?

The word *heaven* is used in three ways in the Bible:

1. first heaven—the atmosphere: the skies above the earth where birds fly, clouds float, and from which we receive dew, rain, and snow (as found in Gen. 8:2; Deut. 11:11; and Isa. 55:10).
2. second heaven—the universe: the celestial realm of the sun, moon, stars, and planets (as found in Gen. 1:1; 15:5; and Ps. 8:3, which says, "When I consider Your heavens, the work of Your fingers, the moon and stars, which You have ordained, what is man . . . ?").
3. third heaven—the dwelling place of God: where God resides, where He is enthroned, where He renders judgment, and the place from which His blessings flow (as found in 1 Kings 8:30;

Ps. 2:4; Isa. 66:1; Rev. 2:7; and Matt. 6:9, which says, "Our Father, who is in heaven").

By virtue of technology, we have been able to visit the first and second heavens through the efforts and achievements of mankind. We can fly in an airplane into the skies of first heaven. Mankind has also walked on the moon and floated in outer space, in the realm of the second heaven. But apart from God's grace, mercy, and forgiveness, we can never reach the third heaven.

In verse 2, when John is supernaturally and spiritually transported up into heaven, he sees a throne and the One who is sitting on the throne—God the Father. We know this is the Father, since the Holy Spirit is distinguished in verse 5, and since Jesus is standing next to this throne in the next chapter (5:6). The throne in heaven is a key topic here in chapter 4. It is mentioned twelve times just in this chapter. Nevertheless, the throne of God is nothing without the God who sits on that throne, and therefore the central theme of heaven, and of this chapter, is God Himself.

What makes heaven, heaven, is the presence of God. Or to put it another way, if God were not there, it wouldn't be heaven. It would be hell, because one of the primary punishments associated with hell is eternal separation from God. As one minister puts it, "In heaven, God will never hide His face, and Satan will never show his."[1]

But with that having been said, our second point, in verse 2, is *God's throne*. This picture of the Lord God seated on His throne reminds us of one of the most important truths that sustain us here on earth: God is on the throne, and therefore God is in control. The believers in the seven churches to whom John wrote were facing intense persecution and suffering for their faith. But the first thing John shares with them about heaven is that God is on the throne.

The message is the same for you and for me. Whatever difficulty you may be facing, whatever trial, whatever issue, whatever disappointment—God is on the throne, and God is in control. The throne symbolizes God's authority and sovereign rule.

Beginning in verse 3, and continuing through verse 5, we come to our third point: *God's glory*. John is incapable of describing the appearance of God, so he is forced to use comparisons. He describes God's appearance as being like jasper and sardius stones.

In chapter 21, the jasper stone is described as being crystal clear, which probably refers to a diamond. The sardius stone comes from the area of Sardis—the location of one of the seven churches—and is blood-red, like a ruby. Perhaps the best way to understand John's use of these two stones to describe the appearance of God is by comparing it to the breastplate of the high priest in the Old Testament. On that breastplate were twelve stones representing the twelve tribes of Israel. These symbolized how the high priest would keep God's people close to his heart in prayer and in sacrificial offerings.

Sardius and jasper were the first and last stones on the breastplate of the high priest. It is worth noting that these two stones are listed here in the order of jasper and sardius. But on the breastplate, sardius was the first stone, while jasper was the twelfth (or last) stone. Perhaps this reversal of order reflects the fact that in the priestly ministry of the Old Testament, the people were looking forward to God's ultimate redemption, whereas here in heaven, we are looking from the other direction, and God's people have already been redeemed.

At the same time, there was a rainbow all around the throne that was emerald green. I wonder whether L. Frank Baum, who wrote *The Wizard of Oz* and created the Emerald City (residence of the great and powerful Oz), got his idea from Scripture. In any case, as with the jasper and sardius stones, we can interpret the rainbow from what we read in the Old Testament.

It's interesting to note that the rainbow is mentioned in both the first and the last books of the Bible—Genesis and Revelation. The rainbow in Genesis, which appeared after the global flood judgment, was the symbol of God's promise that God would never destroy the earth again with a flood (Gen. 9:11–17). The rainbow, therefore, reminds us of God's grace and mercy, as well as how God has kept His promise. The fact that the first verses in this chapter paint us a picture of the rapture and the safe arrival of believers into heaven before God's judgment falls upon the earth is perhaps also symbolized by the rainbow around the throne. The rainbow is a symbol of promise. God has safely delivered His people into heaven, just as He promised; God always keeps His promises.

Now we come to verse 4, and to some fascinating information. "Around the throne were twenty-four thrones, and on the thrones I saw twenty-four elders sitting, clothed in white robes; and they had crowns of gold on their heads." Much discussion has come from this verse in regard to who these twenty-four elders are. Are they angels? Or are they some segment of God's people in heaven? If so, which segment? First of all, these elders are seated on thrones, and nowhere in Scripture do we ever find angels sitting on thrones or ruling. According to Hebrews, the role and responsibility of angels is that of ministering spirits; they do the will of God and minister to God's people (Heb. 1:14). They faithfully obey God in everything—with no questions asked.

The Greek word used here for "elders" is *presbuteros*, from which we get our English word *presbytery*. It is never used of angels in Scripture but only of men. We rarely find angels described in terms of specific numbers either, whereas here we have twenty-four elders on twenty-four thrones. The Bible only tells us there is a countless number of angels.

Also, these elders had crowns of gold on their heads, something never promised to angels. In fact, the promises to receive crowns of gold, to be clothed in white, and to sit on thrones in heaven were given to believers in the seven churches who remained faithful (Rev. 2:10; 3:5, 21). So it's clear that this group is not made up of angels and is therefore human. This leads us to the next question: who are these people? We can't answer this question with absolute certainty; it seems most likely that this group represents God's redeemed people in heaven. Faithful believers are promised to rule and reign with Christ; in verse 6 of chapter 1, we are promised that God "will make us kings and priests."

In the Old Testament, Israel is represented by the twelve tribes; in the New Testament, the church is represented by the twelve apostles. So this group of twenty-four elders undoubtedly represents God's redeemed people, from both Old and New Testaments. Prior to Jesus's death and resurrection, Old Testament believers went to the paradise side of Hades. We see an example of this in the story Jesus told of a believer named Lazarus and an unnamed man who was unsaved. Both went to Hades when they died, but Lazarus went to the side of Abraham's bosom and was in comfort, while the unsaved went to the other side in torment (see Luke 16).

After Jesus rose from the dead and ascended to heaven, He brought with Him into heaven the spirits of all the saints who had died prior to His ascension. And in 2 Corinthians 5:8, we read that when be-lievers are absent from the body (speaking of physical death), they are immediately present with the Lord. So the spirits of all believers, both Old Testament and New Testament saints, are with Jesus in heaven. The twenty-four elders, then, represent all those believers in heaven. Later on, in chapter 21 of Revelation, we read that the heavenly city will have the names of the twelve tribes of Israel on its gates and the names of the twelve apostles on its foundations.

In verse 5 of chapter 4, we read that lightning, thunder, and voices proceed from the throne. Those are all symbols of judgment, and this lets us know that a storm of judgment is about to come upon the earth. I get very excited when I hear the thunder approaching in the distance. I absolutely love thunder and lightning. However, I have to curb my enthusiasm, because in the past, as soon as I heard the thunder, I wanted to go running outside. Obviously, that can be dangerous.

With our technology, we are able to track severe weather—often-times before it strikes—which allows people to prepare. Here in our text, these are storm warnings coming from the throne of God. When this storm of judgment arrives, no one will be running toward the storm but rather away from it. Nevertheless, it will be worldwide, and no one will be able to hide or escape. In the last part of verse 5, John sees the Holy Spirit, represented by seven lamps of burning fire, which are the seven Spirits of God. A better translation would be "the sevenfold appearance of the Holy Spirit" (see Isa. 11:2).

In verse 6, we read about the area in front of the throne, which John says has the appearance of a sea of glass, like crystal. John writes in chapter 21 that there is no sea in heaven, so his words are an attempt to describe that area in front of the throne. I've read some suggestions from commentators as to what this sea of glass represents, and my conclusion is that we don't know. But it is worth noting that in Exodus 24, when Moses, Aaron, and seventy of the leaders of Israel were on Mount Sinai, they saw God and the area underneath God had that same clear, glassy appearance.

Next to the throne were four living creatures. Ezekiel 10 tells us that these are a high order of angels called cherubim. Cherubim are also mentioned in Genesis 3 and Exodus 25. These have the distinct privilege and honor of worshiping God. Day and night, without stopping, they help to lead the heavenly worship of God on the throne. So our fourth point of this passage is *God's choir.*

As we read John's description of the four living creatures, we might be tempted to conclude that these angelic beings are bizarre, or even grotesque. That probably comes from watching too many *Twilight Zone* marathons on New Year's Day, and I truly believe that the exact opposite is true. They reflect the beauty and holiness of God and are therefore very beautiful themselves. The fact that they are full of eyes in the front and in the back means they're probably a lot like mothers: they see everything! These eyes symbolize their full awareness of everything.

They have six wings, and in the Old Testament book of Isaiah—chapter 6—we learn that seraphim angels, very similar to the cherubim, use only two wings for flying. With another two wings they cover their faces, and with the other two wings they cover their feet. This represents the fact that they are seeing a holy God and standing on holy ground before the throne. No wonder they worship God by crying out, "Holy, holy, holy." God is characterized as being love, and light, and life, and mercy, and so forth. But the one word that best captures the essence of God, and all that He is, is the word *holy.*

The act of worship occupies the throne room of heaven, and worship is taken very seriously there. Perhaps we should remember and reflect on that more often. Coming into church late, leaving early, talking to others, texting on a cell phone, daydreaming, doodling, and other such behavior during a time of worship is not taking worship very seriously. Sometimes, the perspective of some believers is that it's okay to miss some or all of the worship time in a church service, because the most important part is the Bible study. But I don't read of any Bible studies taking place in heaven. I *do* read that everyone and everything is worshiping God!

Back in verse 7, the four cherubim are described as having the appearance of a lion, a calf, a man, and an eagle. In the second century, the church leader and writer Irenaeus saw a comparison between this description and the fourfold way in which Jesus is presented in the four Gospels.

- Matthew's Gospel presents Jesus as the Lion of the Tribe of Judah.

82

- Mark's Gospel presents Jesus as a servant, symbolized by the calf.
- Luke's Gospel focuses on the human side of Jesus as a man.
- John's Gospel focuses on His deity, symbolized by the flying eagle.

So as these four cherubim remain close to the throne, worshiping God the Father in His holiness, they also reflect the ministry of God the Son, as portrayed in the Gospels.

In verse 9, we find that whenever those cherubim worship God—giving Him glory, honor, and thanksgiving—the twenty-four elders, who represent believers in heaven, cast their crowns before the throne. Hence the title of this chapter, "Casting Crowns."

I must say that the first time I heard the name of the Christian group Casting Crowns, I thought, "Now that's a great name for a Christian band!" When we get to heaven, and we have received our rewards in the form of crowns, we will be worshiping God. In doing so, we will feel compelled to cast those crowns before the Lord. This act will be prompted by our recognition of God's holiness and that it's all about Him.

So we end this chapter in verse 11, where we read that it is "*You*, O Lord, who is worthy to receive glory and honor and power; for You created all things, and by Your will they exist and were created." We were created by God—to know Him and to worship Him. Therefore, each and every time we worship, we are fulfilling the very purpose for which we have been created. Worship is the purpose for creation and the priority of heaven.

8

The Lion and the Lamb

Revelation 5:1–14

Sam and Charlie were lifelong buddies, with many things in common—most of all, their love of baseball. In their many discussions, they often wondered whether there was baseball in heaven. One day, they made a pact that whoever went to heaven first would find a way to let the other one know whether or not there was baseball in heaven. Not long afterward, Sam passed away and went to heaven. A few nights later, Charlie woke up in the middle of the night when he heard Sam's voice. "Is that you, Sam?" Charlie asked.

"Yeah, it's me!" Sam replied. "Remember that pact we made? Well, I've got good news and bad news for you."

"What's the good news?" Charlie asked.

"There's baseball in heaven!" Sam replied.

"That's so wonderful," said Charlie. "So what's the bad news?"

"Well," Sam replied, "you're the starting pitcher on Friday!"

I seriously doubt there will be baseball in heaven, but as we come to chapter 5 in Revelation, we do learn that there will be thrones, angels, worship, and, best of all, Father, Son, and Spirit. In Revelation 4, we saw God the Creator seated on the throne. Here in chapter 5, we will see Jesus the Savior standing next to the throne.

> And I saw in the right hand of Him who sat on the throne a scroll written inside and on the back, sealed with seven seals. Then I saw a strong angel proclaiming with a loud voice, "Who is worthy to open the scroll and to loose its seals?" And no one in heaven or on the earth or under the earth was able to open the scroll, or to look at it. So I wept much, because no one was found worthy to open and read the scroll, or to look at it. But one of the elders said to me, "Do not weep. Behold, the Lion of the tribe of Judah, the Root of David, has prevailed to open the scroll and to loose its seven seals." And I looked, and behold, in the midst of the throne and of the four living creatures, and in the midst of the elders, stood a Lamb as though it had been slain, having seven horns and seven eyes, which are the seven Spirits of God sent out into all the earth. Then He came and took the scroll out of the right hand of Him who sat on the throne. Now when He had taken the scroll, the four living creatures and the twenty-four elders fell down before the Lamb, each having a harp, and golden bowls full of incense, which are the prayers of the saints. And they sang a new song, saying: "You are worthy to take the scroll, and to open its seals; for You were slain, and have redeemed us to God by Your blood out of every tribe and tongue and people and nation, and have made us kings and priests to our God; and we shall reign on the earth." Then I looked, and I heard the voice of many angels around the throne, the living creatures, and the elders; and the number of them was ten thousand times ten thousand, and thousands of thousands, saying with a loud voice: "Worthy is the Lamb who was slain to receive power and riches and wisdom, and strength and honor and glory and blessing!" And every creature which is in heaven and on the earth and under the earth and such as are in the sea, and all that are in them, I heard saying: "Blessing and honor and glory and power be to Him who sits on the throne, and to the Lamb, forever and ever!" Then the four living creatures said, "Amen!" And the twenty-four elders fell down and worshiped Him who lives forever and ever.
>
> Revelation 5:1–14

John sees a scroll in the right hand of God. As the chapter progresses, John also tells us what he heard. John doesn't have to sing the popular Christian song "I Can Only Imagine," because he is experiencing firsthand the wonders of heaven. John describes a rolled-up scroll in the right hand of God. This scroll has writing on both the front and the back, and it is securely fastened with seven seals. The obvious question is: what is this scroll? Many have called it the title deed of the earth. Others see it as the record of redemption. Some see it as an overview of last-days judgment. Before we try to answer this question, let's consider the information given to us here.

A scroll was made out of a long piece of papyrus or animal skin, which was rolled up from both ends to the middle. The fact that this scroll has writing on both sides indicates to us that it is complete, and nothing can be added. It is also securely fastened with seven seals. In John's day, this was typical of important Roman documents, particularly title deeds and wills. In verse 2, John witnessed a strong angel with a loud voice presenting the question: "Who is worthy to open the scroll and to loose its seals?"

The identity of this strong angel is not given to us. The Greek word for "strong" means "mighty and powerful." This could very well be an archangel such as Michael or perhaps even Gabriel. In the previous chapter, we began to talk about the different orders of angels as we read about cherubim, which are similar to seraphim. There is another, apparently higher, rank of angels called archangels. Michael is described as being an archangel in the book of Jude. Many commentators also believe that Gabriel is an archangel, but I can't find anywhere in Scripture where it states that he is.

Angels have names, but only three are identified by name in the Bible: Michael and Gabriel, who are holy angels, and Lucifer, the fallen angel who is now the devil. The angel in verse 2 is described by John as a strong angel, and he may possibly be Michael or Gabriel, but we simply don't know for certain. References to angels occur seventy-one times in the book of Revelation—more than in any other book of the Bible. Throughout Scripture, from Genesis to Revelation, angels play a vital role in the plans and purposes of God.

In verse 3, we learn in response to the question posed by this angel that no one in heaven, on earth, or anywhere else in the universe is worthy to open this seven-sealed scroll. Everyone remains silent in response to this question, including the archangels, cherubim, and seraphim—as well as all the heroes of faith such as Abraham, Moses, David, Elijah, Peter, and Paul. In verse 4, this prompted John to weep.

If the angel had asked, "Who is willing to open the scroll?" everyone that I mentioned probably would have stepped forward. The angel didn't ask, "Who is willing?" but rather, "Who is worthy?"

John was not crying quietly to himself; the Greek word means that John was expressing loud, emotional grief. It has been well said that you can tell a lot about people by three things: what makes them laugh, what makes them angry, and what makes them cry.[1] This is the only place in Scripture where we read that there are tears in heaven. When we get to chapter 21, we will read that one of the many blessings of the new heaven is that there will be no more tears (Rev. 21:4).

As John is weeping profusely, one of the elders speaks to him. Notice that it wasn't one of the angels but one of the elders. In the last chapter, we deduced that the twenty-four elders in heaven represent the Old and New Testament saints in heaven. It makes sense that an elder would encourage John to stop crying and then point him to Jesus. God's plan of salvation through Jesus was accomplished on behalf of God's people, not God's angels. Therefore, it seems fitting that one of the redeemed saints in heaven would encourage John by directing his attention toward Jesus.

In heaven, Jesus is the source of hope, as one of the elders says, "Do not weep. Behold the Lion of the tribe of Judah. . . . He [can] open the scroll and loosen the seals." Scripture foretold that the Messiah would descend from the tribe of Judah. Jesus was a descendant of David on both his father's and his mother's side and was from the tribe of Judah (Gen. 49:8–10; Isa. 11:1, 10).

As we come to verse 6, John turns his attention to Jesus expecting to see a lion and instead sees a lamb. If you were choosing a symbol for strength and authority, you wouldn't choose a lamb. During college football season I am always reminded of how good, and of how bad, some college mascots are. If you are playing college football, you don't want a wimpy mascot. A Wisconsin Badger isn't too bad, since badgers are pretty feisty. I give high marks to the Georgia Bulldogs, the Auburn Tigers, and the Iowa Hawkeyes. But some mascots sound less than fierce, and they know who they are.

Jesus is both "the Lion and the Lamb." Nearly thirty times in Revelation Jesus is called the Lamb, and the word literally means a pet lamb. In His deity, in His majesty, in His authority, and in His sovereignty, Jesus is indeed the Lion. But in His humanity and in

His humility, Jesus is the Lamb. The Lion and the Lamb are one and the same Person. Jesus came as a Lamb at His first coming, and He will return as a Lion at His second coming.

Remember that this same apostle John, some sixty years earlier, had seen the risen Lord Jesus in His glorified body before Jesus ascended back into heaven. Now John sees this same Jesus the Lamb, still bearing the marks of the crucifixion. I may be splitting hairs here, but it is my opinion that we will not see His scars from the crucifixion as much as we will see His wounds. In John 20, Thomas had missed the first appearance of the risen Jesus in the upper room with the other disciples. When his fellow disciples told him the good news that Jesus was alive again in His glorified body, Thomas refused to believe until he could see Jesus for himself. Thomas said, "Unless I see His hands and put my finger into the wound from the nails, and put my hand into His side, I refuse to believe" (John 20:25 paraphrased). About a week later, Jesus appeared to the disciples once again, and immediately Jesus addressed the doubts of Thomas, saying to him, "Put your finger here and look at My hands; and put your hand into the wound in My side. Stop refusing to believe and start believing" (John 20:27 paraphrased). So it seems to me that we will not see scars but rather the wounds of His crucifixion. Either way, someone said well that "the only work of mankind that we'll see in heaven is the crucifixion wounds of Jesus."[2]

John continues to describe Jesus the Lamb as having "seven horns and seven eyes." In this vision, John is allowed to see Jesus in full power, represented by the seven horns, and full knowledge, represented by the seven eyes. Seven is the number of perfection. In fact, what we see here are the divine attributes of the Son of God: He is omnipotent (all-powerful), omniscient (all-knowing), and omnipresent (present everywhere).

Then we come to a climactic moment in heaven: Jesus steps forward and takes the scroll from the Father on the throne. The entire scene, from John coming up into heaven to Jesus taking the scroll, has been building toward this moment. Who is worthy to take the scroll and open it up? The answer is Jesus, the Lamb. Who is worthy to loose the seals? The answer is Jesus, the Lion. As we will see in the next chapter, as Jesus opens this scroll, seal by seal, devastating and divine judgments are released on the earth. When the seventh seal is opened, it releases the seven trumpet judgments on the earth. Then after the seventh trumpet sounds, we read about seven bowl judgments.

So we come back to our original question: what is this scroll? Is it the title deed to the earth, the record of redemption, an overview of last-days judgment, or something else? I'm not confident that I can answer this question with absolute certainty, but what I see in the chapters that follow, as each seal is opened, is God's divine judgment on the world and the work of redemption continuing to the millennial kingdom.

In verse 8, when Jesus takes the scroll, the saints in heaven fall down before the Lamb, each one having a harp and golden bowls of incense, as they burst into a new song. When Jesus took the scroll, the weeping ended and the worship began. It was the great Bible expositor Donald Gray Barnhouse who made the observation that there are four things out of place in the universe today:

1. the church, which should be in heaven
2. Israel, which should be occupying all of the land promised to her
3. Satan, who belongs in the lake of fire
4. Christ, who should be seated on His throne reigning[3]

All four of those things will soon be made right when Christ takes the scroll from the Father. The harps that we read about in verse 8 symbolize worship. When I was growing up, and a cartoon character was killed, that character became an angel, floated up to heaven, and began strumming on a harp. Those old cartoons apparently got one out of three right. Cartoon characters do not go to heaven, and when people die they do not become angels. However, we do read about the saints having harps in their hands, so all those Saturday morning hours of watching cartoons weren't a complete waste of time.

The golden bowls full of incense are identified for us in the text as the prayers of believers. This is a vivid reminder to us that God remembers all of our prayers. In Psalm 56, David writes that God keeps all of our tears in His bottle, and here in Revelation 5, we see that He keeps our prayers as well.

In verse 9, the saints in heaven, which include you and me, are singing a new song to the Lamb. The lyrics include the important words, "You are worthy." That's what worship is really all about—declaring the worthiness of God through praise and adoration. The lyrics in verse 9 remind us that Jesus was slain and that it was by His shed blood that we have been redeemed. By the way, the Greek word used for "slain" in verse 6, and again here in verse 9, means "to butcher" and "to slaughter."[4] Jesus wasn't just killed; He was sacrificed on the cross. The price that was required for Jesus to become our Redeemer and to save us was His violent death and bloodshed.

Notice at the end of verse 9 that those He has redeemed with His blood and who are worshiping Him in heaven are those "out of every tribe and tongue and people and nation." Only the church fits that description, so this is additional evidence that the church will be in heaven as the tribulation period commences.

In verse 11, we read about innumerable angels—"ten thousand times ten thousand, and thousands of thousands." The word used here in trying to communicate the number of angels is *myriad*—there were myriads of myriads of angels; that is to say, more than could be numbered. This would be like trying to count the stars at night. *Myriads* is the highest numerical word in the Greek language.

Once again, the subject is angels, so look carefully at verse 12. The angels were "*saying* with a loud voice . . . ." The saints were *singing*, but the angels are saying. Why do I bring this up? This may rock your theology a little bit, but there is no evidence in the Bible that the angels sing! Two of my most respected Bible commentators, Warren Wiersbe and John MacArthur, both concur on this. The only verse in Scripture that might appear to indicate that angels are singing is Job 38:7. However, a closer study of that verse reveals that at the beginning of creation, God says, the stars He created were singing, and the angels were shouting.

You might remember the angels rejoicing at the birth of Christ in the shepherd fields of Bethlehem, but once again, the angels praised God by saying, "Glory to God in the highest," and not by singing. Others might remember Luke 15:10, where we read that "there is joy in the presence of the angels of God over one sinner who repents." But it doesn't say that the angels are singing, and it doesn't even say that the angels themselves are rejoicing. It simply says that "there is joy in the presence" of the angels. It probably means that the angels are rejoicing, as are those who are in their presence, which may be referring to believers already in heaven.

When we think about this discussion, it makes a lot of sense. The angels are not the recipients of God's salvation. God provides salvation and redemption for fallen mankind but not for fallen angels (Heb. 2:16). So while angels praise God and rejoice in Him, they *speak* words of praise. But we, as the recipients of God's salvation, have something to sing about! It appears that singing is the privilege reserved for God's saints, who have experienced firsthand the joy of salvation. When Israel passed through the Red Sea on dry land and reached the other side, they sang the first recorded praise song in Scripture—a song of redemption and deliverance.

In verse 14, we read that the cherubim say "Amen," while the twenty-four elders, representing God's people in heaven, worship God. In professional golf, the most prestigious tournament of the year is undoubtedly the Masters, played each year in Augusta, Georgia. It's a very difficult and challenging course—particularly the eleventh, twelfth, and thirteenth holes, which are so treacherous that they have the longstanding nickname of "Amen Corner." Evidently, golfers need to hold their breath and pray through those three difficult holes. Well, there is an "Amen Corner" in heaven—*amen* simply means "so be it." It is a word of affirmation. The saints are singing and the angels are agreeing.

Sadly, while the church and saints are in heaven worshiping God, it is business as usual for the people on earth, as we will see in the next chapter. As it was in the days of Noah, the people go about their daily lives ignoring all the warning signs of the last days. But one day soon, Jesus will take the scroll and open the seals, and His divine judgment will begin to fall, even as the rains fell in the days of Noah.

9

The Four Horsemen of the Apocalypse

Revelation 6:1–8

A man bought a horse from a retired preacher living out in the open spaces of Wyoming. After the deal was finalized, the pastor told the man, "You need to know something. I trained this horse to take off on the command of 'Hallelujah' and to stop on the command of 'Amen.'" The man didn't give it much thought, figuring that he would retrain the horse. The first time the man took the horse out riding, it wouldn't budge. Eventually, the man remembered what the old preacher had told him, and he said, "Hallelujah." Sure enough, the horse took off immediately.

Before long, the horse started to increase its speed. Suddenly, the man noticed that they were galloping toward the brink of a steep cliff. "Whoa," the man yelled, but the horse kept galloping faster. "Whoa . . . stop . . . halt . . . quit!" the man yelled, but the horse kept going. Finally, the man remembered and yelled "Amen!" and the horse came to a screeching halt, just a couple feet from the edge of the cliff. The man was so relieved he looked up into the sky and said, "Hallelujah!"

Horses and horsemen are mentioned nearly three hundred times in the Bible. I think it is safe to say that the most well-known are in the book of Revelation: the four horsemen that appear at the beginning of the tribulation, as well as the white horse on which the Lord Jesus Christ will ride when He appears at the end of the tribulation.

I don't have much experience with horses, but I have always admired their intelligence and beauty. But as Billy Graham points out in his book *Approaching Hoofbeats*, the four horses and their riders are anything but beautiful. Graham writes, "They are terrible and terrifying. The scenes in which they are described are among the most dreadful in the Bible. Many great painters of history have tried to depict this on canvas—but no artist can fully portray the wonder and horror of these events."[1] Let's now examine what happens on the earth when Jesus opens the seven seals in heaven.

> Now I saw when the Lamb opened one of the seals; and I heard one of the four living creatures saying with a voice like thunder, "Come and see." And I looked, and behold, a white horse. He who sat on it had a bow; and a crown was given to him, and he went out conquering and to conquer. When He opened the second seal, I heard the second living creature saying, "Come and see." Another horse, fiery red, went out. And it was granted to the one who sat on it to take peace from the earth, and that people should kill one another; and there was given to him a great sword. When He opened the third seal, I heard the third living creature say, "Come and see." So I looked, and behold, a black horse, and he who sat on it had a pair of scales in his hand. And I heard a voice in the midst of the four living creatures saying, "A quart of wheat for a denarius, and three quarts of barley for a denarius; and do not harm the oil and the wine." When He opened the fourth seal, I heard the voice of the fourth living creature saying, "Come and see." So I looked, and behold, a pale horse. And the name of him who sat on it was Death, and Hades followed with him. And power was given to them over a fourth of the earth, to kill with sword, with hunger, with death, and by the beasts of the earth.
>
> Revelation 6:1–8

After the blessings of God's divine worship in chapters 4 and 5, we now begin to see God's divine wrath in chapter 6. The next fourteen chapters, or nearly two-thirds of Revelation, are devoted to describing the tribulation period. The greatest sorrow and judgment this world will ever experience is the tribulation. In the Old Testament, it is commonly called "the day of the LORD" (Zech. 14:1). It is also called "the time of Jacob's trouble," because of the severe persecution that Israel will face, particularly in the final three and a half years (Jer. 30:7). For Israel, it will be a time of great trouble but also a time of great conversion.

The coming world leader, called the Antichrist, will make a covenant with Israel and others in the Middle East, bringing about a temporary and false peace. Part of the Antichrist's covenant will allow Israel to rebuild its temple. But as Daniel and Jesus both prophesied, the Antichrist will break that covenant in the middle of the seven-year tribulation and commit what is called "the abomination of desolation." This is when the Antichrist will take possession of the Jewish temple, insert his own image, and require the whole world to worship him as God.

In the New Testament, this seven-year period is commonly called the tribulation and the great tribulation. Oftentimes, the term *tribulation* is describing the first three and a half years, while *great tribulation* describes the final three and a half years. The entire seven-year period depicts what is going to take place on the earth following the removal of God's people in the rapture of the church. The end of the tribulation reaches its climax in the battle of Armageddon and the second coming of Jesus Christ.

As Jesus begins to open the seven seals on the scroll, the opening of each seal brings a specific judgment upon the earth. So we move from joy and jubilation in chapters 4 and 5 to judgment in chapter 6.

About twenty years ago, my wife and I were driving through one of the most beautiful places in the United States, Yellowstone National Park. The natural beauty of that park cannot be overstated, with its majestic trees, mountains, waterfalls, lakes, rivers, and wild animals. To this day, it remains one of the most beautiful places I have ever visited. But as we were driving along, suddenly the landscape went from absolute beauty to burnt devastation. The summer fires of 1988 had turned mammoth trees into smoldering sticks, leaving a black and barren landscape. A series of lightning strikes had ignited fires that burnt nearly 1.5 million acres. The sudden and dramatic difference between that beauty and devastation reminds me of this sudden shift from the heavenly splendor in chapter 5 to the earthly devastation of chapter 6.

For the most part, the opening of the first four seals correlates with the judgments in the first half of the tribulation, while the final three seals connect to the rest of the tribulation. As mentioned before, when the seventh seal is opened, it releases the seven *trumpet judgments*, and the seventh trumpet judgment unleashes the seven *bowl judgments*. So we find that all these judgments are essentially wrapped up within these seven seals.

As the first four seals are opened, the same pattern follows: Jesus breaks open a seal, which prompts one of the four living creatures (or cherubim angels) to invite John to "come and see" the judgments of the last days. Each of these first four judgments is represented by four horses of different colors and their riders.

Amazingly, only two verses are given to describe each of these first four seal judgments. What they describe is not only global but also almost unimaginable. The scene in verses 1–8 toggles back and forth between heaven and earth, shifting between John witnessing the Lord opening the seals and the corresponding outcome on earth.

Each of these first four judgments corresponds to what Jesus described to His disciples in Matthew 24, in the Olivet Discourse. As Jesus and the disciples were on the Mount of Olives, discussing the end times, Jesus laid out for them these various events. The chronological order, here in Revelation, is the same as what Jesus described in Matthew 24.

As Jesus breaks open the first seal, one of the four cherubim calls out with a loud voice that booms like a clap of thunder, and he invites John to come and see. In the Greek, it is not literally "come and see" but simply "Come!" So the statement of the angel appears to be both an invitation to John to view what happens next as well as the command, on behalf of God, for judgment to come forth.

In verse 2, John looked, and what he saw was a white horse with a rider on it. In the rider's hand was a bow, and a crown was given to him as he went out conquering. Over the years, some commentators have explained that this rider on a white horse is the Lord Jesus

Christ. They base this on the fact that Jesus is pictured as riding a white horse in Revelation 19, at His second coming. Since we understand that Jesus is riding a white horse in chapter 19, they conclude that He must also be riding the white horse here in chapter 6.

Many other commentators disagree and, in my opinion, for good reason. First of all, Jesus is in heaven in verse 1, breaking open the first seal. So the white horse rider on earth is not Jesus. Second, while it is clear that the white horse rider in chapter 19 is Jesus, this rider in chapter 6 is not identified. Third, while both riders are wearing crowns, two different Greek words are used. Here in chapter 6, it is a *stephanos*, or victor's crown, like the olive branch given in the Olympic-style games of the first century. But in chapter 19, at the second coming, it is a *diadem*, or royal crown worn by kings, and Jesus is the King of kings. Fourth, this white horse rider has a bow, while Jesus will return at His second coming with the sword of His mouth.

Therefore, this white horse rider at the beginning of the tribulation period is not Jesus Christ, but a counterfeit Messiah called the Antichrist. This comes as no surprise, because Antichrist is exactly that—a demonic imitation of the real Messiah. The Antichrist both imitates and opposes the real Christ. So the tribulation period begins in chapter 6 with the emergence of the Antichrist and concludes in chapter 19 with the return of Jesus Christ.

Notice that this crown is *given* to the rider. Through his political and economic deceptions, along with his promise of peace and prosperity, the Antichrist will be given his authority with global support and cooperation. All genuine believers will have been raptured just prior to this, so even the religious people who remain will unite to support him. He will quickly become the new world leader. This is supported by the fact that the Antichrist has a bow but no arrows. This symbolizes how he will achieve a conquest: not with military power but with demonic deception and cunning. So the first thing to note is *the white horse of false peace.*

In Daniel 9, we are told that a prince will arise in the last days, and he will rise to power by "confirming a covenant with many for one week" (v. 27). The event that will catapult this coming leader into world prominence is his negotiation of a Middle East peace pact between Israel and its neighboring nations. But as we know from Revelation, it will be both a false peace and a very short-lived peace.

One thing that has intrigued me about this scenario is how the Antichrist will rationally explain the sudden disappearance of millions of Christians around the world. Somehow, he will weave it all together into his propaganda. Perhaps he will convince the remaining world population that God has judged the Christians for (allegedly) being too intolerant and too judgmental. Since Christians all over the world will disappear instantaneously, he can explain that God has punished all of them. "God has wiped those born-again troublemakers off the face of the earth," the Antichrist might say, "so we must commit as one to unity in government, unity in religion, and unity in peace."

Then he can tackle the Middle East dilemma by saying, "Everyone is going to have to give and take to make this work. What does Israel want? They want peace, and they want to rebuild their temple on the Temple Mount area. But the Muslims control that area, and their Dome of the Rock stands there. And what do the Arabs and Muslims want? They want those areas in Israel that they feel belong to them—areas like the Gaza Strip and the Golan Heights. So this is what we need to do," the Antichrist might say. "Let Israel rebuild their temple, since there's plenty of room on the Temple Mount area. But in return, Israel must release control of the Gaza Strip and the Golan Heights. Now everyone is happy, and we have peace. Come on now; can't we all just get along?" This is obviously speculation, but it does give us some sense of how things might unfold.

Because people are desperate for peace and want to avoid war at any cost, they will quickly become seduced by the deceptions of the Antichrist, whose demonic influence will cause people to believe his lie. Paul wrote that because people will have refused to believe the truth of God in the gospel, they will be quick to believe the lie of Satan and the strong delusion that is coming upon the world (2 Thess. 2:11–12).

Jesus breaks open the second seal, bringing forth the second horse, which is fiery red. This color is also used to describe Satan the dragon in chapter 12. So once again, this rider is the Antichrist. He immediately brings about the removal of peace from all over the world, as people begin to kill one another. This rider receives a sword with which to fight. This charismatic leader and counterfeit Christ who was able to bring about temporary peace is the same one who takes it away. This is *the red horse of war*. In Matthew 24:6–7, Jesus said, "You will hear of wars and rumors of wars . . . nation will rise against nation, and kingdom against kingdom." The Greek word for the sword that is given to the red horse rider describes a short stabbing sword, like that used by a soldier, or the dagger of an assassin. So rather than typical warfare, this refers more to civil war, rebellion, revolt, assassination, and terrorism. Just as the Antichrist was skilled at deceiving people with false peace, he will be capable of subduing people through military force.

In verse 5, Jesus breaks open the third seal in heaven, which prompts the appearance of a black horse. The rider is holding a pair of scales in his hand. Then the voice of God thunders forth from the midst of the four cherubim who surround the throne, and God declares, "A quart of wheat for a denarius, and three quarts of barley for a denarius, and do not harm the oil and the wine." This third horse is *the black horse of famine*. Jesus foretold of famine in Matthew 24:7.

Global famine is the natural consequence of global warfare. Crops, fields, and food supplies are destroyed during warfare. What little food remains skyrockets in price, so the average person can hardly afford it. My dad used to tell me stories of having very little to eat during the Great Depression. He was quite poor while growing up, and he shared many of his hard-luck stories with me. On one of his birthdays, I found the perfect card to give him. On the front cover it read, "Happy Birthday Dad—I knew you'd appreciate this card." Inside, it read, "I had to walk five miles, uphill, barefoot, in the snow, just to buy you this card." He actually thought it was pretty funny!

The scales in the hand of the Antichrist, riding on the black horse, clearly symbolize the serious food shortage during the tribulation period. So there is no misunderstanding, God Himself even declares that a denarius, which was one day's wage, would barely be enough to buy a quart of wheat. A quart of wheat is barely enough food to sustain one person. So a person will spend his or her entire daily earnings to buy just enough food to feed himself. If someone has a family to feed, his next option is to take that one day's earnings and buy barley instead. Barley was a cheaper, much less nutritious grain, which was given to livestock, but at least one could buy three times as much of it. If a family is larger than three people, they will be splitting those smaller rations even further. Two parents with four kids will attempt to survive on half-rations of barley.

The words, "Do not harm the oil and the wine," are not completely clear. Many commentators explain that those items were associated with luxury, so the phrase means that the rich will continue in luxury while the common person suffers. But another explanation makes more sense to me. Oil was the common item used for cooking, while wine was mixed with water to help purify it. So in context, food staples such as wheat and barley will become scarce, and items such as oil and wine will become critical and must not be harmed or wasted.

This brings us to verse 7, where Jesus breaks open the fourth seal. In verse 8, a fourth horse emerges, and this horse is a sickly pale color. The rider represents death and Hades, or death and the grave. This is *the pale horse of death.* The Greek word here for "pale" is *chloros,* from which we get our English words *chlorine* and *chlorophyll.* It is the color of a decomposing corpse. So we are not surprised to read that the rider on this horse is identified as death and Hades. Death claims the body, and Hades claims the soul.

Worse yet, this death will claim one-fourth of the world's population. Today, there are nearly seven billion people on earth, which means that more than one and a half billion people will be killed when the fourth seal is broken open. The cause of death is fourfold: the sword, hunger, death, and wild beasts. Let's examine each one of these.

1. the sword—We have already discussed the outbreak of war, including civil war—not only nations fighting other nations but neighbors fighting their neighbors. Crime is bad enough today, as people are willing to kill each other over small amounts of money, or the right to some local turf. But imagine what will happen when there is a severe food shortage and it costs everything a person can earn to feed one's family. No one who attempts to obey the law and do the right thing will last very long, so it will quickly become survival of the fittest. It is also quite probable that this "sword" will include capital punish-

ment instituted by the Antichrist's government, which executes anyone who rebels against his authority.

2. hunger and famine—These have also been discussed, and once again, they will reach unprecedented proportions. The more death, the more disease; the more destruction, the greater the food shortage.

3. death—This seems redundant; however, when Jesus described this series of events to His disciples in Matthew 24, the next thing Jesus listed, in chronological order after famines, is pestilence—pestilence and disease. These fit in with war, death, and famine, because pestilence and disease are natural consequences to these events. In recent times, we have seen E. Coli bacteria, Mad Cow disease, and West Nile virus in limited outbreaks. Eventually, some such strains will take off like microscopic wildfires, killing untold numbers of people.

4. wild beasts—On the surface, we're already seeing the increase of wild animal attacks against people, as animal habitats and food supplies continue to shrink. The number of stories in the news about wild bears, mountain lions, and coyotes attacking people and pets continues to increase. When we factor in death, decay, disease, and food shortage, we can easily envision the animal kingdom growing out of control. But below the surface, it is undoubtedly worse, and those wild animals will most certainly include rats. For centuries, rats have been carriers of the most deadly diseases and the destroyers of food supplies.

None of these things is fun to read about. But we must remember some important facts:

1. Genuine believers will never experience these things. We will have been raptured up to heaven, where we'll be worshiping God and rejoicing in our salvation.

2. This is God's divine and righteous judgment. God takes no delight in the death of the wicked. God is not willing that any should perish; God's heart, and God's desire, is for people to be saved. But at some point, those who adamantly refuse and reject God and His gospel message will reap the consequences of their freewill decision.

3. This should prompt us to pray for the unsaved. We all have unsaved family members, friends, co-workers, and neighbors who need our prayers.
4. We should witness to and invite the unsaved to church. I know that this is oftentimes met with ridicule and rejection from the unsaved person, but the stakes are far too high not to try to reach them.
5. Those who have never come to Christ should do so before it is too late. Many people—more than one and a half billion of them—are going to die in the first stages of the tribulation period simply because they refused to come to Christ while they still had the chance. No wonder the Bible declares, "Behold, now is the accepted time; behold, now is the day of salvation" (2 Cor. 6:2 KJV).

10

Heavenly and Earthly Responses

Revelation 6:9–16

Everyone has fears that they deal with, which is not always a bad thing. It has been my experience that people who lack a healthy fear in dangerous situations are the ones most likely to get hurt. There is an old saying, "Only fools rush in where angels fear to tread." In Herman Melville's classic novel, *Moby Dick*, Captain Ahab's first mate says to his crew, "I will have no man in my boat who is not afraid of a whale."[1] His meaning was clear: anyone who did not have a healthy respect for the world's largest mammal was a danger to himself and to his shipmates.

It has always intrigued me how many people will pay to be scared. The entertainment industry has made a fortune off people's fears, in amusement parks with dramatic roller coasters, and in television programs and movies. One activity that never ceases to amaze me is bungee jumping. People pay money to jump from a tower or a bridge with nothing to break the fall except a large rubber band. I don't even trust the rubber band on my morning newspaper!

The best type of fear is the fear of God—which is a healthy reverence and awe for Him (Prov. 1:7). Conversely, the greatest danger out there today is the massive number of people who have no fear of or concern for God. Jesus said, "Do not fear those who [can] kill the body, but cannot kill the soul. But rather, fear Him who is able to destroy both soul and body in hell" (Matt. 10:28). Oswald Chambers said it well: "The remarkable thing about fearing God is that when you fear God, you fear nothing else."[2] When the rapture takes place, God will remove everyone from the earth who fears Him, while leaving all the people who do not fear God on earth to face the judgments of the tribulation.

In the last chapter, we saw the unleashing of the four horsemen of the apocalypse. The result will be a temporary false peace, followed by the outbreak of war and bloodshed, followed by famine—all leading to the death of one-fourth of the earth's population. Now as we continue our study in chapter 6, we will see that the fifth seal gives us a glimpse of events in heaven, while the sixth seal gives us another glimpse of what takes place on the earth. So the title of this chapter is "Heavenly and Earthly Responses." It was Charles Spurgeon who rightly said, "The most terrible warning to impenitent men in all the world is the death of Christ. For if God spared not His own Son, on whom was only laid imputed sin, will He spare sinners whose sins are their own?"[3]

> When He opened the fifth seal, I saw under the altar the souls of those who had been slain for the word of God and for the testimony which they held. And they cried with a loud voice, saying, "How long, O Lord, holy and true, until You judge and avenge our blood on those who dwell on the earth?" Then a white robe was given to each of them; and it was said to them that they should rest a little while longer, until both the number of their fellow servants and their brethren, who would be killed as they were, was completed.
>
> Revelation 6:9–11

When Jesus opens the fifth seal on the scroll, John sees an altar. Under the altar he sees the souls of believers who have been martyred for their faith. These people have been "slain," and the Greek word means "slaughtered." These souls that John sees are the souls of people who have come to faith during the tribulation period and have been executed for their faith. The two reasons given here for their execution are: the Word of God and their testimony. So these tribulation converts were murdered for standing on the Word of God by faith and sharing their testimony. The vast majority of people who become Christians during the tribulation will be put to death by the government of the Antichrist.

One of the reasons we know this refers to martyrs from the tribulation period, and not other martyrs from church history, is that John sees their souls. They have not received their glorified bodies yet. This is a common question that believers have in regard to the end times: when do believers receive their glorified bodies?

When a believer dies today, his or her soul goes to be with the Lord, while the body remains behind and is buried. In 2 Corinthians 5:8, we are taught that to be absent from the body is to be present with the Lord. So at the moment of a believer's death, the spirit and soul separates from the body and goes immediately into God's presence in heaven, but the body remains behind.

We read in 1 Thessalonians 4 that when Jesus comes for believers in the rapture, the dead in Christ will rise first. So what does that mean? Well, we already know that the soul of that deceased believer is with the Lord. So the dead in Christ rising first simply means that their bodies will rise, whereby Jesus will instantly transform them into glorified bodies. That new, eternal body will be joined with the soul.

After the bodies of deceased Christians rise first, all those believers who are still alive on the earth when the rapture takes place will be caught up to Jesus in the clouds, and their bodies will be instantly transformed into glorified bodies. So in response to the question of when believers get new bodies, the answer is: at the rapture. After the rapture, there will be many unsaved people who come to saving faith during the tribulation period, and they will be martyred.

Here then, in verse 9, John sees the souls of those tribulation martyrs under the altar in heaven, and they will not receive their glorified bodies until later. It appears that they will receive those new bodies at the end of the seven-year tribulation. In verse 4 of chapter 20, John once again describes seeing the tribulation martyrs, and it is probably at that time that they are given their new eternal bodies.

Another reason I believe these are the martyrs of the tribulation is the sequence of events in chapter 6. When the first four seals are opened, there is tremendous loss of life on the earth, and then the fifth seal introduces us to this group. Their cry for vengeance is against those who dwell on the earth—which means the people still living in the tribulation were responsible for killing them.

Now this raises two very important thoughts for consideration: one thought for the unsaved and one for the saved. To the unsaved people who would entertain the notion of waiting to see whether the tribulation period really takes place—thinking that they can simply commit their lives to Christ at that point—I say: don't bet on it. Making a genuine commitment to Christ during the tribulation will almost guarantee that you will be hunted down and executed by the government. Here's the bottom-line question: if you can't commit to Christ and live for Him today, what makes you honestly think you can commit to Christ and die for Him tomorrow?

Now to all the genuine believers: as you make attempts to share your faith with unsaved family, friends, and others—as you should be doing—you will experience the disappointment of having people dispute, debate, disagree, and, worst of all, depart without making a commitment. But remember this about the power of God's Word: in Isaiah 55:10–11, the Lord says, "As the rain comes down, and the snow from heaven, and do not return there, but water the earth . . . so shall My word be that goes forth from My mouth; it shall not return to Me void, but it shall accomplish what I please, and it shall prosper in the thing for which I sent it." The Word of God is like a messenger from the Lord, and it never returns empty-handed or without making an impact. Even when it has seemingly been rejected, it remains with those people, and the Holy Spirit will continue to use it in their lives.

And here's the connection to Revelation 6: many of the people who come to faith during the tribulation period will do so when they experience the horrors of the last days, as the Holy Spirit brings to their remembrance the gospel truths that you have shared with them. The Word of God will never return void; it will either bring them to saving faith eventually, or it will bear witness against them and their rejection of the gospel.

In verse 9, we find that these tribulation martyrs are under the altar in heaven. This is probably symbolic of the Old Testament system, in which an animal was sacrificed, and the blood was poured out underneath the brazen altar of sacrifice. In the same way, the blood of these martyrs was shed and their lives were given sacrificially as followers of Christ.

In verse 10, we read that these martyrs are crying out to God, who is holy and true, asking how long it will be before He avenges their blood against those on the earth who were responsible for killing them. The emphasis of these martyrs is on the fact that God is holy and true, and He therefore is the One who will rightly judge and punish those murders on the earth. Their question is not "*Will* You punish them, O Lord?" but rather, "*When* will You punish them, O Lord?"

God's response is to have them rest and wait just a little bit longer. God also informs them that many more are going to join them in heaven from the second half of the tribulation. We also read in verse 11 that these martyrs are given white robes. But since these tribulation martyrs don't have their glorified bodies yet, we see these white robes as symbolic of the grace and righteousness that God has bestowed on them, through their faith in Christ.

> I looked when He opened the sixth seal, and behold, there was a great earthquake; and the sun became black as sackcloth of hair, and the moon became like blood. And the stars of heaven fell to the earth, as a fig tree drops its late figs when it is shaken by a mighty wind. Then the sky receded as a scroll when it is rolled up, and every mountain and island was moved out of its place. And the kings of the earth, the great men, the rich men, the commanders, the mighty men, every slave and every free man, hid themselves in the caves and in the rocks of the mountains, and said to the mountains and rocks, "Fall on us and hide us from the face of Him who sits on the throne and from the wrath of the Lamb! For the great day of His wrath has come, and who is able to stand?"
>
> Revelation 6:12–17

When Jesus opens the sixth of seven seals on the scroll, John reports for us that there is a tremendous earthquake, which is accompanied by the sun turning black, the moon turning blood red, and the stars falling from the sky. Then if all that wasn't terrifying enough, the sky rolls up like a scroll, with every single mountain range and island being shaken and shifted from its position. I cannot envision a more frightening scenario on the earth than what we read here. Forget all those fears and phobias I mentioned earlier—these events will cause people's hearts to fail them for fear. No wonder the writer of Hebrews states, "It is a fearful thing to fall into the hands of the living God" (Heb. 10:31).

When an earthquake strikes today, we usually ask each other, "Did anything in your house fall or get broken?" But when this earthquake strikes, somewhere around the midpoint of the tribulation, every mountain and island will move out of place. People will have much more to worry about than their household knickknacks!

A few commentators have suggested that this earthquake refers to a political and economic shakeup around the world. But with all due respect, the fact that every mountain and island will move, along with the reality that every person is trying to run for cover and hide, supports the obvious fact that this is to be understood in the most straightforward sense. Not only is this earthquake quite literal, but it is also much more powerful and destructive than any previous earthquake known to mankind. It is truly "the big one."

The people still alive on the earth who experience this earthquake will have barely survived the war, bloodshed, famine, pestilence, and disease—and everything else we have read about—when the first four seals were opened. While we may think that things are really getting bad in the world today, the current situation is nothing in comparison with what's going to take place after the church is removed in the rapture and God's divine judgment breaks loose on earth.

In conjunction with and as a result of this huge earthquake, the sun will become black and the moon will turn blood red. Because of the constant threat of war, and because of the buildup of nuclear and other mass-destruction weapons, some commentators have suggested that this perhaps describes the aftermath of nuclear war between countries. That is certainly a possibility.

But in my opinion, the better explanation is the more obvious one: an earthquake of such unimaginable magnitude will surely cause numerous large-scale volcanic eruptions around the world. These eruptions will send vast amounts of ash, smoke, and debris into the atmosphere, causing the sun to appear black and the moon to look blood red in the night sky.

At the same time, Scripture associates darkness with judgment. While Jesus was on the cross for six hours, it was during the final three hours that darkness came over all the land and the judgment for our sins was being poured out on Him. Jesus was taking our hell and our eternal punishment on Himself during that time. Jerry Bridges has stated it this way: "Jesus did not die simply to give us peace and a purpose in life; He died to save us from the wrath of God."[4]

In verse 13, we read that the stars will fall from heaven to the earth like ripe figs falling from a tree. We have a large avocado tree in our backyard, and I'm very grateful for that tree because it usually gives us lots of avocados in the last couple months each year. But then we get into January, and the avocados are quite ripe, and when we have a really windy day, it is not unusual to walk outside and find dozens of avocados on the ground. I've picked up as many as eighty avocados after one night of heavy winds.

Like ripe figs, or ripe avocados, the stars of heaven will fall to the earth, John tells us. However, most stars—even our own sun—are far larger than the earth, so it is unlikely that John is describing actual stars. The Greek word used here for "star" is *asteres*, and while it refers to stars, it can also refer to other objects in space, including asteroids and meteors. Therefore, the likely meaning is that of a meteor shower or asteroids striking the earth.

When I was a kid, our family visited the Meteor Crater while traveling through northern Arizona. That crater is 4,000 feet around the perimeter and 550 feet deep. You could place twenty football fields on the floor of that crater. Now imagine a swarm of meteors like that hitting the earth. The consequences would be devastating.

In verse 14, we read more of John's description of cosmic disturbances, with the sky rolling up like a scroll. In his Old Testament book, Isaiah makes a similar reference to the sky rolling up (Isa. 34:4). Somehow, the atmosphere will dramatically alter in appearance. It's possible that this is referring to all the volcanic ash and smoke in the atmosphere rolling across the sky; we don't know for certain. But what we do know, from verse 15, is these events will affect everyone in the same way—with absolute fear, panic, and terror. At this point, a person's social or economic status will be worthless. Everyone will suffer the same level of fright.

When this sixth seal is broken open by Jesus in heaven, the unsaved people on earth will try to hide behind the very objects that are shaking and moving—the rocks and the mountains. The scene described by John is clearly one of utter chaos and panic. They would rather run from God in fear than run to Him in faith.

The unsaved will cry out to Mother Nature but not to God. They will acknowledge that these judgments are coming from God, and yet we do not read here of any repentance toward God. No one is crying out and saying, "I'm sorry, Lord; please save me!" Instead, they are asking the mountains and rocks to fall on them and kill them so they do not have to face the onslaught of aftershocks, volcanic eruptions, and asteroids hitting the earth. They would rather die than face God's wrath, and that I completely understand. But not crying out to God for mercy—that I cannot understand.

This sobering chapter closes with the rhetorical question—who is able to stand in the great day of God's wrath?—and the obvious answer is: no one . . . apart from the grace of God. As bad as all this is, it's not all bad news! In the next chapter, we are going to find that even in the midst of His judgment, God is still offering salvation and forgiveness. Once again, we are reminded that God takes no delight in the death of the wicked and that God is not wanting anyone to perish. But people must respond to the free gift of salvation, and the offer of His forgiveness.

11

Who Is Able to Stand?

Revelation 7:1-17

Living in Southern California, it's ironic to me that we who have some of the nicest year-round weather in the United States still like to complain about the weather. One of the weather patterns common to this area is the Santa Ana winds. Now, I must confess that blustery and windy days are my least favorite. I prefer heat, cold, and even rain to windy days. I already have enough trouble just trying to keep my limited amount of hair all together in the same general area. And for the record, I'm not balding; I'm just taller than my hair!

My wife and I recently traveled by train to Louisiana, and we were able to see some of the positive and negative effects of the wind. As we traveled through the Palm Springs area, for example, we saw acres of wind turbine generators, or windmills. As weird as they may look, each windmill produces 300 kilowatts of electricity per hour. That is the amount used by the typical household in one month.[1] It's a great, positive way to harness the wind.

However, as our travels continued toward Louisiana, we passed through the city of Houston and saw some of the damage from

Hurricane Ike and the devastating winds that it produced. We saw large trees, billboards, and light posts on the ground, as well as roofs and windows missing from several buildings. At the home of one of my relatives in New Iberia, Louisiana, we saw the damage from her neighbor's giant oak tree, which was blown down onto the back of her house as a result of Hurricane Gustav. As we come now to the seventh chapter of Revelation, we're going to read about a time in the near future when God will cause all wind on the earth to cease, and this will not be a good thing.

Chapter 7 is a parenthesis, or a pause, if you will, between the opening of the sixth and seventh seals on that scroll in heaven. In some ways, chapter 7 is the eye of the storm. When we get to chapter 8, the seventh seal is broken open by Jesus, producing judgments far worse than what we have already seen, and they will unfold in rapid succession upon the earth.

During this interlude in chapter 7, we learn the answer to the question posed at the end of chapter 6: who is able to stand? Surprisingly, the answer will be two very large groups of people. We will find out who these people are, but let's begin by reading Revelation 7:1–3.

> After these things I saw four angels standing at the four corners of the earth, holding the four winds of the earth, that the wind should not blow on the earth, on the sea, or on any tree. Then I saw another angel ascending from the east, having the seal of the living God. And he cried with a loud voice to the four angels to whom it was granted to harm the earth and the sea, saying, "Do not harm the earth, the sea, or the trees till we have sealed the servants of our God on their foreheads."
>
> Revelation 7:1–3

Here in verses 1–3, we first see *the angels' activities.* After the opening of the first six seals, and the catastrophic events associated with them, John tells us that he saw four angels standing at the four corners of the earth, holding back the wind. Whether we realize it or not, God has put the wind on the earth for our benefit and blessing, and everyone still living in the world at the time the wind ceases is quickly going to recognize that fact.

Over the years, Bible skeptics have attacked John's words here, suggesting that the Bible is teaching that the earth is flat and has actual corners. However, long before scientists ever discovered that the earth is round, Isaiah the prophet declared that God "sits above the circle of the earth" (Isa. 40:22). The Bible never declares the earth to be flat.

John's reference to "the four corners of the earth" is nothing more than a reference to the four compass points: north, south, east, and west. The Greek word used here, and also in chapter 20, for "four corners" can also be translated as the "four quarters" of the earth.[2] John also refers to the "four winds," which simply means all the winds on the earth, regardless of their direction—north, south, east, or west.

So during this interval between the opening of the sixth and seventh seals, four mighty angels are holding back the winds. The Greek word translated as "holding" refers to exerting great effort to restrain something.[3] The winds are struggling and straining to break free, but these angels are exerting great effort in holding them back. Sometimes when my wife and I are walking our dog, Ripley, on his leash, we'll cross paths with other dog walkers. A few times, we've crossed paths with a very petite woman in our neighborhood who walks her very large dog on a leash. Whenever we pass her, I watch her straining to hold her dog back as he struggles to get free and come say hi to us. I always say a little prayer that she doesn't lose her grip on his leash. That's the picture here; these angels are straining to hold back the winds.

That the wind would stop blowing around the world may not sound very serious, until we stop and think about the dramatic effects. For one, air pollution would hang over every city and would not blow away. Second, and much more important, if the winds were to stop, it would also stop raining. As ocean water evaporates into the atmosphere, it is carried by the wind over the land masses, where it cools, condenses into clouds, and then returns to the earth in the form of rain. If the winds were to stop completely, the evaporated water from the oceans would simply rise straight up into the atmosphere and remain there. This would produce an immediate worldwide drought and add to the famine and lack of water already taking place during the tribulation.

I should confess to you, and state for the record, that I have been guilty of complaining about the wind on many occasions over the years. My understanding of these verses has helped me to decrease my complaining, but sometimes I forget. In many ways, the wind is like the lungs of our planet and is critical to our survival. When we get to chapter 11, we will read that there will be no rain for three and a half years, and it is undoubtedly connected to the lack of wind that we read about here.

Imagine for a moment what will happen when the winds stop and it becomes dead calm. There will be no breeze, no movement of leaves in the trees, and no movement of clouds, and the ocean waters will become completely calm. It will be as if the Lord has turned off the engine of the earth. But make no mistake, this is the eye of the storm and a temporary interlude to God's continuing judgment.

Earlier, I mentioned both the positive and negative effects of the wind. In the same way, there are both positive and negative effects connected to this event—when God commands His angels to hold back the wind. We've just discussed some of the negative effects, but in verses 2 and 3 we see a positive reason for the Lord doing this. Let's read them again and continue through verse 8.

> Then I saw another angel ascending from the east, having the seal of the living God. And he cried with a loud voice to the four angels to whom it was granted to harm the earth and the sea, saying, "Do not harm the earth, the sea, or the trees till we have sealed the servants of our God on their foreheads." And I heard the number of those who were sealed. One hundred and forty-four thousand of all the tribes of the children of Israel were sealed: of the tribe of Judah twelve thousand were sealed; of the tribe of Reuben twelve thousand were sealed; of the tribe of Gad twelve thousand were sealed; of the tribe of Asher twelve thousand were sealed; of the tribe of Naphtali twelve thousand were sealed; of the tribe of Manasseh twelve thousand were sealed; of the tribe of Simeon twelve thousand were sealed; of the tribe of Levi twelve thousand were sealed; of the tribe of Issachar twelve thousand were sealed; of the tribe of Zebulun twelve thousand were sealed; of the tribe of Joseph twelve thousand were sealed; of the tribe of Benjamin twelve thousand were sealed.
>
> Revelation 7:2–8

This pause in God's judgment is, in fact, part of His mercy. During this interlude, God is going to send His angels to select and seal

144,000 Jewish believers on the earth for some particular service. This brings us to our second point in this chapter, which is *the sealed servants*. We now meet the first of two large groups of people who will stand in the last days: this intriguing group of 144,000.

This group consists of 144,000 Jews. Not only do we know that they are all Jews, but we also are given the tribes of Israel from which they are descended. They are called "servants" in verse 3, and we will discuss what their service might be in just a moment. But I would point out that the Greek word used here for "servant" is *doulos*, a frequent New Testament word meaning "bondservant."[4] This shows us that they are already believers when selected and sealed for this service. They were not saved prior to the rapture; otherwise, they would have gone up with the church at that time. Instead, they have come to saving faith in the early part of the tribulation and are now sealed by the Lord for His service.

We are told fifteen times in verses 3–8 that they are sealed unto the Lord, and in verse 3 we read specifically that they will receive this seal on their foreheads. In Scripture, a seal refers to both ownership and protection. They are sealed as belonging to God, and the Lord will protect them in the course of their service. Later on in the tribulation, the Antichrist will imitate this seal of the Lord's servants, and he will require the world's citizens to receive his special mark on their foreheads or right hands. As New Testament believers today, we have also been sealed by the Holy Spirit in our hearts, as we're told in Ephesians 1:13. The Holy Spirit living inside us is our guarantee that God will bring us safely home to heaven.

Now we may wonder how the Lord will protect those 144,000 servants while others are experiencing worldwide judgment. The Scripture is full of examples of how God is able to keep those who belong to Him safe in times of judgment, including Noah, Lot, Rahab, and the Israelites at the time of Egypt's ten plagues. In the same way, God will protect these servants during the tribulation period, even as His judgment continues to fall.

There is no mistaking the fact that these 144,000 servants are Jews. I must affirm this because many religious groups—usually cults—have tried to claim that they are the 144,000 here in Revelation. Jehovah's Witnesses have long claimed that this represents the number of their group that will go to heaven. When their membership surpassed the 144,000 mark, they were forced to revise their theology to say that the 144,000 were those elite members who would go to heaven, while the other members would live in bliss on the earth.

Even some well-meaning Christians have tried to suggest that the promises of Israel are now the promises of God for the church, so they have attempted to apply the significance of this group to the church. But these are physical Jews, and to make that point even more clear, the various tribes of Israel from which they are descended are listed. Let me also point out that only God knows from which tribe each Jew is descended. When the Jewish temple was destroyed, so were all of the genealogical records. Therefore, no Jew today can prove from which tribe he or she is descended.

But here's the bottom line: who, in their right mind, would want to be a part of this 144,000? Think about it. If you claim to belong to this group, then what you are plainly stating is that you're not a Christian. Every genuine believer will be raptured to meet the Lord and will remain with Him in heaven during the seven-year tribulation. So to be a part of this group of 144,000, you would have to be an unsaved Jew, miss the rapture, come to faith in the tribulation period, and then be chosen by God for this special service. I don't want to be a part of the 144,000. I want to be a part of the raptured saints in heaven worshiping the Lord when the tribulation begins!

During the tribulation, God will give Israel the opportunity to accomplish what it had failed to do previously—to be God's missionary light in these final days before Christ returns. Many more Jews will be saved—far beyond these 144,000—but this group will have the privilege of a very special service.

So what will that service be? To find the answer, let's resume our reading.

> After these things I looked, and behold, a great multitude which no one could number, of all nations, tribes, peoples, and tongues, standing before the throne and before the Lamb, clothed with white robes, with palm branches in their hands, and crying out with a loud voice, saying, "Salvation belongs to our God who sits on the throne, and to the Lamb!" All the angels stood around the throne and the elders and the four living creatures, and fell on their faces before the throne and worshiped God, saying: "Amen! Blessing and glory

and wisdom, thanksgiving and honor and power and might, be to our God forever and ever. Amen." Then one of the elders answered, saying to me, "Who are these arrayed in white robes, and where did they come from?" And I said to him, "Sir, you know." So he said to me, "These are the ones who come out of the great tribulation, and washed their robes and made them white in the blood of the Lamb. Therefore they are before the throne of God, and serve Him day and night in His temple. And He who sits on the throne will dwell among them. They shall neither hunger anymore nor thirst anymore; the sun shall not strike them, nor any heat; for the Lamb who is in the midst of the throne will shepherd them and lead them to living fountains of waters. And God will wipe away every tear from their eyes."

Revelation 7:9–17

Our third and final point for this chapter is *the people's praise.* These verses introduce us to the second large group that I mentioned—this multitude of tribulation martyrs. Who is able to stand in the days of God's wrath? The answer is the 144,000 Jewish servants, as well as this multitude of tribulation martyrs.

The question is sometimes asked: will anyone be able to be saved after the rapture has taken place? The definitive answer is not only will people be saved, but multitudes of people from all around the world will be saved. In the midst of God's great wrath and judgment, we find God's great mercy and grace. So large is this multitude of martyrs in heaven that John describes this group as being "a great multitude which no one could number." This great outpouring of evangelism and salvation—far greater than the world has ever experienced—will take place after the rapture and during the seven years of God's judgment. It is a remarkable thing that the period of greatest judgment in the world will also be the time of the greatest salvation in the world. Now, it is commonly taught that these 144,000 servants will be evangelists, and yet nowhere in chapter 7 are we told what they are going to be doing. So what makes most Bible teachers and commentators agree that these 144,000 servants will be given the special service of mass evangelism?

There are a couple good reasons. For one, John states that after seeing the 144,000 servants sealed by God, he then sees this great multitude of people coming up into heaven. This strongly indicates

116

that the first group has something to do with the second. The obvious and logical conclusion is that the 144,000 brought this multitude to saving faith, and the only way to do that is by preaching the gospel.

Another reason we believe this group will minister as evangelists is that Jesus said the gospel would be preached to the whole world just before the end. In Matthew 24, Jesus gave His disciples the order of tribulation events, and we've seen them unfold in that order, beginning in chapter 6. The next event in sequence, according to Matthew 24:14, is when Jesus said, "And this gospel of the kingdom will be preached in all the world as a witness to all the nations, and then the end will come."

The results of that evangelism will be nothing short of phenomenal. Imagine the rejoicing in heaven over seeing people from every part of the world, from every language, and from every nationality. Let us never forget that "God so loved the *world*, that He gave His only begotten Son" (John 3:16). So in response to the question, "Who is able to stand?" the answer is this: those whom the Lord appoints to preach and those who respond by faith.

This great multitude will be wearing white robes, which symbolize the righteousness of God. In their hands will be palm branches, which symbolize victory and celebration. When Jesus came riding into Jerusalem on the Sunday before His crucifixion, He was greeted by people waving palm branches and shouting, "Hosanna!" (John 12:13). In verse 10, we find that this group will be shouting, "Salvation belongs to our God," and that is very similar in meaning to Hosanna, which means "save now."

In verses 11 and 12, these tribulation martyrs are with the angels and the New Testament saints who came up in the rapture and are worshiping the Lord with another sevenfold anthem of praise. The choir just keeps on getting bigger and bigger! In verse 13, one of the twenty-four elders asks John the identity of these new arrivals in heaven. This elder is making the point that this group is completely different from those who were already in heaven. This is reinforced by the fact that John did not know the answer to this question. The elder then identifies this group of new arrivals as martyrs who have come out of the tribulation period. These martyrs are now joining the martyrs who are already there from the earlier days of the tribulation.

In verse 15, we read that these martyrs, and all the saints for that matter, will be around the throne of God and that God will dwell among us. As you look more closely at verse 15, you find that we will be serving God night and day in the temple. Of course, we're all curious as to what type of service we will be rendering in heaven. Since some of that service takes place in and around the temple, and since God has made us kings and priests in His kingdom, it's safe to say that we will all be doing some ministry work in heaven. I, for one, am excited to know that we'll have ministry service in heaven, since the opportunities I've already received here on earth have brought me great joy.

In verse 16, we also learn that we will be free from trials and difficulties such as hunger, thirst, and suffering. On the one hand, this is a direct reference to the martyrs who came to Christ during the tribulation and were suffering hunger, thirst, and persecution. But this promise is for all believers throughout all the ages. In this life, everyone has suffered to some degree as a result of our own sins. But in heaven, there will be no more suffering.

According to verse 17, Christ will continue to be our Shepherd in heaven. He will lead us to fountains of living water, and God will wipe away every tear from our eyes. Now as great as all that sounds, the greatest joy of heaven (and what makes heaven, heaven) is the presence of God. The greatest gift we will receive in heaven is the presence of God, and the greatest absence in heaven will not be the absence of our suffering or our tears but rather the absence of what has caused all that suffering and tears—which is sin.

You and I are not only living in the last days but also living in the days when the Christian faith is being debated, degraded, and denied. At the same time, the church and the gospel message have oftentimes become diluted. For faithful believers, it can become discouraging. But what we read about here—the great outpouring of salvation upon the earth after we're gone and wonderful blessings of heaven—should bring us great joy and encouragement as we await Christ's imminent return.

12

The Terrible Trumpets

Revelation 8:1–13

I don't know whether it's just a natural part of getting older or whether society has just become extremely noisy, but more and more I find myself craving peace and quiet. It's probably a combination of the two—I'm getting older and society is getting noisier. Between the booming car stereos, roaring motorcycle engines, and yard leaf blowers, I find myself wanting to run away from the noise. Recently, I was having lunch at a restaurant, and some guy started having a conversation on his cell phone walkie-talkie. Everyone in the restaurant could hear the irritating back-and-forth conversation, and I can only conclude that he was absent on the day God was passing out common sense.

Now, silence is not always good—such as when married couples disagree and give each other the silent treatment. This happened for one couple as they were traveling a long distance by car. Nothing was said for over an hour, and the atmosphere in the car was very tense. As they drove past a farm with pigs, mules, and goats, the husband broke the silence and said to his wife, "Must be your relatives!"

Without looking over at her husband, the wife calmly responded, "Yup, they're all my in-laws!"

Thus far in our glimpses of heaven through the eyes of the apostle John, we've read about continuous praise, worship, and shouts of joy. But that suddenly changes as we arrive at chapter 8.

> When He opened the seventh seal, there was silence in heaven for about half an hour.
>
> Revelation 8:1

From everything we've seen so far, we know that heaven is not a quiet place. But the text here tells us that there was silence for about half an hour. One commentator has suggested that this may well be the longest silence heaven has ever experienced, since heaven is a place of such joyous praise and worship.[1] I would have to disagree. I imagine that heaven was completely silent during those final three hours on the cross, as the penalty for our sins was being poured out upon Jesus. Either way, we would agree that silence in heaven is unusual.

Four important experiences are recorded by John in this chapter, and here in verse 1, we read about *the pause.* John does not describe for us what brought about this pause in heaven—and it is the only silence ever mentioned in Revelation. Since this final seal is broken and the scroll is now completely opened, we can presume that the writing on the scroll, which describes the remaining judgments, is fully visible. If that is the case, then the judgments that remain are so startling in nature that they bring about a stunned silence in heaven.

Saints and angels alike are holding their collective breath in anticipation of the seven trumpets that are about to sound forth and the judgments that follow. The expectation is so intense that it brings to mind the expression, "You could hear a pin drop."

> And I saw the seven angels who stand before God, and to them were given seven trumpets. Then another angel, having a golden censer, came and stood at the altar. He was given much incense, that he should offer it with the prayers of all the saints upon the golden altar which was before the throne. And the smoke of the incense, with the prayers of the saints, ascended before God from the angel's hand.

Then the angel took the censer, filled it with fire from the altar, and threw it to the earth. And there were noises, thunderings, lightnings, and an earthquake. So the seven angels who had the seven trumpets prepared themselves to sound.

Revelation 8:2–6

The second experience John records for us is *the prayers*. In verse 2, John states that he sees seven angels standing before God with seven trumpets. Notice that John refers to them as "the seven angels." In other words, they are a distinct group—not just any seven angels. Who this specific group of angels is we are not told.

This special group of angels appears to be of a higher order, since they are standing in the very presence of God. One of these seven angels might be Gabriel, because when he appeared to Zacharias (the father of John the Baptist) in Luke 1, he identified himself as "Gabriel, who stands in the presence of God" (Luke 1:19). I would guess, then, that these are archangels and would include Gabriel and Michael.

In verse 3, we begin to read about an angel who has a golden censer, standing before the throne, and who is offering incense along with the prayers of the saints. In the Old Testament, it was the responsibility of the priests, each morning and evening, to relight the incense on the altar inside the tabernacle. They would do this by using a censer, or a fire-pan, to gather hot coals from the brazen altar in the court-yard. They would then transport those coals into the tabernacle to light the incense. The purpose of the burning incense was twofold: it served as an offering to the Lord, and it symbolized the prayers of God's people. In Psalm 141:2, David said, "Let my prayer be set before You as incense."

Some commentators have tried to suggest that this angel in verse 3 (who is not one of those seven angels in verse 2) is Jesus. I don't agree with that, for a couple of reasons. For one, Jesus is the One who is breaking open the seals on the scroll in verse 1. Second, after seeing those seven angels in verse 2, John speaks in verse 3 of "another angel," and the Greek word used for "another" means "another of the same kind."[2] Since Jesus is not an angel but rather Creator of the angels, it can't be Him.

In verse 4, we read about how incense is mixed with the prayers of the people and is then placed on the altar before the throne of

God. Then the smoke of that mixture rises before God. Since the smoke of that fire represents the prayers of God's people, the act of throwing this fire down upon the earth symbolizes the fact that God's judgment are—to some degree—a response to those prayers. There is one prayer that God's people have been praying throughout the centuries and that has not yet been answered. It's included in the prayer Jesus shared with His disciples, and we all know the words: "Thy kingdom come, Thy will be done, in earth as it is in heaven" (Matt. 6:10 KJV). In the meantime, this description of prayer in heaven provides us with some important truths that will strengthen and encourage us in our prayer life today:

1. *Never underestimate the power of prayer.* We read that the prayers of the saints, or God's people, are before the Lord in heaven. Prayer is the means by which we make our requests known to God. But more importantly, the purpose of prayer is to align ourselves with the will of God. It's like the people whose boat is sinking in the ocean, and they throw their rope onto an island rock, out in the waters. As they pull on the rope, are they pulling the rock toward them, or are they pulling themselves toward that rock?

   In the same way, when we pray, we are not pulling God's will toward us as much as we are pulling ourselves toward His will. Oftentimes, our desires and our requests are in alignment with God's will. So in Scripture, we find many examples of the power of prayer. In the Old Testament, for example, we remember how Hannah was childless, and how she wept and prayed before the Lord for a child, and God blessed her with Samuel, as well as other children (1 Sam. 1). In the New Testament, we remember how Peter was being kept captive by Herod and was set for execution in the morning. In the meantime, believers were gathered and praying for Peter. God supernaturally released Peter and allowed him to continue his ministry to the church (Acts 12). Never underestimate the power of prayer.

2. *God's timing is not always our timing.* Back in Revelation 6, we read how some of the martyrs in heaven were crying out to God, asking Him to bring judgment and justice against those on earth who were responsible for executing them. God's re-

sponse wasn't no but rather "wait just a little bit longer." As the great British preacher G. Campbell Morgan was fond of saying, "God's delays are not His denials." Our prayer requests are oftentimes in alignment with the Lord's will, but we must wait on His timing.

3. *God's will shall be done*. When we get to chapter 20, we will see God's kingdom come and His will being done, and it is called the millennial kingdom of Christ. Prayer requires patience and perseverance. At the same time, there is a genuine peace that comes from praying and—best of all—from knowing that God's will shall be done. Psalm 27:14 encourages us to "wait on the LORD; be of good courage, and He shall strengthen your heart; wait I say, on the LORD!" The word David uses for "wait" includes patience as well as eager expectation.

So the seven angels who had the seven trumpets prepared themselves to sound their instruments. The first angel sounded his trumpet: And hail and fire followed, mingled with blood, and they were thrown to the earth. And a third of the trees were burned up, and all green grass was burned up.

Revelation 8:6–7

The third experience John records for us is *the punishment*. God's wrath against unrepentant mankind on earth continues with the breaking open of the seventh seal. All the judgments that follow are part of this final seal that Jesus opens. The seventh seal is the seven trumpet judgments, and the seven trumpet judgments progress into the seven bowl judgments. Following another powerful earthquake at the end of verse 5, we read in verse 6 that each of the seven angels has a trumpet, and each trumpet blast will signal another judgment and barrage of punishment on the earth.

The seven trumpet judgments are divided into two groups. The first four are directed by God at the environment, and they bear some resemblance to the plagues against Egypt in the book of Exodus. The other three are spread over the next three chapters, and they fall more directly on humanity. We're also going to see that while these judgments are quite severe, they are not the final judgment of the unsaved. In fact, the first four trumpet judgments target and affect one-third of the environment. The fact that each judgment affects precisely one-third of its intended target demonstrates that these events are not random but divine in nature. It also demonstrates that God is still giving people the chance to repent.

We constantly hear about the dangers of global warming, which suggests that the earth's average temperature is rising and will eventually bring global havoc and melt the polar ice caps. But the average world temperature in the last hundred years has risen only one degree, and over the last two thousand years, it has actually gone down. However, from a biblical standpoint, the danger is real. I say that because when we get to the bowl judgments in Revelation 16, they will include an intense increase in the sun's heat, resulting in people being scorched. Such an increase in heat will undoubtedly melt the polar ice caps and raise the ocean levels significantly. Now that's a genuine threat of global warming that comes directly from God, and it is the consequence of man's sin and rebellion—not from aerosol hairspray or backyard barbeques.

In verse 7, the first angel sounds the first trumpet, signaling a storm of hail and fire from the skies, which will burn and destroy one-third of the remaining trees and green grass. It is worth noting that after God created the dry land, the first things He brought forth from the earth were the green grass and the trees (Gen. 1:11), and here they will be the first to be destroyed in the trumpet judgments. At the same time, this judgment is very similar to the seventh plague in Egypt, when God brought "hail and fire," as recorded in Exodus 9. It is also very much like the judgment God rained down on the wicked cities of Sodom and Gomorrah (Gen. 19).

In the middle of verse 7, we read that the elements of this judgment will be "thrown to the earth." So it may be that this hail, fire, and blood mixture will be sent down directly from heaven. However, another possible explanation concerns the earthquake mentioned in verse 5. If this second earthquake is anything close to the magnitude of the first earthquake we read about in chapter 6, then what we may have here are widespread volcanic eruptions. The lava shooting up into the air and falling back to the earth would be red, or the color of blood. The molten lava would also burn the trees and the grass. The smoke and ash entering the atmosphere from those volcanic eruptions would trigger unusual hail and lightning storms. John's mention of fire may refer to the lightning of a severe electrical storm.

This much we do know: this catastrophe would radically affect the already depleted food supply of the world, as more crops would be destroyed. This would also diminish the grass and vegetation needed to feed the animals, from which we get so much of our meat and milk. Trees and plants are also vital to the stability of the land and soil.

> Then the second angel sounded: And something like a great mountain burning with fire was thrown into the sea, and a third of the sea became blood. And a third of the living creatures in the sea died, and a third of the ships were destroyed.
>
> Revelation 8:8–9

First of all, and very importantly, we need to note that John says something "like" a great mountain burning with fire was thrown into the sea. John did not see an actual mountain hurling through the atmosphere but rather something "like" that.

Though we can only speculate, the suggestion of a huge asteroid or meteor slamming into the earth seems very likely. I have read how scientists have tracked several asteroids capable of entering our atmosphere—some of them nearly five hundred miles wide. People will undoubtedly see this object for some time as it approaches the earth from space. Television cameras will be focused on it, and all the news stations will broadcast the approach and splashdown of this enormous object. The impact will be massive; the shear fright and terror will be intense, and the destruction will be unimaginable.

Let's remember that the oceans cover nearly three-fourths of our planet. The Atlantic Ocean makes up roughly one-third of the ocean waters. That gives us some idea of how much area will be affected. In fact, it's entirely possible that this event will take place in the Atlantic Ocean.

This judgment will have three specific effects. First, we are told, one-third of the sea will become blood. This reminds us of the first plague that God brought about in Egypt by the hand of Moses, when the Nile River was turned to blood (Exod. 7). Here in Revelation 8, one-third of the ocean waters will become blood, perhaps caused by the mineral composition of the asteroid.

125

Second, one-third of the sea life will be killed, which will contribute significantly to the bloodlike appearance of the ocean waters. This loss of sea life is probably the result of the asteroid's impact, as well as the waters being poisoned by its mineral composition. The loss of so much sea life will further deplete the already thin food supply, as the ocean is a major source of food for the world. The stench and pollution will create many other significant problems.

And as if all that wasn't bad enough, one-third of all the ships will be destroyed. A likely scenario is that there will be a gigantic tsunami created by the impact of the huge asteroid hitting the ocean. We remember the giant Southeast Asian tsunami of 2004 that generated hundred-foot waves and killed over 225,000 people. That tsunami was triggered by a 9.1 magnitude earthquake in the Indian Ocean. In this scenario, a tsunami-type tidal wave seems all but certain. Can you imagine the thousands of ocean liners, merchant ships, naval vessels, and private boats that will capsize and be destroyed in a short period of time? It will be like *The Poseidon Adventure* for thousands of ships.

In verses 10–11, the third trumpet is sounded:

> Then the third angel sounded: And a great star fell from heaven, burning like a torch, and it fell on a third of the rivers and on the springs of water. The name of the star is Wormwood. A third of the waters became wormwood, and many men died from the water, because it was made bitter.
>
> Revelation 8:10–11

Before the people of the earth have much time to recover from the last trumpet blast, another one occurs and another object from the heavens comes falling to the earth. The last object was referred to as being solid, like a burning mountain. This next object is referred to as something more like a burning lamp or torch. The last object crashed into the sea, while this next one evidently falls apart as it nears the earth, scattering its debris over various lakes and rivers.

We could speculate as to what this "star" might be, but it sounds very much like a comet, especially when you consider its description by John as "burning like a torch" and "coming down from heaven." It is also quite possible that the earth will pass through the tail of an enormous comet, such as Halley's Comet. Halley's Comet would not need to veer very far from its normal path for that to happen.

If it is indeed something like a comet, or a meteorite falling apart, it will spill all over the earth, poisoning one-third of the freshwater supply. The Greek word for "springs" at the end of verse 10 is translated as "wells" in the New Testament. So besides all the exposed fresh water being infected, this poison will apparently also seep down and contaminate the water tables below the surface.

Verse 11 tells us the name of this star, and it is Wormwood. You might be thinking that you didn't know stars had names, but as Psalm 147:4 tells us, God "counts the number of the stars; He calls them all by name." Wormwood is a Middle Eastern plant with a strong, bitter taste, so the word *wormwood* is used in the Bible as a reference to bitterness and sorrow. This wormwood will turn the waters to poison, and people will die when they drink from them.

Now let's read in verse 12 about the fourth trumpet judgment in this chapter:

Then the fourth angel sounded: And a third of the sun was struck, a third of the moon, and a third of the stars, so that a third of them were darkened. A third of the day did not shine, and likewise the night.

Revelation 8:12

Here in verse 12, when the fourth trumpet sounds, the sun, moon, and stars are struck, and one-third of their light is diminished. How this will happen is not stated, but the same God who said, "Let there be light," can certainly cause that light to diminish by one-third. This judgment is reminiscent of the ninth plague in Egypt, when God caused three days of darkness (Exod. 10).

The wording used in this verse may mean that the number of daytime hours will be reduced by one-third or (more likely) that all available light will be reduced by one-third. This would affect solar heating and cause a radical drop in temperature. So much for global warming! If this does indeed turn out to be a reduction in solar heat, that sudden drop in world temperatures will generate violent, unpredictable weather conditions and devastating storms.

And I looked, and I heard an angel flying through the midst of heaven, saying with a loud voice, "Woe, woe, woe to the inhabitants of the earth, because of the remaining blasts of the trumpet of the three angels who are about to sound!"

Revelation 8:13

There is a brief interlude between the first four and the last three trumpet blasts. The fourth experience, which John records for us in this chapter, is *the proclamation*. An angel will fly throughout the skies, proclaiming with a loud voice, "Woe, woe, woe." Sounds just like the evening news! Each of these three woes represents one of the three remaining judgments. The wording and the warning given here indicate that the final three trumpet judgments will be even worse then the first four.

Some Greek manuscripts translate this verse to say that this flying messenger was an "angel," while others translate it as an "eagle." I believe that both texts are probably correct, and the best explanation is found in verse 7 of chapter 4. There we read about the "four living creatures," which are cherubim, and the fourth one was described by John as having the appearance of a "flying eagle." So it is quite possible that this angel flying through heaven is that cherub angel who had the appearance of an eagle.

Let me also say something about the phrase "the inhabitants of the earth." That phrase is used twelve times in Revelation, and it refers to more than just people still living on the earth. It refers to those unsaved people who "make the earth their home," emphasizing how they are living for this world. This is the opposite of those people who have placed their faith in God and, as a result, have their citizenship in heaven. In Philippians 3:20, Paul says of believers, "Our citizenship is in heaven, from which we also eagerly wait for the Savior."

When it comes to spiritual citizenship, a person is either a citizen of heaven, making his or her way through this world and headed home to that city whose builder and maker is God, or a citizen of the earth, living for the things of this lost and dying world. It's one or the other—there is no middle ground, and there is no spiritual dual citizenship.

13

Something Wicked This Way Comes

Revelation 9:1–21

A passenger in a taxicab leaned forward to ask the driver a question, and while doing so, he tapped him on the back of the shoulder. The driver screamed, lost control of the taxicab, nearly hit a bus, and drove up over the curb before coming to a stop. For a moment, everything was silent in the cab until the shaken driver finally said, "I'm really sorry, but you scared the living daylights out of me!" The startled passenger apologized and said he didn't realize that tapping him on the shoulder would frighten him like that. The driver replied, "No, it's not your fault. Today is my first day driving a cab—for the past twenty years I've been driving a hearse!"

Many people are jumpy and fearful about a lot of things these days, whether it be the stock market, the housing market, the job market, or the supermarket. When we throw in other concerns—war, terrorism, and crime—there are plenty of things that people find frightening. But all that pales in comparison with the sheer terror and horror connected with the events of the tribulation period. As we arrive now at the ninth chapter of Revelation, and the details of the fifth and sixth trumpet judgments, we're going to see a picture of what this world will look like when all hell breaks loose—and I mean that in the most literal sense. As for this chapter, the title of an early 1960s Ray Bradbury novel kept coming to my mind as I studied Revelation 9: *Something Wicked This Way Comes*. Let's now read the first two verses:

> Then the fifth angel sounded: And I saw a star fallen from heaven to the earth. To him was given the key to the bottomless pit. And he opened the bottomless pit, and smoke arose out of the pit like the smoke of a great furnace. So the sun and the air were darkened because of the smoke of the pit.
>
> Revelation 9:1–2

The fifth angel sounds his trumpet, and John sees "a star fallen from heaven to the earth." In our study of chapter 8, the third trumpet judgment also involved a falling star, which will strike the earth and poison one-third of the freshwater supply. However, here in chapter 9, we have something quite different. Notice that at the end of verse 1, John describes seeing a falling star but then says, "And to him was given the key to the bottomless pit." This star is not an object from space but rather a person. The fact that he has fallen from heaven to earth, and then proceeds to unlock and open the bottomless pit, tells us that this is none other than Satan. Oftentimes, in Scripture, angels are described as stars. When we study chapter 12, we will find a reference to Satan's original fall from heaven, when he took with him one-third of the stars, or angels (Rev. 12:4). Those angels who joined Satan in his rebellion against God all became fallen angels, or demons. Jesus also made reference to Satan's original fall from heaven when He said to His disciples, "I beheld Satan as lightning fall from heaven" (Luke 10:18 KJV).

Now since John is seeing this vision from the tribulation period, this would not be a reference to the original fall of Satan from heaven, as described in the Old Testament books of Isaiah (chap. 14) and Ezekiel (chap. 28). In fact, in the Greek, the verb John uses is in the past tense. So rather than seeing a "falling star," John saw a "fallen star," or a fallen angel—referring to Satan. The second half of verse 1 tells us that the key to the bottomless pit was then given to him. "Bottomless," in the Greek, is *abussos*. It is used seven times in Revelation, and it means "pit of the abyss."[1]

This is where the most vile and wicked demons are now confined. In 2 Peter 2:4, we read, "God did not spare the angels who sinned, but cast them down to hell and delivered them into chains of darkness, to be reserved for judgment." So while many demons today are free and carrying out the agenda of Satan, many other very wicked demons are confined in the abyss. The abyss is not the home of these vile demons but rather their prison, and they absolutely hate being confined there.

Remember the legion of demons that had possessed the man living among the tombs in Luke 8? When Jesus cast those demons out of that man, they begged Jesus that He might not send them into the abyss. Those demons did not want to be confined there; Jesus permitted them to enter into a herd of swine instead. The abyss is the same place where Satan will be chained and confined during the thousand-year millennial kingdom of Christ (Rev. 20:1–3).

So where is this abyss located? Well, we see Satan coming down to the earth and opening up this pit, which releases the smoke that darkens and pollutes the air. Clearly then, this demonic prison pit is somewhere in the center of the earth. The word *abyss* comes from root words that mean "without depth." So the translation of "bottomless pit" is fitting, since this pit is somewhere inside the earth and is truly bottomless. No matter what direction you approach it from, once you've passed through it, you would be heading back up to the earth's surface; therefore, it would be bottomless and "without depth."

So the abyss, where the most vile and wicked demons are confined, is either a part of Hades or in close proximity to Hades, in the center of the earth. Jude describes the inhabitants of the abyss as those "angels who did not keep their proper domain" (Jude 6). Those angels who are incarcerated in the abyss would include those fallen angels from Genesis 6 that somehow engaged in physical relations with women on the earth. Therefore, they have been confined there for thousands of years. We can't even

131

begin to imagine how eager they are to be released and to wreak havoc on the earth.

So one part of God's judgment against the people on earth will be to give the key that opens the abyss over to Satan, who will immediately release those wicked demons. Truly we can say, "Something wicked this way comes." Since Satan will be given the key to this abyss, and since these demonic creatures, in turn, will rise out of the abyss, many have speculated that there must be some sort of portal or shaft that leads into this pit.

Some years ago, I was standing in line at the grocery store, and I glanced over at the tabloid newspapers next to the checkout counter. I saw a headline that read, "Shaft to Bottomless Pit Discovered in Siberia." I picked up that paper and read the silly story about a group of religious scientists who had reportedly discovered the shaft to the abyss and were making arrangements to open it. I thought to myself that if this were true, the next headline would read, "It seemed like a good idea at the time!" Trust me when I tell you that you wouldn't want to open up the portal to the abyss.

Verse 2 begins to explain why. When Satan opens this abyss of the demons, a thick vile smoke rises from it, causing the air to become dark and polluted. The air pollution in Southern California is nothing in comparison with this demonic smoke and stench!

> Then out of the smoke locusts came upon the earth. And to them was given power, as the scorpions of the earth have power. They were commanded not to harm the grass of the earth, or any green thing, or any tree, but only those men who do not have the seal of God on their foreheads. And they were not given authority to kill them, but to torment them for five months. Their torment was like the torment of a scorpion when it strikes a man. In those days men will seek death and will not find it; they will desire to die, and death will flee from them. The shape of the locusts was like horses prepared for battle. On their heads were crowns of something like gold, and their faces were like the faces of men. They had hair like women's hair, and their teeth were like lions' teeth. And they had breastplates like breastplates of iron, and the sound of their wings was like the sound of chariots with many horses running into battle. They had tails like scorpions, and there were stings in their tails. Their power was to hurt men five months. And they had as king over them the

angel of the bottomless pit, whose name in Hebrew is Abaddon, but in Greek he has the name Apollyon. One woe is past. Behold, still two more woes are coming after these things.

Revelation 9:3–12

The demons that emerge from the abyss are described by John as being like a great swarm of locusts. This is reminiscent of the eighth plague that came upon Pharaoh and the Egyptians. People who have lived in the midwest United States, or in the Middle East, are familiar with the destructive abilities of locusts. It is noteworthy that the average life span of locusts is five months—usually running from mid-spring to late summer. These locust-like demonic creatures will also bring their terror for a period of five months.

John is not describing locusts as we know them but rather a locust-like army of the most perverse demons in existence. They will swarm upon the earth just like locusts, and they will overwhelm people just like locusts. But John describes for us how these demons will not behave like locusts, in that they will not harm the remaining grass and trees or any green thing.

Satan has a different agenda for these demons, which is to inflict pain on the unsaved people of the earth. To that end, they are given the power of scorpions, by which they sting people, causing excruciating pain. But they are not given the ability or authority to kill people. This divine limitation reminds us of when Satan afflicted Job in the Old Testament. Although God allowed Satan to torment and test Job through great suffering, Satan was not allowed to kill Job.

The end of verse 4 tells us that this judgment is against those who do not have the seal of God upon them. Therefore, we know that the people protected will include the 144,000 Jewish servants of God from chapter 7, since they received the seal of God on their foreheads. We would like to think this divine protection will extend to everyone who has come to faith in Christ, although we are not specifically told that. When the plague of locusts swarmed down on Egypt, in Exodus, God protected His people.

The pain caused by the sting of these demons will be so intense that unsaved people will try to commit suicide in order to escape their unbearable pain. But as part of this judgment, God will supernaturally intervene and people will not be able to die. However they

133

try to kill themselves—whether it be ingesting poison, jumping from buildings and bridges, or hanging themselves—they will all fail. In fact, those failed attempts will only bring further pain and suffering, as people are injured in the process of trying to kill themselves.

What we are reading is a very vivid picture of what eternal judgment will be like. This is a preview of coming attractions for everyone who refuses to embrace Christ and receive His forgiveness for sin. Satan is there, and all of his worst demons are there with him. They are inflicting excruciating pain and suffering on people, but no one has the ability to die or to make that suffering stop. That is precisely what eternal judgment will be like, according to Scripture—including the furnace, fire, smoke, and darkness that we've been reading about.

But let me take this opportunity to reiterate that this is not God's desire. In Ezekiel 33:11, the Lord says, "I have no pleasure in the death of the wicked, but [desire] that the wicked turn from his ways and live." And Matthew 25:41 shows us that the place of eternal judgment and everlasting fire has been prepared by God for the devil and his angels. The lake of fire was created and intended for Satan and the demons. But every sinner who rejects Jesus and God's forgiveness for sin, and thereby chooses to follow Satan, will follow the devil into that same eternal judgment.

Notice that it is Satan who has released his most vile demons to inflict torment on the people of the world. God is certainly allowing it, but it is Satan who is carrying out this worldwide wave of suffering. And whom is he doing this to? Make no mistake about it: it is his own unsaved followers. We've all heard people reject the gospel and then say, "I'm looking forward to partying with all my friends in hell." Well, take another look, because this is not a picture of Satan hosting a giant backyard barbeque, with kegs of beer and loud music. This is a vivid picture of torture and torment, and this is exactly how Satan treats his followers. This is in contrast with Jesus, who promises us a place that has no sickness, no sorrow, and no suffering.

In verses 7–10, John attempts to describe these demonic creatures, but obviously they are like nothing he has ever seen before. Therefore, John attempts to select various characteristics to try to give us an idea of what these creatures are like. The bottom line that we can glean from these verses is that these demonic, military-like creatures can swarm and fly like locusts; they look like horses; they sting like scorpions; and they have human-looking faces. In Proverbs 30:27, Solomon writes, "The locusts have no king, yet they all advance in ranks." Unlike the insect-type locusts, these locust-like demons do have a king. In all likelihood, this is referring to Satan himself. However, some commentators believe this may refer to a high-ranking demon who was in the abyss and who serves directly under Satan. They point out how verse 11 states that these demons "had a king over them, who is the angel of the bottomless pit," perhaps indicating that this demon king rose up out of the abyss along with the other demons.

The name of this demon king in Hebrew is *Abaddon*, and in the Greek his name is *Apollyon*. Both names mean "destroyer," which is a point in favor of the argument that this demon king is Satan, since Jesus stated that Satan has come only to kill and to destroy (John 10:10). Let's resume our reading in verse 13.

> Then the sixth angel sounded: And I heard a voice from the four horns of the golden altar which is before God, saying to the sixth angel who had the trumpet, "Release the four angels who are bound at the great river Euphrates." So the four angels, who had been prepared for the hour and day and month and year, were released to kill a third of mankind. Now the number of the army of the horsemen was two hundred million; I heard the number of them. And thus I saw the horses in the vision: those who sat on them had breastplates of fiery red, hyacinth blue, and sulfur yellow; and the heads of the horses were like the heads of lions; and out of their mouths came fire, smoke, and brimstone. By these three plagues a third of mankind was killed—by the fire and the smoke and the brimstone which came out of their mouths. For their power is in their mouth and in their tails; for their tails are like serpents, having heads; and with them they do harm.
>
> Revelation 9:13–19

When the sixth trumpet is sounded, John hears a voice from the midst of the golden altar, which is the voice of God, giving the command to the sixth angel to release the four angels who are bound at the great River Euphrates. Now, who are these four angels? Back in chapter 7, we read of four angels who were holding back the wind from blowing upon the earth, but they were not being restrained.

Here in chapter 9, these four angels have been restrained and are now being released. This description is very much like the demons in the abyss who were confined but now have been released. In Scripture we never read of any holy angels being bound, so these are more demons.

The location of these four fallen angels is at the great River Euphrates. Pastor John MacArthur, in his Revelation commentary, reminds us that the Euphrates was one of four that flowed out of the Garden of Eden, as recorded in Genesis 2:14. He points out that this would be near the place where the first lie was told, where the first murder was committed, and where rebellious mankind built the Tower of Babel.[2]

A second army is now being assembled to attack the inhabitants of the earth. The first was an army of demons, who were like locusts and scorpions, among other things. Now we have a second demonic army. There are two stunning facts about this second army: they will number two hundred million, and they will kill one-third of the earth's remaining population. While this second army has the characteristics of a human military force, the overall details are much more supernatural than they are natural.

The wording used by John in verses 17–19 needs to be considered carefully. For example, the horses described here are said to have heads like lions. Also, from their mouths come fire, smoke, and brimstone. John describes them as having tails like serpents. Some Bible students believe that John was trying to describe a military army here, but when you review the chapter as a whole, it seems more likely that he was describing another army of fallen angels.

In a passage with similar imagery, when Elijah was caught up into heaven, there was "a chariot of fire . . . with horses of fire" (2 Kings 2:11). Also, when the servant of Elisha had his spiritual eyes opened in 2 Kings 6:17, he saw "horses and chariots of fire." When the Lord returns at His second coming, He is pictured as coming with the armies of heaven on white horses (Rev. 19). So it is not uncommon in Scripture to read about spiritual armies on horses. But the main point remains that whatever this army, it will kill one-third of mankind.

When the fifth trumpet sounded, people desperately wanted to die, but they could not do so. However, when the sixth trumpet blows, death returns with a vengeance. If we do the math on the deaths that result from the seal judgments and this trumpet judgment, we find that well over half the world's population will have been killed by this point—close to the midpoint of the tribulation. In World War I, around sixteen million people died. In World War II, about seventy million people lost their lives.[3] But here at this point, upwards of two billion people will die.

> But the rest of mankind, who were not killed by these plagues, did not repent of the works of their hands, that they should not worship demons, and idols of gold, silver, brass, stone, and wood, which can neither see nor hear nor walk. And they did not repent of their murders or their sorceries or their sexual immorality or their thefts.
>
> Revelation 9:20–21

The fact that over half the world's population has been raptured or killed, or that 144,000 evangelists are proclaiming the only message of hope, or that all hell is breaking loose will have no effect on those who are still alive, except to harden their hearts even more. Here then is John's fivefold picture of how these unsaved people will respond:

1. demonic worship—The sin listed first and foremost is demonic worship, which really explains the other sins. What we have here is a violation of the first two foundational commandments: you shall have no other gods before the Lord, and you shall not make or worship idols (Exod. 20). As Warren Wiersbe describes it, "Here are dead sinners worshiping dead gods! Their gods will not be able to protect or deliver them, and yet these people will continue to reject the true God."[4] Satanic worship will be at an all-time high as people fully reject God and openly pledge allegiance to Satan.
2. murder—This is violation of the sixth commandment of God. It will take place in a variety of ways. The government of the Antichrist will be hunting down and murdering anyone who refuses his mark and who follows Jesus. The demonic armies will carry on an all-out slaughter. And the people themselves, living under Satan's heavy demonic influence, and in a desperate clash over scarce food supplies, will murder one another.
3. sorceries—The Greek word used for "sorceries" is *pharmakeia*, from which we get our English words *pharmacy* and *pharma-*

ceutical.[5] Drug use will be rampant, especially since demon possession and drug abuse go hand in hand. People will be ingesting drugs by the handfuls in the vain attempt to escape the severe and hopeless realities of the tribulation period.

4. sexual immorality—The Greek word used for "immorality" is *porneia*, from which we get our English word *pornography.*[6] Every conceivable form of sexual perversion will be commonplace at this point. Many of the things taking place today, such as the widespread distribution of pornography, abortion on demand, the offer of free condoms to high school students, and the drive to legalize homosexual marriage, are all paving the way to what we read about here in the tribulation period.

5. thievery—Once again, with depleted food and water supplies, it will be every person for himself. Looting will become commonplace. Every unsaved person will resort to lying, stealing, and deceiving.

In the midst of all this bad news, there is still plenty of good news:

1. God remains in complete control, and nothing is going to prevent God's will from being done—neither the sins of mankind nor the schemes of the devil.
2. The church will be safe in heaven during these terrible days, worshiping God and preparing to return with Jesus to the earth when He sets up His millennial kingdom and personally reigns.
3. All the wrongs in life will eventually be made right, and in the days to come we will most definitely see God's will being done on earth, even as it is in heaven.

14

A Message from God

Revelation 10:1-11

One day, as the Lord was looking down upon the earth and watching the rapid decline, He decided to dispatch one of His mighty angels for a firsthand report. When the angel returned, he reported that 90 percent of the people were being bad, while 10 percent were being good. Later, the Lord sent down another mighty angel, and he returned with the same report: 90 percent were being bad, but 10 percent were being good. So the Lord decided to send an email to those 10 percent who were being good, to strengthen and encourage them. And do you know what that email said? . . . Oh . . . I'm sorry . . . You didn't get that email?

In Revelation, angels are mentioned more than seventy times, and their ministry is very prominent. We have read about angels in every chapter of Revelation thus far, and chapter 10 is no exception. We don't think about angels very often, but when we get to heaven, they'll be everywhere. We remember that angels are God's messengers, and they minister to the church. Angels do a perfect job of glorifying the Lord and focusing on His message. That is the case here in chapter 10, and while these verses have a lot to say about one particular mighty angel, the focus is still on God's message.

In this chapter, we'll see:

- the message for John
- the message for the world
- the message for us

Let's read the first four verses of chapter 10.

> I saw still another mighty angel coming down from heaven, clothed with a cloud. And a rainbow was on his head, his face was like the sun, and his feet like pillars of fire. He had a little book open in his hand. And he set his right foot on the sea and his left foot on the land, and cried with a loud voice, as when a lion roars. When he cried out, seven thunders uttered their voices. Now when the seven thunders uttered their voices, I was about to write; but I heard a voice from heaven saying to me, "Seal up the things which the seven thunders uttered, and do not write them."
>
> Revelation 10:1–4

The opening scene here is in contrast with the opening scene in chapter 9. That chapter begins with the opening of the abyss, which releases an army of locust-like demons. But here in chapter 10, we begin with a holy angel coming out of heaven.

John sees another "mighty angel," and as we read these details, we're probably not surprised to hear that many commentators and Bible students believe this is Jesus. After all, he comes down from heaven, he is clothed with a cloud, he has a rainbow around his head, his face is like the sun, and his feet are like pillars of fire. We have seen similar references to Jesus in Revelation. And let me state for the record that this *could* very well be a description of the Lord Jesus Christ. I have a different opinion, and I'll explain why.

First off, John calls him an angel throughout this chapter. As I've mentioned before, the Greek word for "angel" simply means messenger. While angels are indeed God's messengers, Jesus is not a messenger in that same sense. Someone might argue that Jesus made appearances in the Old Testament and was identified there as "the angel of the Lord." While that's true, that was prior to His incarnation on earth and His ministry at the cross. Nowhere in the New Testament is Jesus ever referred to as an angel. In fact, in Revelation, Jesus is always given a specific title of honor or deity, such as "Alpha and Omega," "Holy and True," "Son of God," and so forth.

Second, John writes that he saw "still another mighty angel." In the previous two chapters, John described six mighty angels sounding their trumpet judgments. Now here in the very next verse, John sees "another mighty angel," and the Greek word John uses for "another" means "another of the same kind." Jesus never was, and never will be, an angel. As God, Jesus is the Creator of the angels.

I would also point out that in the Bible we never read that Jesus is going to come down to the earth at the midpoint of the tribulation period. All of the Scriptures about the end times describe Jesus coming at the end of the tribulation, at His second coming. But why, then, do we read some descriptions in the first few verses that sound similar to the descriptions of Jesus found in the earlier chapters? I think Pastor Jon Courson, in his Revelation commentary, puts his finger on the answer: just as the face of Moses shone with God's glory from being in His presence for forty days, so this mighty angel who comes down to the earth from heaven, and from the presence of the Lord, is also reflecting the glory of the Lord.[1] As we spend time with the Lord—in His Word, in worship, in prayer, and in fellowship—we hope people can look at us and know we have been with Jesus as well.

In verse 2, this angel has a book in his hands. The Greek word used for "book" is a derivative of the Greek word for "scroll."[2] Seeing that the seal judgments and the first six trumpet judgments have taken place, and that we have this interlude at the midpoint of the tribulation, we can conclude that this book contains the remaining judgments of the second half of the tribulation. This angel cries out, and John describes the sound as being like that of a lion roaring.

In addition to the angel's voice sounding like the roar of a lion, it was followed by another voice that sounded like seven peals of thunder. In Psalm 29:3, David writes, "The voice of the LORD is over the waters; the God of glory thunders." So there is little doubt that this thundering voice is that of the Lord.

In verse 4, something quite interesting takes place. As John is about to record what the thundering voice of God has said, another voice from heaven commands John not to write it down but rather to seal it up. It's only my opinion, but I would guess that the thundering voice was that of God the Father, while the second voice from heaven telling John not to record what he has heard is that of the Lord Jesus. The second voice is possibly another angel, but when it comes to instructions for revelation, those commands have normally come from the Lord Jesus.

Our first point here in verses 1–4 is *the message for John.* John heard the message clearly and, as he had been doing all along, was preparing to write what he heard. The purpose of this entire book is to reveal. However, in this one instance, John is commanded not to record what he has heard, making it the only words in Revelation that are sealed.

In spite of God's clear words here, some of the cults have claimed to know what God said. However, it is a very foolish practice to insert a comma where God has placed a period. God told John to seal it up. Period. End of discussion. So why is this incident even mentioned? It is like someone saying to you, "You'll never believe what so-and-so said." When you ask, "What?" he or she replies, "Sorry, but I can't tell you." (Then you say, "Come over here so I can slap you!") In the same way, John says, "God's voice thundered and said the most amazing thing!" We ask, "What, John? What did God say?" "Sorry, can't tell you." Obviously, it wasn't John's intent to tease us; he is simply recording these details as they unfold. As believers, we don't live on explanations; we live on God's promises. This message in verse 4 was only for John, and not for us. We can ask John about it when we get to heaven, but don't be surprised if John smiles and says, "It's none of your business."

Now we come to our next section—*the message for the world*:

> The angel whom I saw standing on the sea and on the land raised up his hand to heaven and swore by Him who lives forever and ever, who created heaven and the things that are in it, the earth and the things that are in it, and the sea and the things that are in it, that there should be delay no longer, but in the days of the sounding of

the seventh angel, when he is about to sound, the mystery of God would be finished, as He declared to His servants the prophets.

Revelation 10:5–7

Like someone being sworn to oath in a court of law, this angel raises his hand to heaven and swears an oath by the name of God. One writer states that the practice of raising the right hand in court, and swearing an oath to tell the truth as a witness, originated from these words in Revelation 10.[3]

The truth being sworn to by the angel is that "there should be delay no longer." God has been delaying and waiting, because He is long-suffering toward the lost, and has been allowing more time for people to be saved. At the same time, He allows the earth to become riper and riper for judgment. Now at the midpoint of the tribulation, God says, "No more delays." The seventh trumpet is about to sound, and the final judgments of the tribulation are about to unfold. God's message to the world is "no more delays."

We read in verse 7 that "the mystery of God," given in Scripture through the Old Testament prophets, is about to be finished. Even when prophets such as Isaiah, Ezekiel, and Daniel wrote about the last days, they did not understand the full meaning of what they were writing. This is part of what the Bible describes as "the mysteries of God."

Now when we hear the word *mysteries*, we probably think of books written by great mystery writers, such as Agatha Christie. I enjoy reading mysteries, and I enjoy mystery movies. In Scripture, the word *mystery* often refers to those Old Testament plans and purposes of God that were not previously understood but are explained and revealed in the New Testament. For example, the Old Testament speaks of God's plan of salvation including the Gentiles, but it wasn't understood how Gentiles, who were not God's chosen people, could be saved. But now we know that Christ's death on the cross provided forgiveness of sins and salvation, which are available to all people by faith, whether Jew or Gentile. This mystery did not begin to be understood until after the church was established in Acts. The mystery spoken of here in Revelation refers to the last days, the second coming of Christ, and the establishment of His kingdom. The full understanding of that is about to unfold at this point of the tribulation.

In verses 8–11, we find *God's message for us.*

> Then the voice which I heard from heaven spoke to me again and said, "Go, take the little book which is open in the hand of the angel who stands on the sea and on the earth." So I went to the angel and said to him, "Give me the little book." And he said to me, "Take and eat it; and it will make your stomach bitter, but it will be as sweet as honey in your mouth." Then I took the little book out of the angel's hand and ate it, and it was as sweet as honey in my mouth. But when I had eaten it, my stomach became bitter. And he said to me, "You must prophesy again about many peoples, nations, tongues, and kings."
>
> Revelation 10:8–11

The voice from heaven, which is undoubtedly the voice of God, instructs John to go and take the little book from the hand of the angel. As John asks the angel to give him the book, the angel essentially tells John, "Eat the book, and as you do, it will taste sweet like honey in your mouth, but it will become bitter as it reaches your stomach."

Just as the angel had described, when John ate the little book, it was sweet in his mouth but became bitter in his stomach. The act of eating the little book was intended to symbolize an important truth for John, and for us as well. It was one thing for John to see the book in the angel's hand and to hear the words spoken from it. But it was quite another thing for John to personally ingest the word into his body.

As you and I are ingesting the book of Revelation into our hearts and minds, it should have exactly the same effect. As we taste the Word of God in Revelation, it is sweet in our mouths, in the sense that we get excited about the Lord's imminent return. We want the Lord to come back. We want the Lord to execute judgment. We want for all the wrongs to be made right. Those truths taste very sweet in our mouths, like honey.

But as we consume these words, they turn bitter in our stomachs. This speaks of our realization that Christ's return closes the door on the ministry of the gospel. It means that all unsaved people are going

144

to suffer immensely. It means that our unsaved families and friends are going to suffer as well. Suddenly, the sweet truths of Revelation begin to turn bitter in our stomachs.

But there's yet another reason why this is God's message for us. In verse 11, the angel says to John, "You must prophesy [or, literally, continue to prophesy] about peoples, nations, tongues, and kings." John needed to complete his commission from the Lord to record the events of the last days. For us, as believers today, we must remain faithful to proclaim both the good news and the bad news of the gospel. We must include the bitter truths along with the sweet. John's words were for all peoples and nations—some saved and some unsaved. The gospel that is very good news to the person who believes is also very bad news for the person who refuses to believe. We have a responsibility to tell people about heaven and to warn people about hell.

Far too many churches are telling people that God loves them, which is the sweet truth, but they are not telling people that they're sinners in need of a Savior. Like John, as we consume the Word of God, we must speak the complete truth to all people. And that truth is, indeed, bittersweet.

15

The Temple
and the Two Witnesses

Revelation 11:1–19

I'm not sure that I should share this with you . . . but I enjoy killing hornets and wasps. I have no issues with bees because they pollinate our flowers, but hornets are nothing more than squatters. They continuously attempt to build their nests underneath the eaves of our house. But one of God's greatest little inventions is hornet knock-down spray, and every time I'm at the home improvement store I pick up a couple cans, whether I need them or not.

This spray allows you to stand back a few feet and spray the hornets' nest from a safe distance. When the spray hits the nest, the hornets become really angry for about two seconds, and then they die. I absolutely love this stuff! The only downside is that by the time I've knocked down the nests under our eaves I'm just starting to get an adrenaline rush, but the fun's already over. I get excited when our neighbors go on vacation, because then I take my knock-down spray can with me and check under their eaves. For the record, I've never been stung by a hornet or a wasp.

I recently read an article with a headline that asked simply, "Karma?"[1] It seems that a Japanese monk discovered a hornets' nest inside his Buddhist temple and decided to get rid of his uninvited guests. But evidently they don't have hornet knock-down spray for sale in Japan. So this monk took a stick, wrapped some old rags around it, lit the rags, and made a torch. He held the lit torch up to the nest, but before he could destroy the nest, the hornets flew out and started chasing him. The monk panicked and dropped his torch while being chased around his Buddhist temple. In the process, the temple caught on fire and burned to the ground. The bad news for that monk, besides the fact that his temple was destroyed, is that he suffered burns on his face and hands. But the good news is that he was not stung by any of the hornets—so the monk and I both have that going for us!

As we come now to Revelation 11, we're going to talk about a different temple: the Jewish temple that will stand during the tribulation period. In verse 1, John's role changes from being an observer and recorder to being personally involved.

> Then I was given a reed like a measuring rod. And the angel stood, saying, "Rise and measure the temple of God, the altar, and those who worship there. But leave out the court which is outside the temple, and do not measure it, for it has been given to the Gentiles. And they will tread the holy city underfoot for forty-two months."
>
> Revelation 11:1–2

The Jewish temple was destroyed in AD 70, just as Jesus had prophesied in Mark 13:2. Today, more than 1,900 years later, the Jewish people still do not have a temple. In fact, the Jewish people have been able to reestablish themselves as a nation only recently—in 1948. Throughout the years, the question has oftentimes been asked, will the Jewish people ever rebuild their temple? And the answer is definitely yes! Not only does the Bible make this clear, but preparations are being made in Israel right now.

In Israel today, you can visit the Temple Institute, where preparations are being made for the rebuilding of the temple. They've finished remaking all the temple utensils, as well as the garments to be worn by the priests. They're preparing for reinstituting animal sacrifices, and they're making everything according to what was written in the Old Testament.

Scripture tells us that the third temple will be built in the near future. In Daniel 9:27, the rebuilding of the temple is strongly implied. Daniel speaks of how the Antichrist will make a covenant with Israel for a period of seven years. He speaks of how the Antichrist will bring a sudden and unexpected end to the Jewish sacrifices in the middle of the tribulation period. The fact that the Jews will be sacrificing once again tells us that the Jewish temple will be rebuilt. Jesus also speaks of this in Matthew 24.

But we can remove any doubt by what we read here in Revelation 11:1–2. Here the apostle John is instructed to measure the temple, the altar, and the people who are worshiping there. So the Jewish temple will definitely be rebuilt. For John personally, we should remember that the temple in his day had been destroyed by the Romans just twenty to twenty-five years earlier. John was recording this vision in the last part of the first century. So John, who had lived with the temple much of his life, is now allowed to see the future temple and to measure it.

Of course, the ongoing question is, how can the Jews rebuild the temple on the Temple Mount, seeing that it is controlled by Muslims and that the Dome of the Rock is already there? Some Bible students have attempted to explain this away by spiritualizing this temple, seeing it not as an actual temple structure but something spiritual and symbolic. However, John would have a difficult time measuring something if it wasn't there, so that suggestion makes no sense.

The Dome of the Rock shrine is considered the third holiest site in Islam, after Mecca and Medina. Muslims believe that the prophet Muhammad, along with the angel Gabriel, ascended to heaven from the rock that sits in the middle of the domed shrine—hence the name, Dome of the Rock. Many Jews and some Christians believe the rock marks the place where Abraham offered up Isaac.

So, again, how will the Jewish temple be rebuilt on the Temple Mount, seeing that the Dome of the Rock is there? Some believe that in order for the temple to be rebuilt, the Dome of the Rock must be removed. Therefore, they conclude, the Dome may be destroyed in some military conflict. While this is possible, I don't see it playing out that way.

When we visited the Temple Institute in 1999, another pastor and I were speaking with a representative there, and her name was Hadassah. We asked Hadassah how she and the others at the Temple Institute believed that the temple would be rebuilt, seeing that the Dome of the Rock is there. Her response was, "We don't know exactly how it's going to happen, but somehow we believe that God will make a way for us Jews, as well as many others, to worship there." I happen to agree with Hadassah.

On another of my trips to Israel, some friends and I were able to visit the Arab-controlled city of Bethlehem. We hired an Arab guide, and this allowed us to enter the city. We would not have been able to enter Bethlehem with a Jewish guide. One of the places we wanted to visit was Rachel's tomb. Rachel, the beloved wife of Jacob, was buried near Bethlehem, as Scripture tells us. However, while the city of Bethlehem is Arab controlled, Rachel's tomb is still Jewish controlled. So as we drove near Rachel's tomb, we saw a twelve-foot fence around the site. Our Arab guide looked at us and said, "I can't take you in to see Rachel's tomb; you would need a Jewish guide to get in." Of course, a Jewish guide couldn't get us into Bethlehem, so it was a catch-22, and we never saw Rachel's tomb. But the experience was not wasted, because that Jewish-controlled tomb, surrounded by an Arab-controlled city, gave me a visual understanding of how the Jewish temple could be rebuilt on the Temple Mount in close proximity to the Dome of the Rock.

A few decades ago, a professor from the Hebrew University in Jerusalem, Dr. Asher Kaufman, had his research work about the Temple Mount published. After many years of painstaking investigation, Dr. Kaufman declared that the former Jewish temples did not rest on the spot where the Dome of the Rock stands but to its north.

There is now a small gazebo-like structure to the northwest of the Dome of the Rock. According to Kaufman's findings, the Holy of Holies of the first two temples was located exactly where that gazebo stands today. The Muslims have a name for that gazebo: the Dome of the Tablets. So it seems quite possible that on that spot stood the Holy of Holies, which held the ark of the covenant, which contained the stone tablets on which were written the Ten Commandments.

It seems very likely to me that the Jewish temple could be rebuilt on that spot, more than a hundred yards from the Dome of the Rock but still on the Temple Mount area. To preserve peace, and to allow both religious groups the opportunity to worship, a large wall could be erected between those two places of worship. Daniel 9:27 states that the Antichrist will barter a peace agreement in the Middle East, and his peace plan may very well allow for Jews to rebuild their temple right next to the Dome of the Rock.

That scenario fits well with the first two verses of Revelation 11. Let's read them again.

> Then I was given a reed like a measuring rod. And the angel stood, saying, "Rise and measure the temple of God, the altar, and those who worship there. But leave out the court which is outside the temple, and do not measure it, for it has been given to the Gentiles. And they will tread the holy city underfoot for forty-two months."
>
> Revelation 11:1–2

The Greek word used here for "temple" is not the word used in reference to the entire temple complex. Instead, it's the Greek word used only in reference to the Holy Place. So it refers to that first room, in which you would find the altar of incense, the table of showbread, and the golden lampstand (or menorah). Then there was the smaller, adjacent room beyond the veil called the Holy of Holies. Inside was the ark of the covenant, with the mercy seat on top. This area is what John is instructed to measure in verse 1. The act of measuring signifies evaluation, and in this case, God is evaluating the worship taking place here. Several respectable commentators interpret these worshipers as being saved Jews, worshiping God at the temple. I have a different opinion, and I'll explain why.

John is instructed to measure the temple, but he is also instructed to measure the altar—the brazen altar in the courtyard directly in front of the temple. We know it's not referring to the altar of incense inside the temple, because only the priests could enter the Holy Place, and not the worshipers. The brazen altar, in front of the entrance to the Holy Place, is where the animal sacrifice was brought.

Then John is instructed to measure or evaluate the worshipers themselves. These worshipers are at the brazen altar, which means they've brought animal sacrifices, so they have reverted back to the Old Testament system. Therefore, they are not worshiping God as New Testament believers but as Old Testament Jews who have not yet accepted Jesus as their Messiah.

In verse 2, John is instructed not to measure the area just outside the rebuilt temple. According to what we've been discussing, this could very well refer to the Dome of the Rock and all the other Muslim structures. The last half of verse 2 speaks about the holy city, which refers to Jerusalem, as being trampled underfoot for the next forty-two months (or three and a half years). This would be the forces of the Antichrist overrunning the city.

Seeing that John was instructed to measure the worshipers at the temple, we should ask ourselves, "How do we measure up as worshipers of God?" Paul reminds us in 1 Corinthians 6 that our bodies are the temple of God, where the Holy Spirit resides. So when God measures the temple of our lives, how do we measure up?

"And I will give power to my two witnesses, and they will prophesy one thousand two hundred and sixty days, clothed in sackcloth." These are the two olive trees and the two lampstands standing before the God of the earth. And if anyone wants to harm them, fire proceeds from their mouth and devours their enemies. And if anyone wants to harm them, he must be killed in this manner. These have power to shut heaven, so that no rain falls in the days of their prophecy; and they have power over waters to turn them to blood, and to strike the earth with all plagues, as often as they desire. When they finish their testimony, the beast that ascends out of the bottomless pit will make war against them, overcome them, and kill them. And their dead bodies will lie in the street of the great city which spiritually is called Sodom and Egypt, where also our Lord was crucified. Then those from the peoples, tribes, tongues, and nations will see their dead bodies three-and-a-half days, and not allow their dead bodies to be put into graves. And those who dwell on the earth will rejoice over them, make merry, and send gifts to one another, because these two prophets tormented those who dwell on the earth. Now after the three-and-a-half days the breath of life from God entered them, and they stood on their feet, and great fear fell on those who saw them. And they heard a loud voice from heaven saying to them, "Come up here." And they ascended to heaven in a cloud, and their enemies saw them. In the same hour there was a great earthquake, and a tenth of the city fell. In the earthquake seven thousand people were killed, and the rest were afraid and gave glory to the God of heaven. The second woe is past. Behold, the third woe is coming quickly.

Revelation 11:3–14

When Paul was preaching the gospel in Lystra, as recorded in Acts 14, he made the statement that God never leaves Himself without a witness (Acts 14:17). Scripture certainly bears this out. From Noah in the flood, to Lot in Sodom, to Elijah on Mount Carmel, to John the Baptist in the wilderness, and all the way to the 144,000 Jewish evangelists in the tribulation period—God always leaves Himself a witness to the truth.

Many years ago, I was the sole eyewitness to a brutal murder. However, the entire event was also overheard by another person, on a pay phone, and on the basis of our two testimonies in court, all of the persons responsible for committing that murder were convicted and sentenced. Here in Revelation 11, we learn about two unique witnesses that God will raise up during the tribulation period. The identities of these two witnesses are not given to us, and, as you might imagine, their identities have been the subject of much discussion over the years.

While we are not given the identities of these witnesses, we are given quite a bit of information about them. In verse 3, God declares that He will give His power to His two witnesses. This is a good reminder to all of us that we are witnesses of God and that everything we do, if it is to succeed spiritually, must be done in His power. The Greek word used here for "witnesses" is *martus*, from which we get our English word *martyr*.

For many of God's people throughout history, being witnesses to God's truth cost them their lives. While that may not be the case for many believers today in the physical sense, it should definitely be true for all believers in the spiritual sense. As Jesus said, "If anyone wants to become My disciple, you must deny yourself, take up the cross, and follow Me" (Matt. 16:24 paraphrased). So all of us are called to be spiritual martyrs.

It appears that the ministry of these two witnesses will be focused on the land of Israel and the city of Jerusalem in particular. So while the 144,000 Jewish evangelists we met in chapter 7 will

152

minister all over the earth, it seems that these two will remain in the Holy Land.

The ministry of these two witnesses is to prophesy for 1,260 days. To prophesy, in the New Testament sense, means to speak forth the truth. The message of these two witnesses will be twofold—warning people about the judgments still to come in the second half of the tribulation, as well as proclaiming the gospel and exhorting people to turn to God by faith in Jesus. This is the same message we are called on by God to share as His witnesses today: the bad news of God's judgment for sin, and the good news of salvation that God offers through faith in Christ.

This period of 1,260 days equals forty-two months, or three and a half years. The fact that God describes their ministry in terms of days, rather than in months or years, is probably significant. It may be emphasizing that these two witnesses will not be preaching occasionally, or once a week, but rather every day for 1,260 days.

Like the prophets of old, these two witnesses will be dressed in sackcloth. Sackcloth is heavy, coarse, and definitely not fashionable or comfortable. Sackcloth is intended to symbolize mourning for sin, repentance, and humility. The next description of these witnesses, in verse 4, is that they are the two olive trees and the two lampstands before God. This wording is very similar to what we read in Zechariah 4. In that chapter, Zechariah describes a vision of two olive trees on either side of a lampstand standing before the Lord. An angel explains for him that they represent two "anointed ones." Most likely, they are the faithful spiritual leaders of that day: Joshua and Zerubbabel, whom the Lord raised up to build the second temple after Israel's seventy years of captivity in Babylon.

In verses 5–6, we read that God will protect and preserve His two witnesses during their three and a half years of ministry. If anyone tries to harm these two, we read, fire will proceed from their mouths and devour their enemies. Now, before we start getting a mental picture of Godzilla stomping down the streets of Japan, this is not to be taken quite so literally. In keeping with previous examples in Scripture, this would mean that these two witnesses, in God's power, would call down fire from heaven, as well as command the rain not to fall, turn bodies of water into blood, and call forth various plagues.

Let's turn now to a discussion of the identities of these two witnesses. On the one hand, if God wanted us to know who these two witnesses were for certain, He would have had John record it for us here. But at the same time, there's no mistaking the similarities that we find to Moses and Elijah. There have been other suggestions such as Joshua and Zerubbabel, because of the references to olive trees in verse 4, or Enoch and Elijah, since they are the only two people in the Bible who went directly into heaven and did not die. Since Hebrews 9:27 states that "it is appointed for men to die once," some have suggested that these witnesses are Enoch and Elijah, who will finally die as martyrs during the tribulation period.

I don't find that theory very compelling. After all, in the rapture, millions of people will be caught up simultaneously and will go to heaven without having to die. So if we take that line of reasoning away, there's no case for Enoch being one of these two witnesses. On the other hand, a very strong case can be made to suggest that these two witnesses will be Moses and Elijah.

In Matthew 17, we read that Moses and Elijah appeared on the mount of transfiguration with Jesus. In the Old Testament, Moses represents the law while Elijah represents the prophets. We also recall that God raised up Moses at a time when a type of Antichrist, Pharaoh, was attempting to obliterate the Jewish people—similar to what will take place in the tribulation. In the same way, God raised up Elijah in some of the darkest days of Israel's history, when wicked King Ahab and his wife, Jezebel, along with the prophets of Baal, were threatening to destroy all true worship of God in the Holy Land.

Then there are the miraculous works, mentioned in verses 5 and 6, which bear a striking similarity to the miraculous works of Moses and Elijah in the days of their ministries. Calling down fire, for example, took place in the ministries of both Moses and Elijah. The end of verse 5 declares that anyone who wants to harm these two witnesses must be killed in this manner. This means that God will supernaturally kill anyone who tries to stop them. It's God's version of the Witness Protection Program!

In verse 6, we read that these two witnesses have power given to them by God so that no rain falls. This reminds us of Elijah and how he declared to King Ahab that no rain would fall in the land, except at his word. There was indeed a severe drought. Interestingly, it did not rain on the land in Elijah's days for three and a half years—exactly the length of ministry for the two witnesses in the tribulation.

The two witnesses will also have the ability to turn water into blood, as Moses did in the first plague against Pharaoh and Egypt. With one-third of the world's water supplies already poisoned, as we read in chapter 8, the lack of rain and the turning of water into blood will greatly intensify the shortage of freshwater. Verse 6 ends with the notation that these witnesses will be able to strike the earth with all sorts of plagues, just as Moses did in Egypt.

One final piece of support for Moses and Elijah being these two witnesses is found at the end of Malachi's prophecy, which closes the Old Testament. In the final three verses, Malachi includes these words of the Lord: "Remember the Law of Moses, My servant. . . . Behold, I will send you Elijah the prophet before the coming of the great and dreadful day of the LORD" (Mal. 4:4–5). How interesting that the final words of the Old Testament make clear reference to Moses and Elijah, who later appear with Jesus on the mount of transfiguration.

In verse 7, we read that "when they finish their testimony, the beast that ascends out of the bottomless pit will make war against them, overcome them, and kill them." No matter how many times people attempt to kill them—and I'm sure there will be numerous attempts—those attempts will always fail, until their ministry is finished. The Antichrist, who is called "the beast" here for the first time in Revelation, is satanically energized from the very pit of the abyss. After three and a half years, and once their mission is accomplished, God will allow the Antichrist to prevail. The Antichrist will do what no one else has been able to do: kill the two prophets. This will undoubtedly go a long way in generating tremendous support for this satanic world leader, as he will finally rid the world of those two menaces to society.

In verse 8, we are told that their bodies will lie in the streets for three and a half days, as the Antichrist will not allow them to be buried. The act of not burying the bodies is intended to bring disgrace. We know that the city in which their bodies will lie is Jerusalem, because the end of this verse tells us that it is the same city where "our Lord was crucified." The very streets where Jesus was savagely beaten and tortured, and then dragged to His crucifixion, will be where the bodies of His two witnesses will lie dead and desecrated. The sacred and holy city, where these two witnesses ministered, will become the place of their murders and humiliation.

The name *Jerusalem* means "dwelling of peace," or "place of peace." Jerusalem is to be the capital city and centerpiece of the Holy Land, where God's people dwell. But at this point, things are so bad that God calls Jerusalem "Sodom and Egypt," spiritually speaking. Sodom is the Old Testament city synonymous with perversion; Egypt is the Old Testament city synonymous with idolatry.

Verse 9 provides an interesting piece of information: everyone around the world will see the bodies of these two witnesses lying in the streets of Jerusalem. This is why it is so exciting for us to study the book of Revelation in these last days. For centuries, spiritual leaders told their congregations that Revelation was impossible to understand, and for many people it has been considered a closed book. Even to this day, the mind-set prevails in some churches that we cannot understand Revelation.

What we read here in verse 9 is just one example of how things have become so much clearer in these last days. Just sixty years ago, it would have been considered impossible for the entire world to witness a single event, as we read here. But thanks to satellite technology, this is now commonplace. Within minutes of world events, television networks are on location, broadcasting live and sending the pictures out to homes all around the world. I can almost envision this on CNN: while reporters give their updates and interviews, somewhere on the screen the image of these two dead bodies will remain in the background for three and a half days.

In the meantime, we read in verse 10, this will create a worldwide celebration that rivals Christmas. This is the only time that people on the earth rejoice during the tribulation—when God's two prophets are killed. Around the world, people will be celebrating, partying, rejoicing, and exchanging gifts. I'm going to speculate that the Antichrist will go on global network television and explain that these two men were responsible for calamities and catastrophes on earth, but now they're dead.

Perhaps the Antichrist, in an attempt to banish any trace of Christmas and the birth of Christ, will declare a new world holiday that includes the exchanging of gifts. Maybe he'll call it anti-Christmas.

156

Imagine the whole world, full of unsaved people, celebrating a new holiday that's based on the death of God's two faithful prophets. Then imagine God in heaven, on His throne, looking down upon the earth and watching this celebration. What will God's response be? Let's read verses 11–14 again.

> Now after the three-and-a-half days the breath of life from God entered them, and they stood on their feet, and great fear fell on those who saw them. And they heard a loud voice from heaven saying to them, "Come up here." And they ascended to heaven in a cloud, and their enemies saw them. In the same hour there was a great earthquake, and a tenth of the city fell. In the earthquake seven thousand people were killed, and the rest were afraid and gave glory to the God of heaven. The second woe is past. Behold, the third woe is coming quickly.
>
> Revelation 11:3–14

The party is over! At this point, many people are beginning to wonder what the return policy is on the gifts they bought. Those who are intoxicated from partying are undoubtedly going to sober up very quickly. After three and a half days, suddenly and quite unexpectedly, the two witnesses receive life once again from God, and they stand up on their feet.

In verse 11, we read that the great joy of the people suddenly becomes great fear after the two witnesses come back to life. Then in verse 13, we read of a great earthquake that rocks the city, causing a tenth of the city to fall down and seven thousand people to die. The end of this verse tells us that the response of the remaining people will be to give glory to God. This has prompted many commentators to wonder whether this is genuine repentance or simply recognition of God's involvement. I might suggest that it's both; some will be genuinely repentant while others will simply be afraid. We do know, according to Zechariah's prophecy, that the spiritual eyes of the Jewish people will be opened, especially in the second half of the tribulation, and they will recognize Jesus as their Messiah.

Remember the story that Jesus told in Luke 16 about the saved beggar named Lazarus and the unsaved rich man? When that unsaved man arrived in Hades and was in torment, he cried out to Abraham and asked whether someone could be sent back to earth to warn his family and friends about that place of torment. The response of Abraham was intriguing, especially when we place it alongside this chapter.

Abraham said, "They have Moses and the prophets; let them hear them." As we stated earlier, Elijah represents the prophets in the Old Testament. Then that tormented, unsaved man in Hades replied, "No, father Abraham; but if one goes to them from the dead, they will repent." But Abraham said to him, "If they do not hear Moses and the prophets, neither will they be persuaded though one rise from the dead" (Luke 16:29–31).

It makes you wonder whether that story told by Jesus was perhaps a veiled reference to this eleventh chapter in Revelation. The story by Jesus certainly points back to Moses and his ministry, but does it also perhaps point forward? If Moses is one of the witnesses, then the inhabitants of the earth will hear him proclaiming God's truth. Although Moses would rise from the dead—if it is indeed Moses here—as Abraham predicted, most people will fail to believe. Certainly Jesus rose from the dead, and the majority of people still refuse to believe.

> Then the seventh angel sounded: And there were loud voices in heaven, saying, "The kingdoms of this world have become the kingdoms of our Lord and of His Christ, and He shall reign forever and ever!" And the twenty-four elders who sat before God on their thrones fell on their faces and worshiped God, saying: "We give You thanks, O Lord God Almighty, The One who is and who was and who is to come, because You have taken Your great power and reigned. The nations were angry, and Your wrath has come, and the time of the dead, that they should be judged, and that You should reward Your servants the prophets and the saints, and those who fear Your name, small and great, and should destroy those who destroy the earth." Then the temple of God was opened in heaven, and the ark of His covenant was seen in His temple. And there were lightnings, noises, thunderings, an earthquake, and great hail.
>
> Revelation 11:15–19

After a long interlude, the seventh trumpet will be sounded, signaling the beginning of the end and the final three and a half years of the tribulation. In verse 15, we read that "the kingdoms of this world have become the kingdoms of our Lord." The remaining judgments will take place in rapid succession, and then Jesus Christ will return to set up His kingdom on earth, followed by the kingdom of God in eternity.

In verse 16, the believers in heaven, represented by the twenty-four elders, return to worshiping God—especially in light of the fact that God's kingdom is about to come, on earth as it is in heaven. This prompts great praise, worship, and rejoicing in heaven. In this chapter, we were reminded of what makes the unsaved world rejoice and celebrate: when God's will appears to fail. In contrast, what makes the believers and angels in heaven rejoice and celebrate is when God's will succeeds. Like the hosts of heaven, our response should also be to worship God.

In verse 19, we read that the temple of God will open up in heaven and the ark of the covenant will be seen. To this day, people love to discuss and debate the whereabouts of the ark of the covenant. Archaeologists are still searching for it, and one day they may find it on earth. But we also remember that the ark of the covenant, made by Moses, was simply an earthly replica of the real ark, which resides in heaven. The ark reminds us of God's presence and God's faithfulness to His people in every generation.

16

A History of Hatred

Revelation 12:1–17

After a long illness, a woman passed away and arrived at the pearly gates of heaven. While she was waiting for Peter to greet her, she peeked in and saw a beautiful banquet table. Sitting inside were some of her family and friends who had gone before her. When Peter came by, the woman said to him, "This is such a wonderful place! How do I get in?" Peter replied, "It's very simple. You just have to spell a word." "What word?" the woman asked. "Love," Peter answered. The woman correctly spelled l-o-v-e, and Peter welcomed her into heaven.

About six months later, Peter came to the woman and asked her to watch the gates for a few hours. While the woman was at the pearly gates, her ex-husband arrived. "I'm surprised to see you," the woman said. "How have you been?" "Oh, I've been doing pretty well since our divorce," the ex-husband told her. "I married my secretary, and then I won the lottery. So I sold the little house you and I used to live in and bought a big mansion. Then my new wife and I traveled all around the world. We were on vacation in Switzerland, and I was skiing when I fell and hit my head—and here I am. So how do I get in?" "You just have to spell one word," the woman told him. "What word?" her ex-husband asked.

"Czechoslovakia."

As we come now to the twelfth chapter in Revelation, the apostle John describes for us a vision from heaven, and fortunately for us, we don't even have to spell Czechoslovakia!

Here in Revelation 12, some significant things begin to take place. For one, we are set to begin the second half of the book of Revelation—eleven chapters completed, and eleven chapters to go. Second, this chapter brings us to the beginning of the second half of the tribulation period. Third, chapters 12 and 13 will start to introduce us to an unholy trinity: Satan, who is described as a fiery red dragon and the serpent of old; the Antichrist, a demonic world leader and false messiah; and the False Prophet, whose ministry is a counterfeit imitation of the Holy Spirit's ministry. God is the great Creator and Originator, while Satan is the great imitator and impersonator.

Chapter 12 presents us with an overview of Satan's hatred toward God and toward God's people, the Jews. For this reason, I've titled this chapter "A History of Hatred." John's vision in Revelation 12 takes us both backward and forward in history. So let's begin.

Now a great sign appeared in heaven: a woman clothed with the sun, with the moon under her feet, and on her head a garland of twelve stars. Then being with child, she cried out in labor and in pain to give birth. And another sign appeared in heaven: behold, a great, fiery red dragon having seven heads and ten horns, and seven diadems on his heads. His tail drew a third of the stars of heaven and threw them to the earth. And the dragon stood before the woman who was ready to give birth, to devour her Child as soon as it was born. She bore a male Child who was to rule all nations with a rod of iron. And her Child was caught up to God and His throne. Then the woman fled into the wilderness, where she has a place prepared by God, that they should feed her there one thousand two hundred and sixty days.

Revelation 12:1–6

Chapter 12 opens with two signs in heaven. These are the first and the second of seven signs recorded in Revelation.[1] The first of these two signs is a woman with child, clothed with the sun, moon, and twelve stars. Clearly, the woman described here is symbolic and not to be taken literally, because no woman would be clothed with planets and stars. So, then, who does this woman represent? Attempts have been made by various religious groups to identify this woman. One major denomination claims that this woman is the virgin Mary. As we will see in just a moment, the Child in these verses is indeed the Lord Jesus, so this assumption is understandable.

However, this interpretation is ruled out by several factors. In verse 1, this woman appears in heaven. Mary was not in heaven prior to her death. Remember that when she was ready to give birth to Jesus, she was a teenager living in Nazareth who traveled with Joseph to Bethlehem. And Mary was certainly not clothed with stars and planets. In verse 6, we're told that this woman will flee to the wilderness during the second half of the tribulation period. Also, in verse 13, this woman is persecuted by satanic forces during the tribulation period. None of those facts would apply to Mary, the mother of Jesus.

Another theory is that she represents the church. This type of thinking shows how quickly people can get off track when they don't compare Scripture with Scripture. In Acts 2, we find that the church was established after the birth, death, resurrection, and ascension of Jesus. The church didn't give birth to Jesus; Jesus gave birth to the church. Jesus Himself said, "I will build My church" (Matt. 16:18).

Then we have the bizarre explanations made by some religious groups in identifying this woman. For example, Mary Baker Eddy, founder of Christian Science, made the ridiculous claim that she was the woman described here in Revelation 12 and that the child was the religion of Christian Science. She also claimed that the great red dragon represented those who would seek to destroy her new religion. What amazes me about this is not that she would make such a bizarre claim but that anyone would believe it! When Dr. Harry Ironside was asked to comment on Mary Baker Eddy's "interpretation" of these verses, he said, "I do not need to take up the time of sane people."[2] I think that sums it up!

The clue to the identity of this woman is actually given to us in verse 1. She is described as being "clothed with the sun," with "the moon under her feet," and wearing "a garland of twelve stars" on her head. There is another place in Scripture with that same description, and it's in Genesis 37. Young Joseph had two dreams. In one of those dreams, he saw the sun, the moon, and eleven stars bowing down to him. When he shared that dream with his family, they immediately understood that the sun symbolized his father Jacob, the moon represented his mother, and the eleven stars were his eleven brothers, all bowing down before Joseph. His family really resented that dream. (Some dreams are better kept to ourselves!) However, this prophetic dream was fulfilled later in Joseph's life, when his family bowed before him in Egypt.

Here in Revelation 12:1, we can see how this symbolism connects us back to Jacob and his family. As we know, God changed Jacob's name to Israel, and the descendants of Jacob's twelve sons became known as the twelve tribes of Israel. Therefore, this woman represents Israel, and Jesus was born a Jew and a descendant of the Jewish tribe of Judah. Warren Wiersbe likes to remind us that many of our spiritual blessings today as Christians have come to us through the Jewish people. These include the Scriptures, the Savior, the prophets and apostles, and the church—which began with Jewish believers, on a Jewish holiday, in the Jewish city of Jerusalem.

Before we move on, let me also mention that this is one of four symbolic women found in the book of Revelation:

1. Jezebel (church at Thyatira)—symbolizes immorality (Rev. 2:20)
2. the woman with child—symbolizes Israel (Rev. 12:1)
3. the great harlot—symbolizes false religion (Rev. 17:1)
4. the bride of Christ—symbolizes the church (Rev. 19:7)

In verse 2, the woman representing the nation of Israel is going to give birth to Christ. In verse 5, the Child is described as One who will "rule all the nations with a rod of iron" and who ascends to His throne in heaven. These are clear references to Jesus. The fact that she (Israel) cries out in great pain represents the fact that the Jewish people were under intense oppression at the time of Christ's birth, courtesy of the Romans. It also symbolizes Israel's longing for her Messiah to come and establish His kingdom, as prophesied in the Old Testament.

In verse 3, the second sign appears, and it is a fiery red dragon. There is no guesswork needed here as to the identity of this dragon, because verse 9 clearly points out that this is Satan. The red coloring refers to bloodshed, just as the red horse rider did back in chapter 6. We'll get into more detail in the coming chapters, but for now, we will note that the seven heads and ten horns symbolize world kingdoms and kings.

In verse 4, the text takes us way back to before the days of Eden and makes reference to the original fall of Satan. John writes that one-third of the stars of heaven fell to the earth with Satan at that time. A few lines later, in verses 7 and 9, these stars are identified as Satan's angels—the demons. Originally, God created millions, if not billions, of holy angels. Satan, known as Lucifer, became filled with pride and wanted to become like God and to be worshiped by the angels (Isa. 14). God cast Lucifer out of heaven, and one-third of the angels joined him in his rebellion and are now demons. Satan's name of Lucifer is found only in Isaiah 14:12; *Lucifer* is the Latin word for the planet Venus.

In the middle of verse 4, we fast-forward thousands of years to the birth of Christ. Satan, who is called the dragon, stood before the woman who represents Israel, ready to devour and destroy the Christ child. We read about this in Matthew, when Satan used King Herod in an attempt to destroy the baby Jesus in Bethlehem. Herod succeeded in killing all the other male babies in the city, but not Jesus. Joseph was warned by an angel of the Lord in a dream to flee with Mary and Jesus to Egypt, and so they escaped.

In verse 5, Israel gave birth to that male Child, and in the not-too-distant future, Jesus will rule the nations. This will be His millennial kingdom—something we will discuss in great detail when we get to chapter 20. The end of verse 5 makes reference to how Jesus ascended to heaven following His resurrection and returned to His throne—symbolizing completion of His work of redemption.

Then we come to some interesting information in verse 6, where we fast-forward at least 2,000 years, from the birth of Christ to the days of the tribulation period. We read here that the woman who represents Israel will flee into the wilderness, to a place prepared by God. There, the Lord will protect and provide for her for 1,260 days (three and a half years), which is the second half of the tribulation. It is worth noting John's use of the wording "a place prepared by God." This phrase appears just one other time, in John's Gospel.

Jesus told His disciples in the upper room, "I go to prepare a place for you," speaking of dwelling places in heaven. Just as Christ has gone to prepare a place for believers in heaven, so God has prepared a place for Israel in the wilderness during the second half of the tribulation.

Jesus talked about the persecution of Israel during the tribulation in Matthew 24:16. He said, "Let those who are in Judea flee to the mountains." There has been much speculation as to where the Jews will flee. You may have heard how some Bible scholars believe the hiding place for the Jews will be in the place called Petra. Of course, as Bible students, our first response should be is there any biblical support for that theory? The answer is yes.

In the latter part of Daniel 11, we read details about the Antichrist and his campaign during the tribulation. In Daniel 11:41, we read, "He shall also enter the Glorious Land, and many countries shall be overthrown; but these shall escape from his hand: Edom, Moab, and the . . . people of Ammon." This is a very interesting verse, because we read that the Antichrist will essentially conquer all of the Middle East, including the Holy Land of Israel, but not Edom, Moab, and Ammon. Today, the Old Testament areas of Edom, Moab, and Ammon are occupied by Jordan.

Jordan is the country neighboring Israel on the east, and not all that far from Jerusalem. Jesus said that Israel would flee to the mountains in the wilderness. Just south of the Dead Sea, and across the border into the wilderness of Jordan, are the red-rock hills and fortress-like enclosures of Petra. I was eager to visit Petra, and I was not disappointed when I did in 2008. It's a large, enclosed area, with hundreds of caves and hiding places.

And war broke out in heaven: Michael and his angels fought with the dragon; and the dragon and his angels fought, but they did not prevail, nor was a place found for them in heaven any longer. So the great dragon was cast out, that serpent of old, called the Devil and Satan, who deceives the whole world; he was cast to the earth, and his angels were cast out with him. Then I heard a loud voice saying in heaven, "Now salvation, and strength, and the kingdom of our God, and the power of His Christ have come, for the accuser of our brethren, who accused them before our God day and night, has been cast down. And they overcame him by the blood of the Lamb and by the word of their testimony, and they did not love their lives to the death. Therefore rejoice, O heavens, and you who dwell in them! Woe to the inhabitants of the earth and the sea! For the devil has come down to you, having great wrath, because he knows that he has a short time."

Revelation 12:7–12

Satan and his demons were cast out of heaven thousands of years ago, in the sense of heaven being their dwelling place. However, while heaven is no longer Satan's dwelling place, he continues to have access to heaven. He goes there to accuse believers before God. But even that will come to an end here at the midpoint of the tribulation period.

A war between the holy and fallen angels will break out in heaven. The time is coming when God will no longer allow Satan to enter heaven with his accusations against God's people. God will give the order to Michael the archangel, telling him it is time to take out the trash! And I'm guessing that Michael will have been looking forward to this moment for quite a long time. Michael and the holy angels will go to war with Satan and the fallen angels. It's very possible, and even probable, that Satan himself was an archangel. If so, this war will be led by two opposing archangels. It is worth noting that Michael's name means "Who is like God?" and that's a good response to Satan, who said, "I will be like God!"

Michael and Satan are very familiar with one another and have fought in times past. I'm not exactly sure how angels fight one another. It is doubtful that they would use weapons, as we do. Maybe it will be one big cosmic food fight—the demons throwing deviled eggs, and the angels throwing angel food cake! What we do know for certain is that Michael and the angels will prevail, and Satan will be cast out of heaven permanently.

Verse 8 states that Satan and his demons "will not prevail" in this fight. These words translate as "were not strong enough" to defeat Michael and the holy angels. In verse 10, we are told exactly what Satan was doing in heaven: "Accusing the brethren before our God day and night." The name *Satan* means "adversary," while *devil* means "to accuse and to slander."

In verse 9, we have more descriptions of Satan: he is called "the great dragon" and "the serpent of old." The use of the word *dragon*

166

to describe Satan is found only in Revelation. The Hebrew word for "dragon" is translated in the Old Testament as "monster."[3] The title "serpent of old" takes us back to the Garden of Eden, when Satan deceived Eve. So in Genesis, he's the serpent, and in Revelation, he's the dragon. And his continuous activity is to "deceive the whole world." He is a liar and the father of lies (John 8:44).

After Satan is defeated by Michael and the angels and is cast out of heaven, it brings a collective shout of joy from the saints in heaven, who declare, "Salvation, and strength, and the kingdom of our God, and the power of His Christ have come." Once Satan is permanently banished from heaven, at the midpoint of the tribulation, it won't be long until God's kingdom is established on earth. It also means that it won't be long until Satan is locked up in the abyss for a thousand years and then cast into the lake of fire for eternity.

In verse 11 (a great verse), we have the believer's defense against the accusations and attacks of Satan. The saints in heaven and on earth overcome Satan in the same way: by the blood of the Lamb, by the word of their testimony, and by their willingness to die for their faith. How do we overcome Satan in our lives today?

- by what Christ did on the cross—"by the blood of the Lamb": It's the sacrifice of Jesus, and His shed blood, that cleanses us from all sin and shields us from the accusations of the devil. As Romans 8:1 reminds us, "There is . . . now no condemnation to those who are in Christ Jesus." Charles Spurgeon said, "I have a great need for Christ, and I have a great Christ for my need."[4]

- by what Christ did in our hearts—"by the word of their testimony": He forgives us as we repent of our sins and turn to Him by faith, and then we share our testimony. This speaks of confessing our faith and of never being ashamed of the gospel. Once again I find myself quoting Spurgeon: "It's not your hold of Christ that saves; it's His hold of you!"[5]

- by what Christ does in our lives—"they did not love their lives": It is Christ who empowers us to live by faith, even unto death. While most of us will probably never need to die for our faith, we are all instructed to die to ourselves, in the sense that Jesus is truly our Lord and Master (Matt. 16:24).

All that we read in verses 7–11 brings two opposite results, as we see in verse 12. In heaven, there is tremendous rejoicing that Satan has been permanently cast out of heaven and that the saints are secure in Christ. But back here on earth, woe to the people, because Satan's wrath is great. He knows that his time is short, so he will unleash his full demonic powers upon the world.

> Now when the dragon saw that he had been cast to the earth, he persecuted the woman who gave birth to the male Child. But the woman was given two wings of a great eagle, that she might fly into the wilderness to her place, where she is nourished for a time and times and half a time, from the presence of the serpent. So the serpent spewed water out of his mouth like a flood after the woman, that he might cause her to be carried away by the flood. But the earth helped the woman, and the earth opened its mouth and swallowed up the flood which the dragon had spewed out of his mouth. And the dragon was enraged with the woman, and he went to make war with the rest of her offspring, who keep the commandments of God and have the testimony of Jesus Christ.
>
> Revelation 12:13–17

After Satan and the other fallen angels were cast out of heaven as their dwelling place, Satan's first attack was on Adam and Eve. Appearing as that "serpent of old," Satan deceived them into disobeying God. This brought the sin that had already taken place in heaven down to the human race on earth. In His foreknowledge, God already knew that this would happen; in His mercy, love, and grace, God provided a plan of salvation from the very beginning. Peter describes it for us this way: You have been redeemed "with the precious blood of Christ, as of a lamb without blemish and without spot. He indeed was foreordained before the foundation of the world, but was made manifest in these last times for you, who through Him believe in God, who raised [Jesus] from the dead, and gave Him glory, so that your faith and hope are in God" (1 Peter 1:19–21).

Satan has also known, then, that God would provide a Savior and a Lamb who would die to take away the sin of the world. Satan also knew that this Savior would come through God's chosen people, the Jews. So throughout biblical and secular history, Satan attempted to destroy the Jewish people, prompting the birth of anti-Semitism.

The word *Semitic* originally referred to all the descendants of Shem, the eldest son of Noah. Abraham, father of the Jews, was descended from Shem, and therefore he was Semitic. Anti-Semitism is prejudice and persecution against the Jewish people.

Satan's plan was straightforward: annihilate and obliterate the Jews so the Savior could not come. So Satan used his antichrists—men such as Pharaoh and Haman—to try to carry out his plan. Then when the time had arrived for the birth of the Savior, Satan used King Herod in an attempt to kill the Christ child.

On the cross at Calvary, Jesus died for our sins; at His resurrection, He conquered Satan and death. For two thousand years, Satan has continued his attempts at annihilating the Jewish people, using modern antichrists such as Josef Stalin and Adolf Hitler. Jesus the Savior has already come and achieved victory, so Satan is attempting to destroy Israel, Jerusalem, and the Jewish people in a vain attempt to obliterate any Israel for Christ to rule and reign over. As Bible students, if we understand this, then we can better understand what is happening in the Middle East today and why.

Here in Revelation 12, we find that after Satan and his demons are permanently expelled from heaven, he will recognize that time is very short until Christ's return. Therefore, he will initiate an all-out campaign to wipe out Israel and the Jewish people. If we thought anti-Semitism was bad before, just wait until the second half of the tribulation period. The Greek word for "persecute," in verse 13, essentially means "to pursue, to chase, and to hunt down."[6]

Zechariah 13 speaks of this time. Listen to what the Lord says through this prophet. "'And it shall come to pass in all the land,' says the LORD, 'that two-thirds in it shall be cut off and die, but one-third shall be left in it: I will bring the one-third through the fire, will refine them as silver is refined, and test them as gold is tested. They will call on My name, and I will answer them. I will say, 'This is My people'; and each one will say, 'The LORD is my God'" (vv. 8–9).

During the second half of the tribulation, two out of every three Jews will die at the hands of the Antichrist. It will be Satan's last-ditch effort to destroy the nation of Israel before the Lord's return. The two-thirds who die will be those who refuse to accept Jesus the Savior, despite the fact that 144,000 Jewish evangelists have preached and proclaimed Jesus. The one-third surviving Jews who are protected by God are those who have trusted God by faith.

In verse 14, we read of God protecting Israel on the wings of "a great eagle." Some Christians have speculated that perhaps this eagle refers to the United States of America, because our national symbol is the eagle. They think the United States might rescue Israel in her hour of need, because we have been supportive of Israel in times past. Unfortunately, that is probably wishful thinking, and Scripture indicates otherwise. This reference to "the wings of an eagle" has been used a few times previously in the Old Testament with regard to Israel, and in each case it was referring to God's own personal care and protection (see Exod. 19:4; Deut. 32:9–12). The same thing will no doubt be true in this situation.

We also read that Israel will be *nourished* "for a time, times, and half a time"—a clear reference to the last three and a half years of the tribulation period. "Nourished" is the same word in Greek that is translated "feed" in verse 6.[7] This reminds us of the first time Israel was in the wilderness, in Exodus, and God supernaturally fed His people with manna from heaven. Now as Israel returns to the wilderness, God will once again supernaturally feed His people. It also reminds us of the time the Lord supernaturally fed Elijah in the wilderness, by having ravens bring him bread and meat, morning and evening (1 Kings 17). For all we know, God may rain down manna from heaven again or feed His people through the birds of the air.

In verses 15–16, Satan will intensify his attack against Israel by spewing out some sort of flood. Whether this is water or a reference to military troops, we don't know for certain. Since the Antichrist is a military world leader, it could be referring to a flood of military attacks in an attempt to kill the Jews. If Petra is that hiding place in the wilderness, then the one-third of surviving Jews will hide there with God's protection and provision, while the other two-thirds will be outside Petra and outside God's protection.

Verse 16 tells us that the earth will open its mouth and swallow this flood. If this is speaking of a flood of water, then God will cause that water to go into the ground before it reaches His people. If it's referring to military troops, then this may be a great earthquake or sandstorm that swallows the attacking army. When a man named Korah led a rebellion against Moses, God caused the ground to open and swallow the rebels alive (Num. 16). Let us not forget how God also drowned the Egyptian armies in the Red Sea (Exod. 14). In Isaiah 59:19, we read, "When the enemy comes in like a flood, the Spirit of the LORD will lift up a standard against him."

As the dragon's attacks are thwarted by God, he becomes even more enraged. Then, we're told in verse 17, he "makes war with the rest of her offspring, who keep the commandments of God and have the testimony of Jesus Christ." "The rest of her offspring" would include saved Jews as well as saved Gentiles. Remember, the true sons of Abraham are those who trust God by faith, as Paul explains in Romans 4. Anyone who trusts Christ as Savior will become the target of Satan's hatred and persecution.

Revelation 12 not only provides us with important insights into the last days, it also reminds us that God's plans continue, right on course. Satan continues to rage against God's people, but his time is short. During this time, all born-again believers from the church age will be safely in heaven, and God will protect the believing Jews in the tribulation. Not long after this, Christ will return to rule and reign.

17

The Blasphemous Beast

Revelation 13:1–10

In the mid-1970s, a few years before I came to Christ, I saw the horror/suspense movie *The Omen*, starring Gregory Peck. Like many unsaved people, a good chunk of my theology came from books and movies. Now, as a Christian with a Bible, I can look back at movies such as *The Omen* and see how fictitious they were. Recently, I was channel surfing, and *The Omen* was on one of those older movie channels. As I watched some of it, I found myself laughing out loud. I may be one of the few people who watches *The Omen* and actually gets a good laugh out of it.

Now the movie wasn't a total spiritual loss, for a couple of reasons. I read that after the movie came out, in 1976, the sales of Bibles increased dramatically. I think the movie scared a lot of people and got them thinking about God. I also think people became intrigued by the story and perhaps wanted to compare the movie plot with Scripture. At the same time, there was a good biblical moment in the movie, when one of the priests visits Gregory Peck. When they're alone in his study, the priest blurts out to Peck, "You must accept

Christ as your Savior—and you must accept Him now!" We would certainly agree with that exhortation!

As we come now to chapter 13 in Revelation, we arrive at one of the more detailed descriptions of the Antichrist. This chapter gives us the opportunity to consider various questions about the Antichrist, such as whether or not he is alive today, his background, his rise to power, and so forth. I'm not saying that we will be able to answer all those questions, but at least we'll be able to gain some understanding.

> Then I stood on the sand of the sea. And I saw a beast rising up out of the sea, having seven heads and ten horns, and on his horns ten crowns, and on his heads a blasphemous name. Now the beast which I saw was like a leopard, his feet were like the feet of a bear, and his mouth like the mouth of a lion. The dragon gave him his power, his throne, and great authority. And I saw one of his heads as if it had been mortally wounded, and his deadly wound was healed. And all the world marveled and followed the beast. So they worshiped the dragon who gave authority to the beast; and they worshiped the beast, saying, "Who is like the beast? Who is able to make war with him?" And he was given a mouth speaking great things and blasphemies, and he was given authority to continue for forty-two months. Then he opened his mouth in blasphemy against God, to blaspheme His name, His tabernacle, and those who dwell in heaven. It was granted to him to make war with the saints and to overcome them. And authority was given him over every tribe, tongue, and nation. All who dwell on the earth will worship him, whose names have not been written in the Book of Life of the Lamb slain from the foundation of the world. If anyone has an ear, let him hear. He who leads into captivity shall go into captivity; he who kills with the sword must be killed with the sword. Here is the patience and the faith of the saints.
>
> Revelation 13:1–10

Perhaps the first question we should address is this: why would we even bother with a study of the Antichrist, seeing that we won't be here but will have been raptured into heaven when he comes to power? For one, the Bible says quite a bit about the Antichrist here and in a handful of other passages. That means God wants us to understand certain things. Second, as we learn about this future demonic world leader, there will be times when we can use that information in our witnessing, since many unsaved people have questions about the last days. As an unsaved person hearing the gospel back in 1980, I remember having several questions about the last days. And third, I can say that in many respects, I'm looking forward to the coming of the Antichrist, because for believers, it means Jesus Christ is coming even sooner.

The first sentence of verse 1 probably belongs at the end of the last chapter rather than the beginning of this chapter. Please remember that the Bible did not come to us from God in chapters and verses but in letters and records. The translators have helped us a great deal by adding chapter breaks, but they're not perfect. The earliest manuscripts we have translate this first sentence as follows: "Then *he* stood on the sand of the sea." So this sentence belongs at the end of the previous chapter and refers to Satan. Satan is pictured by John as standing on the sands of the world, looking out over the sea of humanity.

John goes on to write, "And I saw a beast rising up out of the sea." In John's vision of Revelation, God is allowing him to see the rise of the Antichrist, coming out of the sea of humanity. Later on, in chapter 17, John is told that the waters represent the peoples and nations of the world (Rev. 17:15). John calls the Antichrist a "beast"—a word that means "wild beast or venomous creature."[1] This describes his vile and violent nature.

The Antichrist will be a demon-possessed man who rises from the sea of humanity. Using both the Old Testament and the New Testament, let's briefly discuss the emergence of the Antichrist with the information we have. In Daniel 7, we have our first detailed description of the Antichrist. Daniel records, among other things, that the Antichrist shall have a "kingdom on earth, which shall be different from all other kingdoms, and shall devour the whole earth, trample it and break it in pieces" (Dan. 7:23). So the Antichrist not only will become a world ruler but also will accomplish what all other kings have only dreamed of throughout history: ruling the entire world.

This was the desire of Pharaoh, Nebuchadnezzar, Alexander the Great, and Hitler, but only the Antichrist will achieve world dominance. Daniel continues and says, "He . . . shall intend to change times and law" (Dan. 7:25), which may refer to anything associated with Christianity. So, for example, the Antichrist may do away with any observances such as Christmas and Easter, as well as remove all religious programs on television, radio, and the internet. He may even amend the laws to ban religious books, especially the printing and selling of Bibles.

In Great Britain, the Anglican Church has decided to be politically correct with the Christmas scenes in their churchyards. So not only do they include Joseph, Mary, Jesus, shepherds, and angels, but they also include a Hindu snowman, a Chinese dragon, and a Jewish temple! I have no idea what those other symbols have to do with Christmas and the birth of Jesus, but the Antichrist will take it a step further and eliminate all of it.

In chapter 8 of his Old Testament book, Daniel writes, "A king shall arise, having fierce features, who understands sinister schemes. His power shall be mighty, but not by his own power [the Antichrist's mighty power comes from Satan himself]; he shall destroy fearfully [or in an astonishing manner], and shall prosper and thrive; he shall destroy the mighty, and also the holy people. Through his cunning, he shall cause deceit to prosper under his rule; and he shall exalt himself in his heart. . . . He shall even rise against the Prince of princes [referring to Jesus and the final battle of Armageddon]; but he shall be broken without human means [Jesus Himself will defeat the Antichrist and his armies]" (vv. 23–25).

Daniel 9 describes the Antichrist and the final seven-year tribulation this way: "He shall confirm a covenant [or treaty] with many for one week [or seven years]; but in the middle of the week [or after three and a half years—at the midpoint of the tribulation] he shall bring an end to sacrifice and offering. And on the wing of abominations shall be one who makes desolate" (v. 27). In other words, the Antichrist will negotiate a peace treaty in the Middle East, around the beginning of the tribulation, that allows Israel to rebuild the temple and to reestablish the Old Testament sacrifices and temple worship. But three and a half years into that treaty, the Antichrist will suddenly invade the Jewish temple—no doubt with full military force—and seize it. He will bring an immediate end to the Jewish sacrifices, and in the ultimate act of abomination—as we will read here in Revelation 13—he will require the world to worship him and his image.

In the eleventh chapter of Daniel, we read that he "shall do according to his own will: he shall exalt and magnify himself above every god, shall speak blasphemies against the God of gods, and shall prosper till the wrath has been accomplished [referring to the seven-year tribulation]. . . . He shall regard neither the God of his fathers, nor the desire of women, nor regard any god; for he shall exalt himself above them all" (vv. 36–37).

The Antichrist will refuse to honor any god—whether it be the true God of heaven or the false gods that people worship today. Instead, he will make himself god and will exalt himself above all others. When Daniel states that he will not regard "the desire of women," it has led some Bible students to conclude that the Antichrist will be a homosexual. That's certainly a possibility, but in context, it probably refers to the fact that the Antichrist will be so consumed with world dominance and receiving the world's worship that he will not care about anything else, including the attention of women.

In Paul's second letter to the Thessalonians, he provides further details concerning the Antichrist: "Let no one deceive you by any means; for [the day of the Lord] will not come until the falling away comes first, and the man of sin is revealed, the son of perdition, who opposes and exalts himself above all that is called God or is worshiped . . . and now you know what is restraining, that he [Antichrist) may be revealed in his own time. For the mystery of lawlessness is already at work; only He who now restrains will do so until He is taken out of the way. And then the lawless one will be revealed . . . the coming of the lawless one is according to the working of Satan, with all power, signs, and lying wonders" (2 Thess. 2:3–9).

This underscores the fictitious nature of movies such as *The Omen*, which deals with the birth and childhood of the Antichrist. Scripture says absolutely nothing about those things but plainly teaches that the identity of the Antichrist will not be revealed until the tribulation period begins. So the question is often asked, "Is the Antichrist alive today?" The answer is that we don't know, although it's certainly possible. What we do know for certain is that the spirit and the sentiment of the Antichrist are alive and well today. If we are indeed close to the rapture of the church and the beginning of the tribulation, then the Antichrist would undoubtedly be alive today.

Even so, his identity will not be made known until the church is raptured, and then the people who remain behind, for the most part, will not care. God is now restraining the rise of the Antichrist to world prominence, but once that restraint is removed, he will emerge. In 2 Thessalonians 2, that restraining force appears to be the power of the Holy Spirit working through the church. Once the church is removed in the rapture, the Antichrist can come forth into world prominence.

Another common question about the Antichrist has to do with his nationality: will he be a Jew or a Gentile? The Scriptures do not provide an ironclad answer to that question, and opinions have been formed on both sides. Those who believe the Antichrist will be a Jew suggest that in order for him to be received by the Jews as their Messiah, he would have to be a Jew. Also, as I quoted from Daniel 11:37, the Antichrist "shall regard neither God of his fathers," and some take that to mean he will be a Jew.

On the other hand, we read here in verse 1 that the beast will rise from the sea, which refers to the sea of humanity, making his chances of being a Gentile much stronger. Throughout Scripture, Antichrist-type leaders who blasphemed God and persecuted His people were primarily Gentiles. Pharaoh was Egyptian, Haman was an Amalekite, Nebuchadnezzar was Chaldean, and so forth. And in Daniel 11:37, the literal translation is that the Antichrist "will not regard the *gods* of his fathers." That points to him being a Gentile, with multiple gods.

One of the more compelling arguments for the Antichrist being a Gentile is found in Daniel 9:26. Daniel is talking about the crucifixion of Jesus, and he says, "Messiah shall be cut off, but not for Himself." (That is to say, Jesus will be put to death, but it will be for our sins.) "And the people of the prince who is to come shall destroy the city and the sanctuary." Daniel goes on to describe that prince, who is the Antichrist. So the people of the Antichrist are the same people who, after Christ was crucified, destroyed the city and the sanctuary.

What group of people, not many years after the crucifixion of Jesus, destroyed Jerusalem and the sanctuary? It was the Romans, led by the commander named Titus, in AD 70, in fulfillment of the prediction made by Jesus Himself. So the final world ruler, and the final world empire of the tribulation period, will likely come out of

Europe. This brings us to verse 1 of Revelation 13, where the beast is described as having "seven heads and ten horns." What are these seven heads and ten horns?

The later chapters of Revelation give us that answer. In Revelation 17:9, John is told that the seven heads are seven mountains, and many commentators believe this refers to Rome—the city commonly described as sitting on seven hills. However, it is more than just Rome, because in the very next verse, John is told that "these are also seven kings. Five have fallen, one is, and the other is yet to come." So these seven heads represent seven world empires.

Historically speaking, we know that the world empires have consisted of Egypt, Assyria, Babylon, Medo-Persia, Greece, and Rome. John was writing these words in the first century, when Rome was the world empire. So in John's own words in Revelation 17:10, "Five empires have already fallen [Egypt, Assyria, Babylon, Persia, and Greece], one still is [the Roman Empire of his day], and the other is yet to come." That is the empire of the Antichrist in the last days.

So the seven heads, here in verse 1, refer to the fact that the empire of the Antichrist will be an accumulation of all those successive world empires all rolled into one. This is born out by John's description of the Antichrist and his last-days empire, in verse 2, which says, "The beast which I saw was like a leopard, his feet were like the feet of a bear, and his mouth like the mouth of a lion." These same descriptions are found in Daniel 7, and they symbolize previous world empires.

- The leopard symbolizes Greece, and the swiftness by which Alexander the Great conquered other nations.
- The bear symbolizes the Medo-Persian empire, characterized by its brute strength.
- The lion symbolizes the Babylonian empire and its fierce nature.

Once again, this simply means that the final world empire, headed up by the Antichrist in the last days, will be a combination and composite of those previous world powers. The "ten horns" that John mentions in verse 1 represent a confederacy of ten kings, who will unite behind the Antichrist. We will discuss that in more detail when we get to Revelation 17.

178

The Antichrist will receive his demonic power and influence, his throne, and his authority from Satan himself. There have been many antichrists in world history—men such as Haman, Herod, and Hitler—but they all take a back seat to the beast of the tribulation period. Not only will he have Satan's full power and authority, but God Himself will have removed all restraints, allowing him to do his very worst. Just as Jesus Christ is God come in the flesh, the Antichrist will be Satan come in the flesh. Even more than Judas Iscariot, Antichrist will be a true son of Satan.

The question is sometimes asked, "How could one man gain control over the entire world?" The answer is found in these verses. The church will have been raptured up to heaven, while God's restraint on earth will be removed. The world's population will consist of unsaved people, and those who come to faith during the tribulation will be put to death by the government of the Antichrist. The Antichrist will have the full power and authority of Satan himself. That is your formula for how one man will gain control over the whole world.

In verse 3, we have information that has generated plenty of discussion. One of the Antichrist's heads is mortally wounded, but his deadly wound is healed, causing the unsaved world to marvel. Something miraculous takes place that dramatically increases the Antichrist's appeal. When we compare this verse with the seven heads in verse 1, it would seem, on the surface, to refer to one of the world empires being revived. Some commentators and Bible students believe this indicates the revival of the Roman Empire.

However, as we carry out the discussion of this mortal wound being healed, we find that it actually refers to the Antichrist himself receiving a mortal wound and miraculously surviving. This is made clear in verses 12 and 14, as well as in chapter 17 (vv. 8 and 11). In verse 14, we are told that this wound will be inflicted with a sword. The Greek word used there for "sword" can refer to a smaller sword, such as a dagger. The Antichrist will be mortally wounded, most likely in an assassination attempt.

At the end of the Old Testament book of Zechariah, we read of Jesus the Shepherd being betrayed and put to death. The passage then speaks of a foolish and worthless shepherd who attacks and destroys the sheep, referring to the Antichrist. Because the people reject the Good Shepherd, God will allow the emergence of a worthless shepherd. It says of the Antichrist, in Zechariah 11:17, "Woe to the worthless shepherd, who leaves the flock! A sword shall be against his arm and against his right eye; His arm shall completely wither, and his right eye shall be totally blinded!" If that verse in Zechariah is talking about the same wound that we read about here in Revelation, as it certainly seems to be, then the Antichrist will receive a critical injury that will cause him to lose his right eye and the use of one arm.

But even more interesting is whether or not the Antichrist will die as a result of this wound. Some believe that he will die and come back to life, while others believe he will appear to die but survive. My first thought was to examine the Greek word for "mortal" wound in this verse, but it refers to death in both the literal and the figurative sense. So that was no help, and it explains why we have the two sides of the discussion.

Here we have the account of how the Antichrist will come back to life in John's words: "I saw one of his heads as if it had been mortally wounded." This perhaps indicates a near death and a miraculous recovery. Let us also remember that the devil is the great imitator; he regularly imitates what God does, on his own demonic level. So, this appears to be intended as a counterfeit resurrection, in contrast with the authentic resurrection of Jesus. Sadly, after Jesus rose from the dead, the majority of the world refused to believe, but when the Antichrist performs a counterfeit resurrection, the world will worship him.

The words of adoration spoken by the people at the end of verse 4 reveal a Godlike reverence for the Antichrist. They say, "Who is like the beast?" In the book of Exodus, after the children of Israel crossed through the Red Sea on dry ground, they sang the first praise song in Scripture. In Exodus 15:11, they sang, "Who is like You, O Lord, among the gods?" So this worship of the beast is continued blasphemy against God.

Notice how these events will increase the worship of Satan himself, in the first part of verse 4. Since the power and authority of the beast are coming from Satan, the people will actually be worshiping the devil, something he has wanted from the very beginning. In many ways today, people worship Satan and don't even realize it.

In verses 5 and 6, the beast will speak unbelievable words of blasphemy against God, as well as God's abode in heaven and the saints who are with God in heaven. The beast will slander anything associated with God, using the most vulgar and profane language and descriptions possible.

In verse 7, the beast will make all-out war against anyone who claims allegiance to Christ—whether Jew or Gentile. You will remember from chapter 12 how Satan is permanently banned from heaven at the midpoint of the tribulation, and in complete rage, he devotes the final three and a half years of the tribulation to annihilating God's people—the Jews, in particular. Here in verse 7, we see him using his Antichrist to accomplish that purpose.

In verse 8, it is made clear that those in the world who worship the beast are the unsaved, whose names have not been written in the Lamb's Book of Life. The phrase that John uses in describing Jesus as "the Lamb slain from the foundation of the world" speaks of how God always knew that mankind would fall and predetermined that He would provide Jesus as our Lamb and Savior. It also speaks of the fact that God has always known who would believe in Him by faith.

In verses 9 and 10, this section closes with a word of exhortation and a word of encouragement. The exhortation is in verse 9, telling us to pay close attention to the details of these things to come. It should cause all who read these words to ask themselves, "Am I listening carefully to what God says, and am I following the Lord with all my heart, soul, mind, and strength?"

In verse 10, we find a word of encouragement for us as believers today and for those who come to faith and suffer during the tribulation. God will bring justice and punishment for all those who harm God's people. Those who lead God's people into captivity will themselves go into captivity. And those who kill God's people will themselves be killed. Knowing that God is in control, and knowing that He will ultimately right every wrong, gives us patience and peace and strengthens our faith.

18

Satan's Worship Leader

Revelation 13:11-18

In the earliest days of creation, Satan was one of the holy angels in heaven. And though we cannot be completely certain, Scripture strongly indicates that Satan was an archangel and that he led the angelic praise and worship of God in heaven (see Ezek. 28:13). But in spite of all this, Satan's heart was filled with pride, and he coveted the same worship that was reserved only for God.

Here in Revelation 13, in the final days before Christ's return to establish His kingdom, Satan is making his last attempt to acquire the worship of the world, something he has wanted from the very beginning. Satan even has his own worship leader, whose sole responsibility will be to coerce and compel the unsaved masses of the world to worship the devil and his Antichrist.

> Then I saw another beast coming up out of the earth, and he had two horns like a lamb and spoke like a dragon. And he exercises all the authority of the first beast in his presence, and causes the earth

and those who dwell in it to worship the first beast, whose deadly wound was healed.

Revelation 13:11–12

In verse 11, John begins to describe "another beast." The first beast is the coming demonic world leader, known as the Antichrist. Here, then, is "another beast," which means "another of the same kind." Like the Antichrist, this is a person who will be possessed by a demon from the abyss. Like the first beast, this second beast will promote the agenda of the devil from a position of global leadership, in the role of second in command to the Antichrist. These demon-possessed world leaders will be two of a kind, working in tandem and with the same agenda—but with different roles.

The first beast, the Antichrist, will become the political and military leader of the world. The second beast will become the religious leader, working directly under the Antichrist. The appearance of this second beast isn't as threatening as the first. The first beast was compared to a leopard and a lion, whereas this second beast is likened to a lamb. The second beast has two horns, whereas the Antichrist was described as having seven heads, ten horns, and ten crowns. In Scripture, horns symbolize authority, so this second beast has less authority than the Antichrist. And his likeness to a lamb tells us that he will be a religious leader, as lambs were associated with religious sacrifices. But the end of verse 11 makes it perfectly clear that while this second beast has the appearance of a lamb, he has the voice of a dragon, and he will be Satan's religious mouthpiece.

Whom did Jesus describe in the Gospels as looking like sheep outwardly but inwardly being ravenous wolves? False prophets (Matt. 7:15). This second beast, then, will be the ultimate false prophet—as well as a false priest. Just as we worship Father, Son, and Holy Spirit, there is the counterfeit trinity of Satan, the Antichrist, and the False Prophet.

Satan wants to be worshiped by people, just as God the Father is rightly worshiped. The Antichrist will be a false messiah, in contrast with Jesus, the true Messiah. And the False Prophet will function in much the same role as the Holy Spirit, but in the demonic sense. The role of the Holy Spirit today is to point people to Jesus and their need for Him. In his demonic imitation, the False Prophet will function in the same role, except that he will be pointing people to the Antichrist and, ultimately, to worshiping Satan.

In verse 12, the False Prophet has the same demonic authority of the Antichrist, but his particular role will be in causing the unsaved world to worship the Antichrist. One of the ways in which the False Prophet will persuade the unsaved world to worship the Antichrist is by pointing to the Antichrist's miraculous "resurrection." As you remember, the Antichrist will receive a serious wound that should end his life, but he miraculously survives. This is described at the end of verse 12 as being the "deadly wound that was healed."

> He performs great signs, so that he even makes fire come down from heaven on the earth in the sight of men. And he deceives those who dwell on the earth—by those signs which he was granted to do in the sight of the beast, telling those who dwell on the earth to make an image to the beast who was wounded by the sword and lived. He was granted power to give breath to the image of the beast, that the image of the beast should both speak and cause as many as would not worship the image of the beast to be killed.
>
> Revelation 13:13–15

The event that will propel the Antichrist into world prominence and global leadership will be his negotiation of a brilliant Middle East peace plan. That takes place at the beginning of the tribulation. The event that will propel the False Prophet into a position of world influence will be how he handles the aftermath of an assassination attempt on the Antichrist. That will take place around the middle of the tribulation. The survival of the Antichrist after this assassination attempt will be so spectacular that many people will believe it to be a resurrection—Satan's imitation of the real resurrection of Jesus.

In verse 13, we read of how the False Prophet will perform great signs or miracles, including fire falling down to the earth. This is a good time to underscore the fact that miracles, in and of themselves, do not necessarily come from God. Miracles present two challenges: was it really in fact a miracle? And if it was, was it really from God? Both Jesus and Paul spoke about "lying signs and wonders," or false miracles (Matt. 24:24; 2 Thess. 2:9). We're reminded of this truth in Exodus. When Moses was performing miraculous signs, two of Pharaoh's magicians were able to mimic a few of those miracles.

These great signs and miracles will deceive the masses, but we see how they are satanic imitations of significant spiritual events. For example, just as Jesus rose from the dead, the Antichrist will have his own mock resurrection. And just as the fire of the Holy Spirit fell upon the apostles on the day of Pentecost, we see the False Prophet causing fire to fall from heaven to the earth. The book of Revelation confirms that the three main weapons of Satan are accusation, opposition, and imitation.

In verses 14 and 15, another bizarre deception of the False Prophet involves commanding the unsaved worshipers to erect an image of the Antichrist. Not only is the image to be worshiped, but the False Prophet will use his demonic powers to give it a voice—a voice that calls for the death of those who refuse to worship the image.

This image and the requirement of the world to worship it remind us of the statue that was erected in the likeness of King Nebuchadnezzar, in the book of Daniel. Nebuchadnezzar called for the construction of a ninety-foot gold statue in his image. The people were commanded to bow down and worship it at the sound of special royal music. As we remember, three young Hebrew men—Shadrach, Meshach, and Abed-Nego—refused to bow down before the image. When the king tried to have them executed in a fiery furnace, God supernaturally protected them (Dan. 3).

During the tribulation, a similar scenario will take place when the image of the Antichrist is constructed and the world is required to worship it or be put to death. Like Shadrach, Meshach, and Abed-Nego, a large segment of Jewish believers will refuse to worship the image. They will flee into the wilderness, where God will protect them from the Antichrist and his attempts to kill them.

As if that image and the worship of it weren't bad enough, the image will be set up inside the sanctuary of the Jewish temple in Jerusalem (Dan. 8:11–14; 2 Thess. 2:4). Daniel, Jesus, and Paul all referred to this event, "the abomination of desolation" (Dan. 9:27; Matt. 24:15; 2 Thess. 2:4). This is a vivid picture of Satan's desire when he was still in heaven and wanted to be worshiped in the place of God. God did not allow that to take place in heaven, so Satan will have the image of his Antichrist placed in the temple sanctuary—the place where God is to be worshiped.

Many believers who die in the second half of the tribulation will be executed by the Antichrist's government for their refusal to bow before the image. But it will not be easy to monitor every citizen and to determine whether or not they are complying with this mandatory worship. So the Antichrist will take it a step further, as we read below:

> He causes all, both small and great, rich and poor, free and slave, to receive a mark on their right hand or on their foreheads, and that no one may buy or sell except one who has the mark or the name of the beast, or the number of his name. Here is wisdom. Let him who has understanding calculate the number of the beast, for it is the number of a man: His number is 666.
>
> Revelation 13:16–18

More and more, we hear references to globalization—global economics, global technology, global government, and so forth. Globalization has been described as "the process by which the people of the world are unified into a single society and function together."[1] Today, when a nation's economy takes a significant downward turn, it adversely affects the economies of other nations. The same is true with the trade markets, so global economics would help to stabilize the world economy. At the same time, there is the ongoing threat of rogue nations getting their hands on weapons that can be used against other nations. When Iran launched its own satellite into space, it brought immediate concerns. All of these challenges are causing leaders and experts to call for globalization, or global and integrated solutions for the world's problems and challenges.

My point is simply this: the world is becoming ripe for the idea of a global government. And apart from the demonic agenda, a lot of these ideas make sense. But from a biblical perspective, we must understand that the only world government God will ever honor and bless is the kingdom of Jesus Christ—the King of kings and the Lord of lords. He will return in the near future to establish His kingdom.

In addition to the threat of execution for failure to worship the image, the Antichrist will force the world to maintain allegiance to him by requiring everyone to receive a government mark. This is commonly referred to as "the mark of the beast." There are no exceptions or exemptions for this required mark, and everyone—whether small or great, rich or poor, free or slave—must take the mark or be put to death. No bribery or bargaining will allow anyone to refuse this mark.

Nevertheless, the vast majority of unsaved people will receive this mark willingly and even gladly. That's because we read, in verse 17, that no one will be able to buy or sell anything—including food, water, clothing, medicine, and fuel—unless they have this mark. But rather than seeing it as a government regulation, most people will see it as a sensible solution and system for a cashless society and for safer financial transactions. People and businesses today are victims of constant theft. And there is a high cost of having to continually print money for circulation.

We're already taking steps away from using cash, as more and more people are using credit and debit cards—making check writing obsolete. But even so, credit and debit cards can be lost or stolen—not to mention being used for fraud and counterfeiting. The same problems exist with driver's licenses and identification cards.

Several years ago, I took my car through a car wash. Unfortunately, the parolee who was vacuuming my car stole my credit card out of the center console. Later that evening, he and his buddy took my credit card to a nearby liquor store. After leaving the liquor store, they went to a restaurant a couple blocks away. This was a bad decision because the owner and several of his employees attend the church where I am a pastor. The parolee partners attempted to purchase several pieces of fresh fish to go, but when they handed the credit card over the counter, the restaurant employee recognized my name on the card. He pretended to walk away and make the transaction but called the police instead. Those two men are no longer parolees; they are detainees of the California prison system.

That's the problem with cash and credit cards: they can be stolen. So the next logical step is to have that information imprinted on the right hand or, if there is some limitation with the hand, on the forehead. Technology today allows us to imprint huge amounts of information on tiny chips or tiny bar codes. The government mark of the beast may very well be a small bar code. It's my opinion that society today is being conditioned and primed for this future branding system through the current popularity of tattoos.

The Greek word for "mark," in verse 16, means "to stamp, etch, or brand."[2] More than an ink stamp, this is a permanent mark etched into the skin. Apart from the demonic aspect of this plan, it makes a lot of practical sense, and therefore, people will accept it willingly.

Here then is another demonic imitation, as we read in Scripture that all genuine believers have been sealed by the Holy Spirit. Ephesians 1:13–14 states that "having believed, you were sealed with the Holy Spirit of promise, who is the guarantee of our inheritance" in heaven. The seal of the Holy Spirit at the moment of our conversion is God's promise that we belong to Him and His guarantee of our salvation. We also read, back in chapter 7, of how the Lord will place His special seal on the foreheads of 144,000 Jewish converts who are appointed to share the gospel. A seal speaks of ownership.

Those who take the mark of the beast become the property of Satan. Although there may be some holdouts for a while, the point will come when everyone who remains on the earth will be marked—with either the mark of the beast or the seal of God. There will be no middle ground, and people will belong either to the Antichrist or to Jesus Christ. Those who have come to faith in the tribulation period, and have not already been put to death, will refuse to take the mark. They will immediately be put to death as martyrs, apart from those believers whom God protects in the wilderness.

The final two verses provide more information in regard to the mark of the beast. Notice in verse 17 that this mark may consist of the name of the beast or the number of his name. The number of the beast is recorded at the end of the chapter, and it is perhaps the most famous—or infamous—number in existence today: 666. If we spot a license plate or a mailbox with the numbers 666, we secretly imagine that Freddy Krueger is driving the car, or Jason from *Friday the 13th* lives at that address. If we're given a phone number that includes the numbers 666, we're fearful of dialing some devil worshiper. If that cup of coffee and low-fat blueberry muffin come out to $6.66 at the register, we immediately add a tin of breath mints, just to change the amount. We've become superstitious about numbers such as 13 and 666. However, we shouldn't get worked up over the number 666.

188

As Paul tells us in 2 Thessalonians 2, the identity of the Antichrist will not be revealed until after the restrainer is removed, which (once again) I believe is referring to the rapture and the removal of the church. Since the number 666 is somehow tied into the name of the Antichrist, we can't figure it out on this side of heaven. The Antichrist will not be revealed until we're gone, and therefore, the number 666 will probably not carry any significance until then.

Now someone who is reading these words might point to verse 18, where John says, "Here is wisdom. Let him who has understanding calculate the number of the beast, for it is the number of a man: His number is 666." As we consider verse 18, we must consider to whom it is directed and to what people it will have application. Since the identity of the Antichrist will not be revealed until after we are gone, and since unsaved people will come to Christ after the tribulation begins and the Antichrist is in power, for whom do you think the words and warning of verse 18 are intended? This is a warning to those in the tribulation.

For hundreds of years, people in the church have been trying to assign numerical value to letters of the Greek, Hebrew, Latin, and English language in an effort to identify the Antichrist. The problem with that, depending on your mathematical formula, is that you can make lots of names come out to 666. As Warren Wiersbe writes, "If you work at it hard enough, almost any name will fit!"[3]

In a more general sense, we understand that 6 is the number of man. Mankind was made by God on the sixth day of creation. Seven is the number of perfection—a divine number, if you will—while 6 falls short of that divine perfection. Another way of looking at this is that 7 is the number of perfection—so 777 emphasizes the absolute holiness of God. The number 666, then, emphasizes the absolute failure and imperfection of mankind—specifically, the Antichrist.

This I am confident of: when the Antichrist comes to power, and when he initiates his government program requiring all citizens of the world to receive his mark, the significance of the number 666 will be perfectly clear to the believers who have come to faith during the tribulation. Those Christians will refuse to take the mark of the beast, while the unsaved world will do so gladly and willingly. Rather than unraveling the mark of the beast, the far more important question is have you been sealed by God for salvation?

19

The Certainties of God

Revelation 14:1–20

A fifth grade teacher in a Christian school asked her class to look at TV commercials and see if they could use them in some way to communicate ideas about God. Here are some of the results:

- God is like a Ford: He's got a better idea.
- God is like Coke: He's the real thing.
- God is like Hallmark cards: He cares enough to send his very best.
- God is like Tide: He gets the stains out that others leave behind.
- God is like General Electric: He brings good things to life.
- God is like Sears: He has everything.
- God is like Alka-Seltzer: Try him, you'll like him.
- God is like Scotch tape: You can't see him, but you know he's there.
- God is like Delta: He's ready when you are.

- God is like Allstate: You're in good hands with him.
- God is like VO-5 hair spray: He holds through all kinds of weather.
- God is like Dial soap: Aren't you glad you have him? Don't you wish everybody did?[1]

As we come now to Revelation 14, we'll look at three main subjects. The first is God's salvation, which reminds us of the American Express slogan: "Don't leave home without it." Then we'll talk about angels flying throughout the skies, proclaiming God's gospel, which is reminiscent of the Verizon slogan: "Can you hear me now?" Finally, we will consider God's judgment being poured out on the earth, which brings to mind the Southwest Airlines slogan: "Wanna get away?"

The title of this chapter is "The Certainties of God." When God assures us of something, it's an absolute certainty. And in this chapter, we are reminded of some very vital certainties. So let's begin our reading together:

> Then I looked, and behold, a Lamb standing on Mount Zion, and with Him one hundred and forty-four thousand, having His Father's name written on their foreheads. And I heard a voice from heaven, like the voice of many waters, and like the voice of loud thunder. And I heard the sound of harpists playing their harps. They sang as it were a new song before the throne, before the four living creatures, and the elders; and no one could learn that song except the hundred and forty-four thousand who were redeemed from the earth. These are the ones who were not defiled with women, for they are virgins. These are the ones who follow the Lamb wherever He goes. These were redeemed from among men, being firstfruits to God and to the Lamb. And in their mouth was found no deceit, for they are without fault before the throne of God.
>
> Revelation 14:1–5

Those who belong to God have the promise and full assurance of a safe arrival in heaven. Here in verse 1, John describes the scene and says, "Then I looked, and behold, a Lamb standing on Mount Zion." Some thirty times in this book, John says "Behold!" and it means "Look for yourself," or in modern vernacular, "Check this out!" And what John is drawing our attention to is Jesus Christ the Lamb standing on Mount Zion.

At this point, the commentators part ways like the Red Sea; they are divided over this reference to Mount Zion. Is this the Mount Zion of heaven or of earth? In Psalm 48, Jerusalem, the city of the Lord, is also called Mount Zion. Then in Hebrews 12, reference is made to the heavenly Jerusalem and the heavenly Mount Zion. So which Mount Zion is being referred to here in verse 1? Some see this as being heavenly Zion, with the redeemed standing with Jesus before the Father. Others see this as the Mount Zion on earth, and they describe this as a preview of the scene when Jesus returns at the end of the tribulation.

I'm of the opinion that this is referring to heavenly Mount Zion, and I'll explain why. In verse 3, and again in verse 5, we read that these redeemed believers are before the throne of God, which tells me this is referring to heaven. In verse 3, we also read that the redeemed are standing before the four living creatures and the elders—who were around the throne of God in heaven, back in chapter 4. Finally, these believers are described at the end of verse 3 as those "who were redeemed *from* the earth." Therefore, I believe this is describing the safe arrival of the 144,000 in heaven. As Jon Courson says, in regard to God's assurance, "We do not see 143,999 witnesses, but 144,000— they all make it through."[2] Their salvation is a certainty, as is ours.

These verses reacquaint us with the 144,000 Jews we met back in chapter 7. There we saw how these Jews were selected by God: 12,000 from each tribe. They were sealed and sent out by God to preach and proclaim the gospel. Immediately after that, we read that there was a great multitude in heaven, of every nation, tribe, people, and tongue, standing before the throne of God. So in chapter 7, the 144,000 are on earth, and here in chapter 14, I believe they are in heaven.

You are probably not familiar with the name Irena Sendler. I wasn't either, until I heard her story. Irena Sendler was born in Warsaw, Poland, in 1910. By 1940 she was working in Warsaw's welfare department in Hitler's occupied Poland. Hitler banished half a million Jews to the ghettos of Warsaw, where many were left to die without proper food, supplies, or medical care. Irena's department responsibilities included dealing with tuberculosis patients, so she had the freedom to come and go as she needed. During that time, she used her freedom to approach Jewish families and plead with them to allow her to take their children out of the area and hide them away. Obviously, it was a traumatic decision for those Jewish parents to let their children go, but they understood that if they didn't, the children would die.

Irena used burlap sacks, coffins, toolboxes, and an ambulance to hide those Jewish children as she got them out of that area. Irena even trained a dog to bark repeatedly whenever the Nazi soldiers would stop her for questioning, in order to cover up the sounds of the crying children. She gave all of those children new names and documents and placed them with Christian families. But not wanting those children to lose their original identities, she made meticulous records of their names and family connections and buried that information in a jar next to an apple tree in her backyard.

Eventually, Irena Sendler was arrested by the Gestapo and placed in a prison camp. She was brutally beaten and tortured and set to be executed. She managed to escape when her friends bribed one of the guards, and she went into hiding until the war was over. Afterward, the first thing Irena did was to dig up that jar by her apple tree. She then worked tirelessly to reunite those children with their parents. Unfortunately, the majority of those parents had been killed by the Nazis or had died from lack of food and medicine.

Irena reunited many of those children with other relatives. When everything was said and done, Irena had helped to rescue over twenty-five hundred Jewish children from certain death at the hands of the Nazis. During the last years of her life, the elderly Irena lived in a nursing home, where—amazingly—she was cared for by one of those Jewish children she had smuggled out of Warsaw: a baby girl who was only five months old at the time. Irena had smuggled her out in a toolbox, with Irena's faithful dog barking at her side, covering up the sounds of the child crying.

In 1965, the Yad Vashem Holocaust Museum in Jerusalem added her name to what is called the "Avenue of the Righteous," where Gentile heroes are recognized for their sacrifices in helping the Jewish people. Irena Sendler's name was placed alongside other names much more familiar to us such as Corrie ten Boom and Oskar Schindler. In 2007, at the age of ninety-seven, Irena Sendler was nominated for the Nobel Peace Prize for her efforts in rescuing those twenty-five hundred Jewish children. But, it is sad to say, she lost . . . to Al Gore

193

and his movie about global warming. About ten years before her death, a play about Irena's life was produced by some high school students in Kansas. It gained national attention in the United States, then Europe, and eventually around the world. The name of that play sums up Irena's story quite well: *Life in a Jar*.

Here in our text, we're reading about 144,000 faithful Jews, whom God appointed to reach the world with the gospel. By God's grace, and through their efforts in the tribulation, they will be responsible for a multitude of people from all over the world getting into heaven by saving faith. Here, then, we are reading about their victory, and they are standing in heaven. And for people like Irena Sendler and Corrie ten Boom, they too will receive a standing in heaven for their faith, as well as recognition for allowing God to use them to help save thousands of Jewish people.

Something we learn in these verses is that the seal on the foreheads of these 144,000 consists of God's name. Back in chapter 7, we only knew that they had a seal, but here we learn that the seal is the Father's name. This is obviously in contrast with the name or number of the beast that the unsaved world will receive on the right hand or forehead.

This is quite a worship service that we read about here. It includes harps, a 144,000-voice choir, and a song that only this choir can sing. In verses 4 and 5, we learn important characteristics of this group that should also characterize us as believers. Let's see if what is said of them can also be said of us. In verse 4, they "were not defiled with women, for they are virgins." Sexual immorality is rampant in the world, and, it is sad to say, the church is by no means immune. This sin will not only continue in the tribulation but also escalate. These believers, however, will be faithful to avoid all sexual impurity. They are described as being virgins, and those words may very well mean exactly that; they will be chosen and called while unmarried and will remain as such, completely devoted to the will of God.

I would also point out that the text here may not be referring to these believers being virgins in the sense of unmarried and celibate but rather that they will be morally virtuous. The Bible is clear that the marriage bed is undefiled (Heb. 13:4), so some or all of this group of Jewish evangelists may be married but will remain sexually and morally pure in the midst of the Antichrist's very immoral society. In 2 Corinthians 11:2, the apostle Paul declares his desire to present believers as "chaste virgins to Christ." That may be the intended meaning here—that these believers will remain spiritually and morally pure.

The second thing we read is that these believers will "follow the Lamb wherever He goes." What a great statement that is, and I hope it can be said of us as well. Jesus said, "If anyone desires to come after Me, let him deny himself, and take up his cross, and follow Me" (Matt. 16:24). When we placed our lives in God's hands by faith and received forgiveness for our sins through the shed blood of Christ on the cross, our lives were purchased and redeemed by God. Therefore, as 1 Corinthians 6:19–20 reminds us, our lives no longer belong to us; they belong to God. This means we are willing to go wherever the Lord wants us to go, and we are willing to do whatever the Lord wants us to do. That does not mean we forfeit our dreams and desires, but it does mean that we commit everything to the will of God.

At the end of verse 4, these 144,000 believers are also referred to as being "firstfruits." Just as the word indicates, "firstfruits" simply means that many more people will come to faith during the tribulation, and that multitude of converts will also arrive safely in heaven. It is quite likely that, during those seven years of unbelievable horror, death, and destruction, the greatest outpouring of salvation in the history of mankind will also take place, as hundreds of thousands of people—if not millions—will come to Christ.

In verse 5, a final characteristic of these believers is that no guile or deceit is found in their mouths, and they are blameless. Unlike the rampant deceit of the Antichrist and his followers, these believers will only speak the truth of God. They will be just like Jesus. Peter said of our Lord, He "committed no sin, nor was deceit found in His mouth" (1 Peter 2:22). In the same way, these believers will also speak words of truth, and they will be blameless—which doesn't mean sinless but that they will live their lives above reproach and without hypocrisy.

Then I saw another angel flying in the midst of heaven, having the everlasting gospel to preach to those who dwell on the earth—to every nation, tribe, tongue, and people—saying with a loud voice, "Fear God and give glory to Him, for the hour of His judgment has come; and worship Him who made heaven and earth, the sea and springs of water." And another angel followed, saying, "Babylon is fallen, is fallen, that great city, because she has made all nations drink of the wine of the wrath of her fornication." Then a third angel followed them, saying with a loud voice, "If anyone worships the beast and his image, and receives his mark on his forehead or on his hand, he himself shall also drink of the wine of the wrath of God, which is poured out full strength into the cup of His indignation. He shall be tormented with fire and brimstone in the presence of the holy angels and in the presence of the Lamb. And the smoke of their torment ascends forever and ever; and they have no rest day or night, who worship the beast and his image, and whoever receives the mark of his name." Here is the patience of the saints; here are those who keep the commandments of God and the faith of Jesus. Then I heard a voice from heaven saying to me, "Write: 'Blessed are the dead who die in the Lord from now on.'" "Yes," says the Spirit, "that they may rest from their labors, and their works follow them."

Revelation 14:6–13

Back in Matthew 24:14, Jesus told His disciples that the gospel must be preached to the whole world, and then the end will come. Some believers have taken that statement to mean that when the church has finally reached every person in the world with the gospel, only then will the Lord finally come back. But that wasn't what Jesus was saying. In context, Jesus was stating that the gospel would reach the entire world in those last days, prior to His second coming. Here in these verses, we see one of the ways in which the gospel will reach the whole world: a holy angel flying throughout the skies proclaiming the gospel.

There is a renewed sense of hope for many people today, and everyone is favorable toward a spirit of hope. But hope is only as strong as the foundation on which it is based. If your hope is in people, politics, or programs, then your hope is resting on a weak foundation that will crumble. Our hope is not in any man we put into authority; it's in the Man we put on the cross. Or as John MacArthur said, "Man's efforts to bring about a better world . . . amount to little more than rearranging the deck chairs on the Titanic to give everyone a better view as the ship sinks."[3] But if your hope is in the Lord and in His gospel, then your hope is secure and on a strong foundation.

In verse 6, we find that same message of hope—the message of the "everlasting gospel"—going out to the unsaved world. The main difference here is the messenger, which is an angel. Throughout church history, God has chosen His people to proclaim the gospel, and not angels. But as the old saying goes, "Desperate times call for drastic measures." The unsaved people of the world are fearful of the Antichrist and are commanded to worship him, so this angel counters that with a gospel message that says, "Fear God and give glory to Him, for the hour of His judgment has come; and worship Him who made heaven and earth, the sea and springs of waters."

So much for mankind's theory of evolution! One anonymous writer must have been smiling when he wrote, "To believe in evolution is to believe that the frog really does turn into a prince."[4] This angel from heaven tells the world to fear God and worship Him, and for two very good reasons: He is the Creator, and His judgment has come! It's worth noting that the first book of the Bible, Genesis, describes God's creation, while the final book of the Bible, Revelation, describes God's judgment. This angel proclaims God as both Creator and Judge.

There's no denying that the world will indeed fear the Antichrist, but the fear of the Lord is a much stronger motivation. Or as Jesus put it, "Do not fear those who kill the body but cannot kill the soul. But rather fear Him who is able to destroy both soul and body in hell" (Matt. 10:28). "The fear of the LORD is the beginning of wisdom," as Solomon said (Prov. 9:10).

In verse 8, a second angel follows the first angel's proclamation of the gospel with the declaration that Babylon, the great city, has fallen. We'll talk more about the symbolism and significance of Babylon in chapters 17 and 18. But let me just say that there is a political and economic Babylon, which refers to the government of the Antichrist. There is also a religious Babylon, which is part of that demonic system as well. At the same time, it appears that a Babylon city will also exist, literally, in these last days. It could mean that the city of Babylon will be rebuilt, or it could simply be a symbolic reference to another city, such as Rome. For now, the point of this second angel's declaration is that if anyone is trusting in the government of the Antichrist to bail him out, spiritually speaking, Babylon has fallen.

In verses 9–11, a third angel follows with the announcement that if any unsaved people go so far as to worship the beast and take his mark upon them, they will have sealed their fate for eternity. To take the mark of the beast is to cross the point of no return. In the middle of verse 10, the eternal punishment from God is described as "the cup of indignation" (*wrath* would be another word). In the Garden of Gethsemane, Jesus willingly accepted the cup of suffering to provide forgiveness for our sins. But everyone who refuses the sacrifice of Christ and chooses to follow the beast will receive God's cup of indignation.

I must comment on verse 11, especially in this day and age. In verse 11, we are unmistakably told that the torment of those who die without Christ will last forever and ever. I don't highlight that fact with any measure of joy, but it does need to be underscored. This is because many unsaved people today have deluded themselves into thinking that they can live without Christ, and then, when they die, they will simply cease to exist. There are even well-meaning Christians who wrongly teach that God will punish, and then annihilate, the unsaved. But what does Scripture say?

In several verses such as this one, the Bible plainly teaches that eternity is eternal—for both the believer in heaven and the unsaved in hell. This prompts many people to ask the age-old question: how can a God of love send people to hell? The short answer is that people choose to go to hell of their own free will. The Bible teaches that every person is a sinner, and our sin separates us from God. Therefore, apart from God's intervention, we would all end up in hell, as we all definitely deserve.

But because He is in fact a God of love, He sent His sinless Son Jesus to the earth to suffer and die in our place. On the cross at Calvary, Jesus took the punishment, the pain, and the penalty of our sins on Himself. Jesus literally took our hell upon Himself so that we might come to Him by faith and receive His heaven. And in God's grace, those who willingly come to Christ and accept His payment for their sins will be forgiven and receive the promise of eternity in heaven with God. The fact that people are going to hell does not mean that God is not loving; it simply means that those people have chosen to reject God's love of their own free will.

In addition to that, in Matthew 25:41, Jesus declares that hell was created for the devil and his fallen angels, and not for people. But if you slap away the hand of God and reject His gift of forgiveness, then you will, of your own choosing, follow the devil and his fallen angels right into hell and into the lake of fire. At the end of Matthew 25, Jesus also makes it abundantly clear that the punishment

198

of hell is everlasting and that life in heaven is eternal; He uses the same Greek word in describing both heaven and hell as eternal and everlasting (see also 2 Thess.1:8–9; Rev. 20:10).

In verse 13, we find a wonderful word of encouragement to those who place their faith in Christ during those difficult days of the tribulation: "Blessed are [those] who die in the Lord from now on." As a pastor who has conducted funeral services for over twenty years, I can tell you that there are good funerals and bad funerals. The funeral service of a committed believer has an underlying joy, for people know that the deceased person is with the Lord and eternally free from pain and suffering. It doesn't mean we don't experience sorrow and sadness, because we definitely do. But the sorrow and sadness are for us, because we'll miss that person until we see him or her again in heaven. But services for people who didn't know the Lord are indeed sad. The death of the unsaved is a great tragedy. At that point, we're trying to reach the unsaved family members and friends while there is still time. Here in these verses, we have an echo of what is recorded in Psalm 116:15: "Precious in the sight of the LORD is the death of His saints." For the believer, death is a blessing in the sense that it releases us into the Lord's presence. For believers having to endure the horrors of the tribulation, it will especially be a blessing.

Then I looked, and behold, a white cloud, and on the cloud sat One like the Son of Man, having on His head a golden crown, and in His hand a sharp sickle. And another angel came out of the temple, crying with a loud voice to Him who sat on the cloud, "Thrust in Your sickle and reap, for the time has come for You to reap, for the harvest of the earth is ripe." So He who sat on the cloud thrust in His sickle on the earth, and the earth was reaped. Then another angel came out of the temple which is in heaven, he also having a sharp sickle. And another angel came out from the altar, who had power over fire, and he cried with a loud cry to him who had the sharp sickle, saying, "Thrust in your sharp sickle and gather the clusters of the vine of the earth, for her grapes are fully ripe." So the angel thrust his sickle into the earth and gathered the vine of the earth, and threw it into the great winepress of the wrath of God. And the winepress was trampled outside the city, and blood came out of the winepress, up to the horses' bridles, for one thousand six hundred furlongs.

Revelation 14:14–20

199

The first three angels were heralding, while these next three angels are harvesting. Incidentally, you'll note that this chapter is saturated with words associated with the harvest: firstfruits, sickle, reaping, ripe, grapes, vine, winepress, and so forth. Today the church is involved in a spiritual harvesting of souls into the kingdom of God, but the day is coming when the Lord will thrust His sickle into a harvest of judgment, as we see illustrated in this chapter. A subtitle for this section could easily be "The Grapes of Wrath."

In verse 14, we have a picture of Christ with a sharp sickle in His hand, symbolizing the divine judgment that is about to continue on the earth below. I find it a bit bizarre that death is oftentimes portrayed in the person of the Grim Reaper, and he (or she) always has that long sickle in hand. I personally have no issues with the Grim Reaper symbolizing death, but the sickle represents judgment, and judgment belongs to God alone.

In verse 15, we have an angel who comes directly from the Father and announces to the Son that the time has come for this judgment to begin. Back in Matthew 13, Jesus explained His parable about the wheat and the tares. The wheat represents the believers, while the tares represent the unsaved. Jesus explained that at the end of the age, the Son of Man will send forth His angels to the earth to gather the tares and to cast them into the fire of torment and suffering. Revelation 14 gives us a vivid picture of that event.

It is important to note that the Father places this judgment in the hands of Jesus. Jesus, who died on the cross to provide forgiveness for our sins, is the same Jesus who will judge the earth—including those who have refused to accept His sacrifice and payment for their sins. At the end of verse 15, we read, "Thrust in Your sickle and reap, for the time has come . . . for the harvest of the earth is *ripe*." So that no one underestimates the long-suffering of God, I would point out that the Greek word for "ripe" literally means "overly ripe, withered, and rotten"—like spoiled fruit that has fallen off the tree.[5]

In this chapter, we see two significant things about the mercy of God:

1. He is sending forth the gospel, even in the final days and minutes.
2. He is holding back His judgment until the earth is overly ripe and can wait no longer.

Never underestimate the love, mercy, and grace of God. At the same time, never underestimate the holiness, righteousness, and judgment of God.

At the end of verse 19, we read how God's wrath and judgment are likened to a great winepress. Symbolically, the angels will gather the grapes of wrath, or the unsaved, and cast them into God's great winepress of judgment. In the first century, a winepress consisted of two vats—one large vat and another smaller vat below it. The gathered grapes were cast into the upper vat, where they were trampled underfoot. During this process, the juice from those trampled grapes would flow down to the lower vat. That word picture is being used here to describe the judgment of the Lord in the final days of the tribulation, and instead of juice flowing, the winepress of God's wrath will be filled with the blood of the unsaved.

In verse 20, this winepress activity of God's judgment will take place outside the walls of Jerusalem. This is in order to preserve the holy city. When this wrath is completed, Christ will return to the Mount of Olives, where He will initiate His millennial kingdom, and Jerusalem will be His headquarters. In verse 20, we also read that the blood of this massive slaughter will reach the height of a horse's bridle—which is upwards of four feet—and the blood will flow approximately 185 miles.

That 185 miles is roughly the distance from the Valley of Megiddo in northern Israel down to southern Israel. The whole land of Israel will become like a giant winepress, with the main battle taking place in the upper vat of Megiddo and the blood flowing down through the land. In spite of the present-day threat of nuclear weapons, this description is of a battlefield slaughter rather than a nuclear exchange. We'll talk more about the last-days battle of Armageddon when we get to chapter 16.

In this chapter, we've seen some of the certainties of God: salvation, the gospel, and divine judgment. These are not "take it or leave it" discussions; these are "take it to the bank" certainties. At the same time, this chapter has confirmed to us that people who end up in heaven do not get what they deserve. It's not justice that brings a person to heaven; it is God's grace and mercy. On the other hand, people who end up in hell are getting exactly what they deserve—what we all deserve. It is, in fact, justice that sends a person to hell. Praise God for His grace and mercy!

20

The Beginning of the End

Revelation 15:1–16:6

In September of 2007, my buddy Ron and I had the opportunity to travel to Green Bay, Wisconsin, and attend the opening-day game of the Packers. It was extra special, because it turned out to be Brett Favre's final season in Green Bay. Sometime during the trip, Ron casually mentioned to me that he had brought along two homemade signs for us to hold up at the game. However, I broke it to Ron (ever so gently) that I hadn't traveled over two thousand miles to Green Bay so I could hold up a sign during the entire game! He assured me that it was our best chance of getting on television, so our family and friends could see us, but that didn't sweeten the deal for me.

So during the game, whenever the roving CBS television cameras came anywhere near us, Ron held up his sign and tried to get us on television. I did notice that the camera guys were always focusing on the craziest fans in the stadium—the ones with green and yellow face paint, bizarre outfits, or no shirts. I finally turned to Ron and told him, "It's a catch-22, my friend. You'll have to act like a complete idiot in order to get on television, and then if you do that, all your family and friends back home will tell you, 'Hey, I saw you on television during the game, and you looked like a complete idiot!'"

In Revelation 15, the apostle John tells us that he saw another great and marvelous sign in heaven, but it isn't like one of those homemade signs you hold up at a football game.

> Then I saw another sign in heaven, great and marvelous: seven angels having the seven last plagues, for in them the wrath of God is complete. And I saw something like a sea of glass mingled with fire, and those who have the victory over the beast, over his image and over his mark and over the number of his name, standing on the sea of glass, having harps of God. They sing the song of Moses, the servant of God, and the song of the Lamb, saying: "Great and marvelous are Your works, Lord God Almighty! Just and true are Your ways, O King of the saints! Who shall not fear You, O Lord, and glorify Your name? For You alone are holy. For all nations shall come and worship before You, for Your judgments have been manifested."
>
> Revelation 15:1–4

As God prepares to unleash this series of seven bowl judgments on the earth, John informs us that in these judgments, "the wrath of God is complete." It's the beginning of the end. The events that we will read about in these next few chapters take place in rapid succession and lead to the second coming of Jesus.

Throughout the pages of Scripture, we find that after much patience and grace on the part of God, His judgment finally comes. We see it in the global flood in the days of Noah. We see it in the destruction of the twin cities of Sodom and Gomorrah. We see it in the days of Pharaoh and Egypt. We see it in King Nebuchadnezzar's invasion of Israel with his Babylonian armies, whereby Jerusalem and the temple were destroyed. Here we see it in the later days of the tribulation period.

In verse 2, John sees "something like a sea of glass mingled with fire." If you've ever been out on a lake when it is perfectly still, those calm waters can resemble glass. Obviously, this is not an actual sea, because the saints are standing on it. But it does look like a glassy sea. We read about this glassy sea area in front of God's throne back in chapter 4. Here we have the added detail that it is "mingled with fire." This either symbolizes the fiery trials of those who make commitments to Christ during the tribulation and then lose their lives as martyrs, or else it symbolizes God's fiery judgment that is about to fall on the earth.

This glassy sea mingled with fire may very well represent both God's deliverance through our fiery trials as well as His judgment. This is a familiar thread that runs through Scripture. For example, the global floodwaters of Genesis were a deliverance for Noah and his family, but they were judgment to the unsaved inhabitants of the earth. The waters of the Red Sea were parted and gave deliverance to Israel, but they also became the judgment waters for Pharaoh's army. Even at the moment of our water baptism, going under the water symbolizes death to our old, unsaved nature, while coming up out of those same waters represents our new life in Christ.

In Revelation, we learn that while God's people will stand on a sea of glass, the unsaved will spend eternity in a lake of fire (Rev. 20). Standing and singing on top of this glassy sea is a special group of people with harps in their hands. The guitar and piano are the most popular instruments here on earth, but if you want to prepare for the worship team in heaven, you might consider taking harp lessons. David's instrument of choice in the Old Testament was the harp.

These believers are the ones who have achieved "victory over the beast, over his image, over his mark, and over the number of his name." If we pay close attention to the wording here in verse 4, we can understand more about these martyrs. In his full demonic power and authority, the Antichrist is going to require the world to worship his image and to receive his mark—and the penalty for refusing to do so will be death. I believe these martyrs standing in heaven on the glassy sea are those who made commitments to Christ in the second half of the tribulation. Back in chapter 7, we read about another great multitude of converts in heaven, from every tribe, nation, and tongue, who were won to Christ by the witness of the 144,000 Jewish evangelists. Those were martyrs from the first half of the tribulation, whereas these are now coming from the second half. These are the ones who gained victory over the Antichrist. And how did they accomplish that victory in God's power? Look again at verse 4: they refused to worship the image of the beast, described as "victory over his image," and they refused to take his mark or his number on their hands or foreheads, described as "victory over his mark and over the number of his name."

In his book titled *Heaven*, Randy Alcorn tells of a young woman named Florence Chadwick, who in 1952 attempted to swim from Catalina Island to the main shore of California. She had already succeeded in swimming the English Channel—the first woman to do so. As she swam in the chilly waters from Catalina, it was quite foggy. Her mother and some others were traveling alongside her in a boat. Florence swam for fifteen hours and then became exhausted. Her mother encouraged her, and told her that she was almost there. But being physically and emotionally exhausted, she felt she couldn't continue, and she urged them to pull her out of the water. Only when Florence was in the boat and proceeding to the mainland shore, did she realize that she had stopped just a half mile short of her goal. At the news conference afterward, Florence told the press, "All I could see was the fog. . . . I think if I could have seen the shore, I would have made it."[1]

Those who make commitments to Christ during the tribulation and are put to death by the Antichrist for refusing to take his mark and worship him, will do so by realizing how close they are to their heavenly destination. The same is true for us today; peace and patience and perseverance in the faith require us to keep our eyes on the Lord and on our destination. It was Charles Spurgeon who said, "By perseverance, the snail reached the ark."[2]

Based on what we've read in chapter 14, combined with what we read here, the strong implication is that everyone on the earth has made a decision at this point. Either they've made their commitment to Christ and have been sealed by God, or they've taken the mark of the beast and are eternally separated from God. At this point, the time will come for the worst judgment ever known to mankind to rain upon the earth.

There will still be many Jewish and Gentile believers left on the earth during that time, and God will protect them from His wrath. Then at the end of the tribulation, those surviving believers on earth will remain. They will join Jesus in the millennium and begin to repopulate the world. When we get to our study of the millennial kingdom in chapter 20, I'll explain that further.

In the meantime, these new arrivals in heaven are standing on the glassy sea, and they're holding harps for worshiping God. We are told that they will sing two songs at that time: the song of Moses and the song of the Lamb. Here in Revelation, the lyrics for the song of the Lamb are provided for us. But where are the lyrics for the song of Moses? They're recorded back in Exodus 15. In fact, the song of Moses is the first recorded praise song in Scripture, while the song of the Lamb is the last recorded praise song.

Let's look at the words of this song again.

> Great and marvelous are *Your* works, Lord God Almighty! Just and true are *Your* ways, O King of the saints! Who shall not fear *You*, O Lord, and glorify *Your* name? For *You* alone are holy. For all nations shall come and worship before *You*, for *Your* judgments have been manifested.

> Revelation 15:3–4, emphasis added

This is exactly how true worship should be: emphasizing God and His works, which include creation and salvation. Evelyn Underhill described worship as "the total adoring response of man to the Eternal God."[3] True worship exalts God and fulfills the very purpose for which we were created. I would summarize worship in a couple of words: reverence and response. Our worship of God must begin with a holy reverence, and continue as a loving response to all that God is and says and does.

Notice a couple things that are not included in this song. For one, nothing is said about any of the sacrifices or efforts of these tribulation martyrs. This song is all about the glorification of God. Second, there are no words of grumbling or grief. None of these singing martyrs is complaining about what they had to go through back on earth. "God reveals Himself, but He rarely explains Himself—we don't live on explanations, we live on the promises of God."[4]

To the people today who want to blame God for all their problems, be reminded that apart from God, you would not have any hope in this world or in the world to come. God is not to be blamed; He is to be blessed, honored, and praised! These saints are singing the song of the Lamb because the Lamb laid down His life for them on the cross and gave them eternal life in heaven.

After these things I looked, and behold, the temple of the tabernacle of the testimony in heaven was opened. And out of the temple came the seven angels having the seven plagues, clothed in pure bright linen, and having their chests girded with golden bands. Then one of the four living creatures gave to the seven angels seven golden bowls full of the wrath of God who lives forever and ever. The temple was filled with smoke from the glory of God and from His power, and no one was able to enter the temple till the seven plagues of the seven angels were completed.

Revelation 15:5–8

We return to our discussion about the third great sign mentioned in verse 1. This sign is the seven angels having the seven bowl judgments. These angels are ministers of God, doing the work of God as He directs them. In verse 5, John describes something that seems to startle him. He is focusing on the magnificent vision of worship when suddenly his attention is drawn to the Holy of Holies in heaven being opened up.

We remember how the Holy of Holies on earth was not accessible to the people—or even to the priests, for that matter. Only the high priest could enter, once a year, on the Day of Atonement. But when Jesus was crucified at Calvary, one of the unique things that happened at the moment of His death was that the temple veil was torn in two. That thick curtain was the separation between the Holy Place and the Holy of Holies. When God tore that veil, it signified that God was providing access to His presence through the sacrifice of His Son Jesus. Now John sees the Holy of Holies in heaven. John was alive while the earthly temple was closed off to the general population, and he was near the cross when Jesus died and the veil was ripped in two. Now in verse 5, he sees the corresponding results of the open temple in heaven.

In verse 6, seven angels emerge from the heavenly temple—a vivid reminder that God's judgments are just as holy as His grace. In the words of Stuart Briscoe, "The wrath of God is as pure as the holiness of God."[5] Here we have the Holy of Holies in heaven, which contains the true ark of the covenant. And the ark contains, among other things, the Ten Commandments. And what is the first commandment of God? "You shall have no other gods before Me." And what are the

207

people on earth doing? Worshiping the Antichrist (13:4). And what is the second commandment of God? "You shall not make any graven images." And what are the people on earth doing? Worshiping the image of the beast (13:14–15). And what is the third commandment of God? "You shall not take the name of the Lord in vain." And what is the Antichrist on earth doing? Blaspheming the name of God and God's holy tabernacle in heaven (13:6). So is this judgment from God holy and righteous? Absolutely—without question!

These seven angels are clothed in garments of pure linen and have gold bands across their chests. This reminds us of the garments worn by the Old Testament priests as they carried out their temple ministry. That's what these angels are doing.

Back in chapter 4, we talked about the identity of the four living creatures, which are a special order of angels called cherubim. Cherubim have the honor and privilege of worshiping God at His throne in heaven. So it's no surprise that they worship God by crying out, "Holy, holy, holy." One of these four cherub angels gives the seven angels "seven golden bowls full of the wrath of God."

The Greek word for "bowls" in verse 7 (some translations say "vials") actually describes shallow and wide saucers. We can almost envision the angels, carefully balancing these shallow saucers filled with God's wrath, ready to spill over. After these seven angels receive their bowls, the temple is filled with smoke, which symbolizes God's presence. In Exodus, after its completion, the tabernacle was filled with the presence of the Lord, and Moses was not able to enter it. In the same way here, we read that the temple was filled with God's glory, and no one was able to enter.

Revelation 15 is, by far, the shortest chapter in the book. But having just studied it, we see that it is an important bridge linking the events of the tribulation's midpoint to these final bowl judgments. So what judgments do these bowls contain?

Then I heard a loud voice from the temple saying to the seven angels, "Go and pour out the bowls of the wrath of God on the earth." So the first went and poured out his bowl upon the earth, and a foul and loathsome sore came upon the men who had the mark of the beast and those who worshiped his image. Then the second angel poured out his bowl on the sea, and it became blood as of a dead man; and every living creature in the sea died. Then the third angel poured out his bowl on the rivers and springs of water, and they became blood. And I heard the angel of the waters saying: "You are righteous, O Lord, The One who is and who was and who is to be, because You have judged these things. For they have shed the blood of saints and prophets, and You have given them blood to drink. For it is their just due."

Revelation 16:1–6

What we will read in chapters 16–19 of Revelation was described by the Old Testament prophets as "the day of the Lord is great and very terrible" (Joel 2:11). We remember that, initially, there were the seven seal judgments that began in Revelation 6. The seventh seal judgment, when opened, released the seven trumpet judgments. In turn, the seventh trumpet judgment unleashed these final seven bowl judgments. So in reality, all the trumpet and bowl judgments are the seventh seal judgment. These seven bowl judgments are far worse and far more devastating than any of the previous judgments. As Jesus said, in Matthew 24:22, "If these days were not cut short, the entire human race would be destroyed" (paraphrased).

Here in verse 1, John describes hearing a loud voice from the temple. Nearly twenty times in Revelation we read about a "loud" or "great" voice speaking. It's almost as if these seven angels are reluctant to pour forth the horrific judgments from their bowls, and God's voice, calling to them from the temple, is saying, "Go ahead and pour out the bowls of wrath on the earth." If those angels were the least bit hesitant, we could certainly understand why.

When the first angel pours out his bowl upon the earth, every unsaved person who has taken the mark of the beast upon him and who worships the beast will be struck with severe and malignant sores. The specific wording strongly indicates that this judgment will target the unsaved but not those who belong to God. That is certainly in keeping with God's series of plagues against Pharaoh and the Egyptians, which did not harm the children of Israel. In fact, this bowl judgment of sores is very similar to the sixth plague—the plague of boils—against Egypt.

Wouldn't it be interesting if the very process that will be used for applying this global mark also ends up being the source of these ma-

209

lignant sores? In other words, since the mark is permanent, and since a few billion people will have to be marked in a very short period of time, it is possible that the government will use some process that is either unsafe or untested. Perhaps that process will include the use of chemicals or elements that will make those people susceptible to the malignant sores that God brings.

Whatever the case, the painful sores being described here are intense, oozing, burning, and incurable. There will be no relief and no remedy. In fact, when the fifth bowl judgment is being poured out in verse 11, the people are still suffering from these sores. In verse 11, we also read the most amazing and sad aspect of these sores and bowl judgments: those unsaved people will continue to curse God and refuse to repent of their sins. This confirms our conclusion that they will have reached the point of no return by this time.

In verse 3, we have the second bowl judgment: all the ocean waters are turned into blood. This is much worse than it sounds. The oceans cover approximately 71 percent of the earth's surface, so nearly three-fourths of the earth will become blood. Every single creature in the sea will die. The loss of all sea life will produce a series of crises.

For one, the already depleted food supplies of the world will be severely diminished. Second, the stench and pollution of those dead sea creatures will contaminate the air. And third, the massive amounts of death and decay in the sea will undoubtedly produce various diseases, which will spread quickly. This judgment bears similarity to the first plague in Egypt, when Moses struck the waters of the Nile River with his staff and God turned the waters into blood. Obviously, this bowl judgment will be far greater in scope and magnitude than that plague.

I've had the blessing of visiting Egypt. I remember our Egyptian guide's name; it was Moses—what else? Nothing like a guided tour with Moses! He was a very nice and knowledgeable young man. One of the many facts that he shared with us was how 96 percent of the people in Egypt live on only 4 percent of the land. The reason is simple: most people in Egypt live along the Nile River because the rest of the country is basically desert.

When Moses told us that, I began thinking about that first plague in Egypt, as recorded in Exodus. Imagine a major water source like the Nile River becoming pure blood. Using the demographics provided by my tour guide, it would have affected 96 percent of the population. Just imagine how many people will be affected when 71 percent of the earth's surface will become blood. The effect of this second bowl judgment is beyond staggering.

The third bowl judgment, in verse 4, takes the global crisis we just described and magnifies it. This judgment will turn the freshwater lakes, rivers, and springs into blood. What will people drink? The angel answers that question in verse 6, when he declares, "For they have shed the blood of saints and prophets and You have given them blood to drink." So there will be no freshwater, and the only drink available, so to speak, will be blood. Then the angel of God who oversees the waters declares, almost like a courtroom verdict, "It is their just due" (or "It's what they deserve").

I can't help but be reminded that God's wrath and judgment are also what each one of us deserves. But God, in His great love, sent Jesus. If anyone reads these words of judgment and feels that God is acting too harshly, please remember that this is exactly what happened to Jesus on the cross. During the crucifixion, and particularly during those three hours of darkness on Good Friday, God poured out His divine wrath and holy judgment for our sins on to Jesus. Christ took our wrath upon Himself so that we might receive His forgiveness and eternal life in heaven. But for those who refuse Christ, the righteous wrath of God still waits for them.

21

God's Righteous Judgments

Revelation 16:7–21

A few years ago, a woman in Yankton, South Dakota, took her stepson to his Boy Scout meeting. At that meeting, the special guest was a local police officer who specialized in narcotics, and he had brought his drug-sniffing German shepherd police dog. As the mother was watching the demonstration from the back of the room, the dog suddenly trotted over to where she was standing, nudged her purse with his nose, and began whining. Sure enough, inside the woman's purse was a bag of drugs, and the Boy Scout meeting ended abruptly with the mother's arrest!

Here in Revelation 16, we read about God's justice, and as we pick up our reading in verse 7, another voice cries out from the altar in heaven, "Even so, Lord God Almighty, true and righteous are Your judgments." Back in chapter 6, we read about some of the tribulation martyrs who had been killed for their faith and whose souls were under the altar in heaven, asking God, "How long, O Lord, holy and true, until You judge and avenge our blood on those who dwell on the earth?" Here now, in chapter 16, we're reading about those people who dwell on earth being given blood to drink, because it is what they deserve. Therefore, it's probably the same voice of those martyrs under the altar, here in verse 7, declaring that God's judgments are true and righteous.

But there is much more judgment to come:

> Then the fourth angel poured out his bowl on the sun, and power was given to him to scorch men with fire. And men were scorched with great heat, and they blasphemed the name of God who has power over these plagues; and they did not repent and give Him glory.
>
> Revelation 16:8–9

The sun, created by God and given to us to provide light, warmth, and energy, will be used by God as an instrument of judgment to bring unbearable heat, pain, and suffering. In the world today, we experience periodic heat waves, and sometimes people have died as a result. But those will pale in comparison with this heat wave, in which mankind will be "scorched with great heat." These people have already been struck with malignant sores, and now this scorching heat will only intensify their pain and suffering.

At the same time, the scorching heat will burn up whatever remaining crops and vegetation there might be. It will also increase everyone's level of thirst and their need for fluids—but God will have already turned the freshwater into blood. So where will people get water to drink? New sources of water may come unexpectedly, but it won't be what people were hoping for. Let me explain: this increase in the sun's intensity will undoubtedly result in the melting of the polar ice caps, as well as mountain snow packs. They will melt so quickly that it will surely result in a deluge of floodwaters.

It has been estimated by scientists that there are enough ice reservoirs around the world to raise sea levels by two hundred feet, if they were rapidly melted. If that information is accurate, you could say good-bye to coastal cities such as New York, New Orleans, Los Angeles, San Francisco, Tokyo, Sydney, and many others. Thirty-five of the forty largest cities in the world today are either coastal or situated next to large rivers.

But the most amazing effect of this fourth bowl judgment is recorded in verse 9, where we read that those who are scorched with this great heat will blaspheme the name of God, who has power over these plagues, and they will refuse to repent. As commentator Lehman Strauss puts it, "If a man rejects the kindness and love of God, then what makes us think that the judgment of God will change his heart either?"[1]

This brings us to verse 10, where we continue our reading:

> Then the fifth angel poured out his bowl on the throne of the beast, and his kingdom became full of darkness; and they gnawed their tongues because of the pain. They blasphemed the God of heaven because of their pains and their sores, and did not repent of their deeds.
>
> Revelation 16:10–11

Back in the 1970s, in the early days of television's *Monday Night Football*, the team of announcers included Don Meredith, the former quarterback of the Dallas Cowboys. Each week, when the point came, somewhere in the fourth quarter, that the outcome of the game was obvious, Meredith would start singing, "Turn out the lights, the party's over." Well here, in the latter stages of the tribulation, God turns out the lights and the party is definitely over!

Like the ninth plague in Egypt, God will punish the people with absolute darkness. The feeling of total darkness is very eerie and unsettling. This darkness, coupled with the malignant sores, will continue to bring unbearable pain to the unsaved people who worshiped the beast. We read that the pain will be so agonizing that it will drive people to gnaw on their tongues. I have a suggestion as to what may be happening here: people are using their tongues to blaspheme God, so God sends them so much pain that it causes them to chew on their tongues.

In verse 10, John states that this darkness will fall upon the throne of the beast, as well as his kingdom. There is uncertainty among commentators as to whether this means the darkness will affect only the city headquarters where the Antichrist is or whether it will be more far-reaching. I have no doubt that it will be a worldwide darkness, because these bowl judgments are a punishment against every unsaved person who has taken the mark and worshiped the beast. The kingdom of the beast is worldwide, as he has required the whole world to worship him.

214

As I read these verses, I can't help but think of Christ on the cross. Earlier I mentioned the incredible thirst that people will experience during these judgments. On the cross at Calvary, as Jesus was taking all of our judgment on Himself, He experienced radical thirst. One of the seven statements He made from the cross was, "I thirst." Then, during the final three hours at Calvary, darkness came over all the land as God's wrath for our sins fell upon Jesus. Here in Revelation, these people will experience that darkness that is associated with God's judgment.

Scripture says that God is light. While Satan masquerades as an angel of light, he is really the prince of darkness. Jesus said, "I am the light of the world" (John 8:12). But John also tells us, "Men loved darkness rather than light, because their deeds were evil" (John 3:19).

What we're reading in Revelation is a vivid preview of hell. Back in Matthew 25:30, Jesus described hell and eternal punishment as "outer darkness" where there will be "weeping and gnashing of teeth." It is also described as a place of "flaming fire" (2 Thess. 1:8). What the Antichrist and his people are experiencing at this point in Revelation is just a foretaste of their eternal destiny in the lake of fire. Eternal punishment and pain will not bring them to repentance or remorse but rather to a place of continual blasphemy. Those who have hard hearts and hate God here on earth will continue to have hard hearts and hate God in eternity.

> Then the sixth angel poured out his bowl on the great river Euphrates, and its water was dried up, so that the way of the kings from the east might be prepared. And I saw three unclean spirits like frogs coming out of the mouth of the dragon, out of the mouth of the beast, and out of the mouth of the false prophet. For they are spirits of demons, performing signs, which go out to the kings of the earth and of the whole world, to gather them to the battle of that great day of God Almighty. "Behold, I am coming as a thief. Blessed is he who watches, and keeps his garments, lest he walk naked and they see his shame." And they gathered them together to the place called in Hebrew, Armageddon.
>
> Revelation 16:12–16

When the sixth angel pours out his bowl of God's wrath, the Euphrates River will dry up. The first reference in Scripture to the

Euphrates is found in Genesis 2. There we read that a river flowed out from the Garden of Eden, and as it divided into four riverheads, one of those was the Euphrates. The Euphrates is still flowing in the Middle East—the longest river in that area, running almost eighteen hundred miles.

The waters of the Euphrates start from Mount Ararat and the melting snows of seventeen-thousand-foot mountain peaks. When the fourth bowl judgment of the scorching sun takes place, it will melt all of that accumulated snow on Ararat, and the Euphrates River will overflow, bringing widespread flooding. Now let me mention again that the Antichrist will have his own city of Babylon as his headquarters. Whether that means the Antichrist will rebuild the city of Babylon, we don't know for certain. It could mean that he will make an existing city, such as Rome, his own Babylon. But if the Antichrist does rebuild Babylon—a distinct possibility—it would undoubtedly be situated near the Euphrates River, as was ancient Babylon.

So when the judgment of scorching heat begins, the snow will melt, the Euphrates River will overflow, and Babylon will be flooded. Then when the plague of darkness comes, the Antichrist will be shut down—having to sit by helplessly, waiting for his next opportunity. Then comes the next judgment, when the Euphrates River suddenly dries up. If the Antichrist's rebuilt city of Babylon is there on the Euphrates, the city will lose much of its power and resources.

But more to the point, the reason God will cause the waters of the Euphrates to dry up is to draw in the kings of the east, as well as the other kings of the world. The Euphrates River is a natural boundary in the Middle East, and it forms a barrier of separation for the Holy Land. So God will dry up that great river, which will entice the kings of the east to begin their military march west toward Israel.

Remember that God separated the waters of the Red Sea, which allowed Israel to escape the pursuing Egyptian armies. But those divided waters also enticed the Egyptian armies to pursue Israel. In the same way, God will dry up the Euphrates River, which will entice military leaders to attack Israel. The motive of those nations may be anti-Semitism and a desire to destroy the Jewish people, or they may be seeking natural resources. For example, just recently, Israel discovered its largest reserve of natural gas off its coast. That natural gas reserve is estimated to be worth fifteen billion dollars. A resource like that could easily draw in other nations, who would invade and attack Israel—especially as natural resources will be so desperately needed.

In verse 12, "the kings of the east" is literally "the kings from the rising sun." Most commentators agree that this refers to the armies of the Orient. A confederacy of nations such as China, Japan, Pakistan, and India will band together and begin their march west toward the Holy Land. However, they will not realize that God is drawing them in for the day of judgment by drying up the Euphrates.

In verse 13, we also find that Satan is contributing to this gathering of armies in Israel. The unholy trinity of Satan, the Antichrist, and the False Prophet will all send forth unclean, frog-like demonic spirits to entice the world. These are not literal frogs, any more than the locust-like demons were actually locusts back in chapter 9. Locusts are swift and destructive, while frogs are foul and unclean, so both symbolize the character of these demonic forces. This does remind us, though, of the plague of frogs that God sent against Pharaoh and Egypt.

These demonic spirits will use deceiving signs and wonders to draw the armies of the world into Israel for battle. Satan's motive is to destroy Israel and the city of Jerusalem. Satan knows that if he can do this, Christ will have no Holy Land to return to and no holy city in which to establish His kingdom.

In verse 15, we have a welcome parenthesis—a word of comfort and encouragement from the Lord:

> Behold, I am coming as a thief. Blessed is he who watches, and keeps his garments, lest he walk naked and they see his shame.
>
> Revelation 16:15

Jesus is encouraging those who have made a commitment to Him, in those difficult days of the tribulation, to remain strong in their faith. He will come like a thief to the unsaved and the ungodly, who are not looking for Him. But God will preserve His faithful followers.

In verse 16, we have the only reference in Scripture to Armageddon. The name *Armageddon* comes from two Hebrew words, *har Megiddo*, which mean "hill or mountain of Megiddo." The ancient city of Megiddo is about sixty miles north of Jerusalem and over-looks the Valley of Megiddo. The entire area has been the site for previous battles recorded in Scripture:

- It was there that Barak defeated the Canaanites (Judg. 4).
- It was there that Gideon defeated the Midianites (Judg. 7).
- It was the battlefield where King Saul lost his life (1 Sam. 31).
- King Josiah also died there in battle (2 Kings 23).

When Napoleon Bonaparte saw that same area, over two hundred years ago, he called it the greatest and most natural battlefield on earth. Napoleon then said, "Here indeed, all the armies of the earth may gather for battle."[2] Following World War II, General Douglas MacArthur stated that the next world war would certainly be Armageddon. According to verse 16, the final great world battle will be fought in "har Megiddo"—the hills and valleys of Megiddo. But this will not be a battle as much as it will be a slaughter, as Jesus returns and quickly crushes the gathered armies of the world. In fact, the word *Megiddo* means "place of troops" or "place of slaughter."

Now, the sixth plague is not the battle of Armageddon; we will read about that battle in chapter 19. The sixth bowl judgment is the drying up of the Euphrates River, which leads to the gathering of the world's armies. So this simply sets the stage for the final battle at Christ's second coming. In the meantime, there is a seventh bowl judgment:

> Then the seventh angel poured out his bowl into the air, and a loud voice came out of the temple of heaven, from the throne, saying, "It is done!" And there were noises and thunderings and lightnings; and there was a great earthquake, such a mighty and great earthquake as had not occurred since men were on the earth. Now the great city was divided into three parts, and the cities of the nations fell. And great Babylon was remembered before God, to give her the cup of the wine of the fierceness of His wrath. Then every island fled away, and the mountains were not found. And great hail from heaven fell upon men, each hailstone about the weight of a talent. Men blasphemed God because of the plague of the hail, since that plague was exceedingly great.
>
> Revelation 16:17–21

The first bowl judgment was poured out on the earth, as we read in verse 2. The second bowl was poured out on the oceans, and the third bowl on all the freshwater rivers and streams. The fourth bowl was poured out on the sun, the fifth on the throne of the Antichrist, and the sixth on the Euphrates River. Now in verse 17, the seventh and final bowl is poured into the air. This reminds us of how Satan is described in Scripture as being "the prince of the power of the air" (Eph. 2:2).

We also read about the voice of God calling out from His throne and from the temple in heaven, declaring, "It is done!" The final words of Christ from the cross as He died were, "It is finished!" Here now, after God's final bowl judgment is poured out, we hear God in heaven saying, "It is done!" At the cross, Jesus finished His sacrifice of suffering and death to provide salvation for all who believe and receive; here in the tribulation, God is done pouring out His final bowl judgments against unrepentant sinners.

In verse 18, we read that a global earthquake will take place, so powerful and so devastating that it will be unlike any other in the history of mankind. We only have to think back to December 26, 2004, when a magnitude 9.0 earthquake struck Southeast Asia, triggering a tsunami and resulting in the deaths of more than 230,000 people. But what John is describing for us here is a global earthquake so powerful and so devastating that no scale will be able to measure it. Once again, we think back to Calvary and remember that an earthquake took place at the moment Jesus died, causing the rocks to split open.

This earthquake will be unique not only because it will be global but, because of its catastrophic effects, whereby islands will disappear, mountains will be leveled, and the entire topography of the earth will be radically altered. What I believe the Lord will be doing, through the effects of this judgment, is renovating and restoring the earth—closer to what it was like in the days of Adam and Eve. Oftentimes on the news, we see footage of large buildings being imploded, and after all the rubble has been cleared, a new and better building takes its place. With this global earthquake, it seems as though the Lord will be demolishing the planet and preparing it for His millennial kingdom, which will begin not long after these events.

The demolition includes a renovation of the holy city of Jerusalem, as we read here in verse 19. The great city will be split up into three parts, while all the other cities of the world will crumble, including the Babylon city of the Antichrist. Today, the old city of Jerusalem is divided into four quarters: Jewish, Christian, Muslim, and Armenian. But in the aftermath of this earthquake, the entire city will be reconfigured into three parts, and not based on any ethnic or religious distinctions.

In Zechariah 14:4, we also read that when Christ returns and stands on the Mount of Olives—the place where He ascended into heaven after His resurrection—the Mount of Olives will be split in two, creating a very large valley.

In verse 21, those who escape the death and devastation of the global earthquake will not escape the hailstorm from heaven. God's seventh plague of hailstones against Egypt, in Exodus, was quite severe. We're told that it was the most severe hailstorm until that time, and the hailstones were mixed with fire. But here in Revelation, this is much worse, as these hailstones will weigh one talent, or approximately a hundred pounds each! Can you imagine hundred-pound hailstones falling from the sky? Forget about the golf-ball-size hailstones that fall in Texas; we're talking about hundred-pound blocks of ice!

But even as people are dying from the earthquake and from the hundred-pound hailstones, notice that they're still blaspheming God. Do you remember what the Old Testament punishment was for blaspheming God? The punishment was being stoned to death—just as we read here (Lev. 24:16). These are indeed "God's Righteous Judgments."

22

Judgment of the Harlot

Revelation 17:1–18

I recently celebrated my birthday. I agree with Jerry Seinfeld when he said, "I'm getting sick of pretending to be excited every time it's somebody's birthday. . . . What's the big deal? How many times do we have to celebrate that someone was born? Every year, over and over . . . all you did was not die for twelve months. That's all you've done, as far as I can tell!"[1] I think the bigger issue today is the large number of people who can't seem to accept the fact that they are getting older. It's pretty scary when people in their senior years are trying to look and act like high school seniors!

Some other things—far more serious—that do not mix are false religion and genuine faith. But since the beginning of time, both have been thriving. Regardless of whether people will acknowledge it, every person was created by God to know Him and to worship Him. But for many, instead of worshiping God, they worship a false god, or a religious system, or the environment, or the constellations, or—in many cases—they worship themselves.

Sigmund Freud, an atheist, described religion as an illusion; it was Freud who said, "When a man is freed of religion, he has a better chance to live a normal and wholesome life."[2] Mahatma Gandhi said, "I consider myself a Hindu, Christian, Moslem, Jew, Buddhist, and Confucian." I think instead of "Confucian" he should have said "confusion"! There are those who deny God as Creator and embrace evolution. I would have to agree with Christian comedian Robert G. Lee, who said, "I have a hard time believing that billions of years ago, [microorganisms] bumped into each other under a volcanic cesspool and evolved into Cindy Crawford!"[3]

As we come now to Revelation 17, we read about the downfall of false religion, symbolized by a harlot. Every person today, and every person living in the final days of the tribulation, will identify with either the harlot of false religion or the bride of Christ. In the previous chapter, we read about God's wrath against Babylon and the kingdom of the Antichrist. In chapter 17, this wrath is against religious Babylon, and in chapter 18, it will be against political and economic Babylon.

> Then one of the seven angels who had the seven bowls came and talked with me, saying to me, "Come, I will show you the judgment of the great harlot who sits on many waters, with whom the kings of the earth committed fornication, and the inhabitants of the earth were made drunk with the wine of her fornication."
>
> Revelation 17:1–2

One of the seven angels who poured out the bowl judgments now shows John "the judgment of the great harlot." I would presume that this is the seventh angel with the seventh bowl, simply because he is describing some of the details of God's wrath against Babylon, which was part of that seventh bowl judgment.

One of the blessings of this chapter is that many of the details are clarified for us—either here or in other chapters of Revelation. For example, the angel tells John that he is going to show him the judgment of the great harlot "who sits on many waters." Later on, in verse 15, the angel tells John, "The waters which you saw, where the harlot sits, are peoples, multitudes, nations, and tongues." So the harlot represents false religion, and the waters reveal to us that this last-days false religion will be worldwide.

When the rapture takes place, all genuine believers will be removed from the earth, but the world will continue with religious business as usual. It's truly a sad and frightening thought that, after the rapture, there will continue to be an abundance of religious services that will include prayers, songs, and words of false encouragement—and none of it will have anything to do with genuine faith in God. A. W. Tozer was right when he said, "The whole world has been booby-trapped by the devil, and the deadliest trap of all is the religious one."[4] So we agree with the exhortation of Vance Havner, when he said, "Don't ever come to church without coming as though it were the first time, as though it could be the best time and as though it might be the last time."[5] The day is coming when our next worship service will be in heaven!

False religion is symbolized here as a harlot—a term used four times in this chapter. This is not a harlot in the sense of a prostitute—although sexual immorality is sometimes part of false religion—but a harlot in the sense of spiritual idolatry and apostasy. When Israel had been spiritually unfaithful in the Old Testament and was worshiping other gods, God characterized His people as playing the harlot (Hosea 9:1). Faithful followers in the New Testament are described as being the bride of Christ, speaking of spiritual purity, whereas the followers of false religion belong to the harlot, speaking of spiritual perversion.

I have three points for this chapter in regard to the judgment of the harlot, and the first is *her allure*. It is with this harlot of false religion that "the kings of the earth commit fornication, and the inhabitants of the earth are made drunk with the wine of her fornication." From the highest places of authority and the palaces of kings to the everyday people around the earth, the seduction of this false world religion will be embraced by all the unsaved followers of the Antichrist. The entire unsaved world will become intoxicated with the religious wine of the harlot.

John continues to describe this vision of judgment:

So he carried me away in the Spirit into the wilderness. And I saw a woman sitting on a scarlet beast which was full of names of blasphemy, having seven heads and ten horns. The woman was arrayed in purple and scarlet, and adorned with gold and precious stones and pearls, having in her hand a golden cup full of abominations and the filthiness of her fornication. And on her forehead a name was written: MYSTERY, BABYLON THE GREAT, THE MOTHER OF HARLOTS AND OF THE ABOMINATIONS OF THE EARTH.

I saw the woman, drunk with the blood of the saints and with the blood of the martyrs of Jesus. And when I saw her, I marveled with great amazement. But the angel said to me, "Why did you marvel? I will tell you the mystery of the woman and of the beast that carries her, which has the seven heads and the ten horns."

Revelation 17:3–7

As the angel continues to reveal details about the great harlot of false religion, he takes John into the wilderness and shows him *her appearance*. In verse 3, the harlot is sitting on a scarlet beast. This is the Antichrist—the beast who rose to power, as we read back in chapter 13. The color of scarlet reminds us of the fiery red dragon, Satan, who gives the Antichrist his demonic powers to rule over the world. This creature is nothing less than Satan incarnate. The other descriptions—the names of blasphemy, the seven heads, and the ten horns—all coincide with the earlier description of the Antichrist.

Here is the ultimate demonic picture: the great harlot sitting on top of the scarlet beast. This is like a rodeo from hell! This tells us that the Antichrist will support the harlot in the tribulation. In other words, the global government of the Antichrist will initially include a one-world religion made up of the unsaved people who follow the beast. Now at this point, you may be wondering, is this one-world religion different from the worship of the image of the Antichrist, under the direction of the False Prophet? These are actually two different stages of false worship and false religion in the tribulation. I'll explain how this unfolds, chronologically, a bit later in this chapter.

In the meantime, the angel continues to show John the harlot's appearance in verse 4, where she is dressed in purple and scarlet and decked out with gold, pearls, and expensive jewelry. Like a high-priced prostitute, the harlot of false religion is dressed in the finest clothing—purple and scarlet being the colors worn by the most affluent people. The expensive jewelry she wears adds not only to her appearance as a high-priced prostitute but also to the fact that her trade of false religion makes her quite wealthy.

In her hand is a gold cup, which once again gives the appearance of wealth and status. But inside her cup are the abominations and filthiness associated with her false religion. Jesus willingly took the cup of suffering so that He could offer us the cup of salvation. In

224

contrast, this harlot of false religion offers the world "a golden cup full of abominations and filthiness."

In verse 5, a name is written on the forehead of the harlot. The great harlot of false religion, all decked out in her high heels, fine clothing, and expensive jewelry, is identified with these words: MYSTERY, BABYLON THE GREAT, THE MOTHER OF HARLOTS AND OF THE ABOMINATIONS OF THE EARTH. In your Scripture memorization program, there would be better verses for you to memorize than this one!

The word *mystery*, in Scripture, refers to something previously unknown but now revealed in the Word of God. There were several spiritual truths that were not understood in the Old Testament but have been revealed and explained in the New Testament. Although Babylon has been mentioned nearly three hundred times in the Bible, we learn here that this harlot does not refer to a literal location of Babylon but rather to a figurative fact—that Babylon represents a system that always has been, and always will be, opposed to God. To help us better understand the meaning behind this title on the forehead of the harlot, let's take a moment to talk about Babylon historically.

In Genesis 10, we read that Nimrod founded the kingdom of Babylon. Although we can't be certain about the meaning of Nimrod's name, some scholars believe that in the Hebrew language it means *Rebel* "rebel" or "to rebel." Whether his name means that or not, Nimrod was a rebel against God and an early type of Antichrist. Eventually, Babylon became the capital city of the Babylonian kingdom.

In Genesis 11, we read how those people built the Tower of Babel, in defiance of God's post-flood commandment for the people to multiply and spread out across the earth. Instead, they sought to establish themselves in Babylon, building a brick tower both as a monument and as a shrine to themselves. Not only were they defying God, but this tower symbolized their desire to live their lives apart from God.

Later on, those same brick towers became known as ziggurats and were part of false religions, oftentimes associated with astrology. As history advanced, Babylon became a world empire, and God used the Babylonians as the means of punishing His people Israel for their continued idolatry. The Babylonian influence of false religion and rebellion against God was part of every world empire. In his first Epistle, Peter sent the greetings of believers in Babylon to fellow believers elsewhere. Peter was in Rome when he wrote his Epistle, and he used "Babylon" as a code name for Rome, to protect the persecuted believers. But Peter's choice of the name "Babylon" is not lost on us, as the Roman Empire, like all the world powers before it, had that Babylonian, anti-God, worldly influence.

Here in Revelation 17, this last-days harlot of false religion embodies all of that Babylonian influence throughout history. In that regard, she is "THE MOTHER OF HARLOTS." The Babylonian system has, in one way or another, given birth to all false religions. And like many false religions, this harlot is drunk with the blood of God's martyrs and saints, as we read in verse 6. It was the unsaved religious leaders who were responsible for handing Jesus over to be crucified. False religions are never content to lead the masses away from God; they are also compelled to persecute God's people.

In verse 6, a distinction is made between saints and martyrs, and this probably means that this Babylonian system of opposition to God is responsible for the death of God's saints throughout history, as well as the martyrs in the tribulation. Regardless, all of this causes John to be both shocked and amazed at what he was seeing. In response to this, the angel tells John not to be so amazed, as he will now explain what all of this means.

"The beast that you saw was, and is not, and will ascend out of the bottomless pit and go to perdition. And those who dwell on the earth will marvel, whose names are not written in the Book of Life from the foundation of the world, when they see the beast that was, and is not, and yet is. Here is the mind which has wisdom: The seven heads are seven mountains on which the woman sits. There are also seven kings. Five have fallen, one is, and the other has not yet come. And when he comes, he must continue a short time. The beast that was, and is not, is himself also the eighth, and is of the seven, and is going to perdition. The ten horns which you saw are ten kings who have received no kingdom as yet, but they receive authority for one hour as kings with the beast. These are of one mind, and they will give their power and authority to the beast. These will make war with the Lamb, and the Lamb will overcome them, for He is Lord of lords and King of kings; and those who are with Him are called, chosen, and faithful." Then he said to me, "The waters which you saw, where the harlot sits, are peoples, multitudes, nations, and tongues. And the ten horns which you saw on the beast, these will hate the harlot, make her desolate and naked, eat her flesh and burn her with fire. For God has put it into their hearts to fulfill His purpose, to be of one mind, and to give their kingdom to the beast, until the words of God are fulfilled. And the woman whom you saw is that great city which reigns over the kings of the earth."

Revelation 17:8–18

In these final 11 verses, we are given a lot of critical information that helps us to understand how the last days of the tribulation will unfold. I know they probably sound confusing. But as we break them down, I think you will get a better understanding of what's going to take place. Let's start with verse 8, where the angel is describing the beast.

The scarlet beast that John saw in this vision is the Antichrist. He will ascend out of the bottomless pit of demons. As we discussed earlier, the Antichrist will be a man who rises from the sea of humanity, but he will be demonically possessed, demonically energized, and demonically directed by Satan. The good news is that his ultimate destination is perdition, a word meaning "destruction" and which refers to the final judgment place of all the unsaved: the lake of fire. A summary of the angel's words is that the Antichrist will rise out of hell and ultimately return to hell.

The angel continues his explanation: the people on the earth who marvel at the Antichrist are those who have rejected God and the gospel of salvation. They are unsaved and unholy, and their names are not found in the Lamb's Book of Life (which contains the names of all the people who belong to God by faith). What causes the unsaved people of the world to marvel at the Antichrist is the phenomenon that "he was, then was not, and then is again." We discussed this back in chapter 13—how an assassination attempt will be made on the Antichrist, inflicting him with a mortal wound. This wound should kill him, but miraculously, he will survive.

As we discussed earlier, he may even appear to die and come back to life, in a demonic imitation of Christ's resurrection. However it pans out, it will amaze the unsaved world, and Satan will use it to help persuade people to worship the Antichrist. But we must never lose sight of the fact that the reason why all of these people so readily accept this lie is that they have already rejected the truth. As G. K. Chesterton once said, "People think that when they do not believe in God they believe in nothing, but the fact is they will believe in anything."[6]

227

In verse 9, the angel continues and says, "Here is the mind which has wisdom: The seven heads are seven mountains on which the woman sits." Historically, there has been only one city associated with seven mountains, and that is Rome, which was built on seven hills. As a result, many people have concluded that the harlot is the Roman Catholic Church. I do not agree with that, for a couple of reasons. For one, this woman is the mother of harlots and all the abominations of the world. So she doesn't refer to one location or to one religion. It's certainly possible that the capital city of the Antichrist in the tribulation will be Rome, or it may be the rebuilt city of Babylon by the Euphrates River.

Second, I would point out that all denominations and all religious systems have multitudes of unsaved people. Any denomination or professed belief or cult or religious system that is not rooted in the true saving faith of Jesus Christ will be a part of the harlot of false religion. To say that this harlot is one particular group or denomination is to miss the much bigger picture.

The first part of verse 9 says, "Here is the mind that has wisdom," and at the very least, it's a tip-off that we shouldn't settle for what seems like the simple or surface interpretation. Rome was clearly built on seven hills, but the angel is urging us to use deeper discernment. And in verse 9, these seven mountains on which the harlot is sitting are also seven kings. "Okay," we might say, "what seven kings?" The angel continues and says that five of these kings are fallen, one is, and the other is still to come. When that seventh king comes, he will rule for only a short time. It is also helpful to remember that John wrote this book of Revelation at the end of the first century.

Those who contend that the seven mountains where the harlot sits refer to the Roman Catholic Church also contend that these seven kings are the Roman emperors of John's day. However, when John wrote this letter in about AD 95, there had already been seven emperors: Julius Caesar, Caesar Augustus, Tiberius, Caligula, Claudius, Nero—and then Domitian, who was in power when John wrote Revelation. So the whole "five down, one up, and one to go" scenario doesn't fit the Roman emperors.

Earlier, when we read the name of the harlot on her forehead, it was, among other things, "Babylon the Great." As we've discussed, that Babylonian, anti-God spirit has been rampant in the world throughout history. So as many commentators see it, these seven kings refer to the seven empires of world history. Those would be Egypt, Assyria, Babylon, Medo-Persia, Greece, Rome, and the last-days empire of the Antichrist, whose reign during the tribulation will be short—just seven years. This also fits because five of those world empires had already come and gone when John wrote these words. The sixth—Rome—was in power in John's day, while the seventh and final empire of the Antichrist is still coming.

It gets even more involved as we read in verse 11 that the beast, or the Antichrist on his way to perdition, is also the eighth kingdom and comes out of the seventh kingdom. We'll need the information in the next two verses to complete the picture: "The ten horns which you saw are ten kings who have received no kingdom as yet, but they receive authority for one hour as kings with the beast. These are of one mind, and they will give their power and authority to the beast." Here's what the angel is describing to John: the seventh kingdom and world empire will be that of the Antichrist. This beast has seven heads, which represent those world empires throughout history. At the same time, the beast also has ten horns, symbolizing power and authority. The angel explains for us that those ten horns are ten kings.

These are not necessarily kings that we recognize today, because the angel states that they have received no kingdom as of yet. It also tells us, at the end of verse 12, that they will receive authority for "one hour"—that is to say, a very short time. The angel also tells us that they are kings "with the beast," and not separate from the beast. Now let's take all the pieces of this puzzle and put the picture together.

Immediately following the rapture of the church and the removal of all genuine believers from the earth, the Antichrist will emerge. The Antichrist will instantly rise to world prominence by negotiating a brilliant peace agreement in the Middle East that makes everyone happy, including the Jewish people, who have a green light to rebuild their temple. During the first three and a half years of the tribulation, the Antichrist will work with a federation of ten nations, and with ten kings, helping to rule the world. They will be something like a United Nations, forming a global government.

One of the ways in which the Antichrist and that ten-nation confederacy will unite the world under one government is by establishing a one-world religion: the harlot. The Antichrist will use the harlot to help unify the nations and the people of the world. Then at the midpoint of the tribulation, the Antichrist will suddenly take possession of the Jewish temple, set up his image inside the temple, and require the world to worship him. Now the harlot of world religions is no longer needed, and the Antichrist will have her destroyed.

In verse 13, we read that these ten kings will give their power and authority to the beast—the Antichrist. So at this point, these kings are no longer ruling alongside the Antichrist but under his authority. This explains to us how the Antichrist will be of the seventh king but also be the eighth king. In the first part of the tribulation, he is ruling with this ten-king confederacy. But after the Antichrist's mock resurrection from the dead, they will relinquish their power and authority to the beast, and he will become the eighth king that emerges all alone as ruler over the world.

The Antichrist will then direct the ten-king federation to destroy the harlot, because he is done using her for his purposes. So we read in verse 16, "And the ten horns which you saw on the beast, these will hate the harlot, make her desolate and naked, eat her flesh and burn her with fire." Here, in regard to the great harlot, the angel describes her annihilation. The devil, along with the Antichrist and the False Prophet, never wanted a one-world religion made up of everybody's religious beliefs and concepts. What the devil has wanted from the beginning is to be exclusively worshiped by all creation, in the same way God is to be worshiped.

Today, we hear so much about religious tolerance and acceptance—you worship your god, and I'll worship my god, and he doesn't worship any god, and she worships the trees! In the meantime, God in heaven says, "I am the Lord God, and you shall have no other gods before Me." The majority of people today believe that everyone should worship whomever or whatever they want, and for the sake of unity, we should all just get along. After all, we're all really worshiping the same god, right? Wrong! But the Antichrist will begin his seven-year reign in the tribulation with the religious platform and promise that all people may worship their own gods—even the Jews. But then . . . surprise! Satan pulls back the curtain, and there's his image, and if you don't worship him, he'll kill you.

The world will be surprised by all this, but God won't be. In fact, He will have been putting all the pieces into place. In verse 17, we read, "For God has put it into their hearts to fulfill His purpose, to be of one mind, and to give their kingdom to the beast, until the words of God are fulfilled." God is not going to allow Satan and the unsaved world to ridicule Him, reject Him, and rob Him of His rightful glory. God wouldn't truly be God Almighty if He allowed that to continue without an intervention of judgment.

Going back to verse 14, we find that the ten-nation confederacy will also be aligned with the Antichrist in his desire to make war with the Lamb. Isn't it amazing that unsaved rulers and people could be so deceived and so deluded as to think they can make war against the Lamb? There is a psalm in the Old Testament that addresses the subject of people fighting against God:

> Why do the nations rage, and the people plot a vain thing? The kings of the earth set themselves, and the rulers take counsel together, against the Lord and against His Anointed, saying, "Let us break Their bonds in pieces and cast away Their cords from us." He who sits in the heavens shall laugh; the Lord shall hold them in derision. Then He shall speak to them in His wrath, and distress them in His deep displeasure: "Yet I have set My King on My holy hill of Zion." "I will declare the decree: The Lord has said to Me, 'You are My Son, today I have begotten You. Ask of Me, and I will give You the nations for Your inheritance, and the ends of the earth for Your possession. You shall break them with a rod of iron; You shall dash them to pieces like a potter's vessel.'" Now therefore, be wise, O kings; be instructed, you judges of the earth. Serve the Lord with fear, and rejoice with trembling. Kiss the Son, lest He be angry, and you perish in the way, when His wrath is kindled but a little. Blessed are all those who put their trust in Him.
>
> Psalm 2:1–12

Coming back to Revelation, according to verse 14, the Antichrist and the ten kings will make war with the Lamb, and the Lamb will overcome them. This refers to the battle of Armageddon, which we'll read about in chapter 19. Jesus will win, because He is Lord of lords and King of kings. At that time, when Christ returns, we will return with Him. "And those who are with Him, are called, chosen, and faithful."

23

Babylon Is Fallen!

Revelation 18:1–24

I heard about a wealthy and materialistic man who was determined to take his money with him when he died. He asked his wife to gather all his money together, put it in a sack, and hang it from the rafters in the attic. He told her, "When my spirit is caught up to heaven, I'll grab the sack on my way up." Well, he eventually died, so the wife raced up to the attic, but the sack of money was still hanging there. She shook her head and said, "I knew I should have hung that sack in the basement."

Many people today not only lack genuine saving faith in God but also have their hope and trust in the world of finance, business, and politics. In Revelation 18, God reveals to us through His Word that the economic, commercial, and political system is going to crash and burn as a result of God's judgment. In Revelation, the last-days global government of the Antichrist is called Babylon. As we studied in the last chapter, Babylon has been around since Genesis 11, when people said, "Come, let us build ourselves a city, and a tower whose top is in the heavens; let us make a name for ourselves" (Gen. 11:4).

The city they built was their capital, Babylon, and the tower was the Tower of Babel. That anti-God, Babylonian world system and influence have permeated every world empire throughout history and will find ultimate fulfillment in the global government of the Antichrist.

Those who place their trust in the economic, commercial, and political system will realize their folly when it all burns down. I'm not being negative or pessimistic; I'm simply conveying biblical truth and reality. So let's begin reading:

> After these things I saw another angel coming down from heaven, having great authority, and the earth was illuminated with his glory. And he cried mightily with a loud voice, saying, "Babylon the great is fallen, is fallen, and has become a dwelling place of demons, a prison for every foul spirit, and a cage for every unclean and hated bird! For all the nations have drunk of the wine of the wrath of her fornication, the kings of the earth have committed fornication with her, and the merchants of the earth have become rich through the abundance of her luxury."
>
> Revelation 18:1–3

Chapter 18 opens with the words, "After these things." So the first and natural question is: after what things? In chapter 17, we looked at the destruction of religious Babylon—the ecumenical harlot and the global religion that cooperate with the Antichrist to seduce the world. Here in chapter 18, we read about the same judgment for commercial, political, and economic Babylon.

John describes seeing another angel coming down from heaven. This is no ordinary angel, as he has "great authority, and the earth is illuminated by his glory." The glory of this angel is so bright that the entire earth is lit up. Some have tried to identify this angel as Jesus, but the text does not support that conclusion. This is "another angel," meaning an angel similar to the one who showed John the destruction of the harlot in chapter 17. Since this angel has great authority, and since his glory illuminates the earth, we could presume that it is probably an archangel—perhaps even Michael.

In verse 2, we learn that this mighty angel has a mighty voice, as he makes a proclamation concerning the fall of Babylon. Notice the repetition of the words "is fallen, is fallen." Why that repetition?

There are a couple of possibilities. It might be referring to the fact that both the city and the system of Babylon have fallen. Or it may be highlighting the dual judgment of religious Babylon and commercial Babylon.

We constantly hear about the need for separation of church and state in our culture. But interestingly, the last-days world leader will actually unite the two. There will be a one-world religion and a one-world government, and they will work together under the global leadership of the Antichrist, until God intervenes and destroys it all.

The real inspiration and influence behind this world system is clearly identified, at the end of verse 2, as being satanic. It is called "the dwelling place of demons, a prison for every foul spirit, and a cage for every unclean and hated bird." The words *prisons* and *cages* are the same in Greek, and that word is referring to Babylon. All the demons who were already living on the earth, all the demons who came down with Satan after their failed battle with Michael in heaven, and all the hordes of exceptionally wicked demons released from the abyss, like a menagerie of the most filthy birds, will be gathered in the capital city of Babylon. This will make Alfred Hitchcock's screen version of *The Birds* look like a documentary about lovebirds, in comparison.

The next time you're standing in line at the grocery store, try saying to the person in front of you, "Did you know that the world system of the future will be inhabited and controlled by foul demons?" It won't take long for that person to take his or her basket of items to another line because he thinks you're crazy. But on the bright side, as you keep saying that to people around you, the line will continue to get shorter, and you'll be out of the grocery store and on your way home a lot quicker!

In verse 3, we're reminded of why God is judging Babylon: "For all the nations have drunk of the wine of the wrath of her fornication, the kings of the earth have committed fornication with her, and the merchants of the earth have become rich through the abundance of her luxury." Throughout history, Satan has used his anti-God, demonic style of government to seduce, deceive, and manipulate the people of the world. Notice that in the last days, this includes all nations. The entire world will be seduced, including kings and merchants, so this system is economic, political, and commercial.

Share

Just as the harlot had seduced the world into false religion, so too has the economic and commercial system seduced the world into living for passion and pleasure. As Paul told Timothy in regard to the last days, men have become "lovers of pleasures rather than lovers of God" (2 Tim. 3:4).

> And I heard another voice from heaven saying, "Come out of her, My people, lest you share in her sins, and lest you receive of her plagues. For her sins have reached to heaven, and God has remembered her iniquities. Render to her just as she rendered to you, and repay her double according to her works; in the cup which she has mixed, mix double for her. In the measure that she glorified herself and lived luxuriously, in the same measure give her torment and sorrow; for she says in her heart, 'I sit as queen, and am no widow, and will not see sorrow.' Therefore her plagues will come in one day—death and mourning and famine. And she will be utterly burned with fire, for strong is the Lord God who judges her."
>
> Revelation 18:4–8

Here in verse 4, God is calling His people to get out from the Babylonian city and system, because they are going to collapse. First came the decree that Babylon is fallen, and now come the details of her destruction. But notice in verse 4, that just before God's judgment rains down on Babylon, God's people are being warned to separate themselves—or else they will be caught up in her judgment. Does this warning sound familiar? How about when God rained down fire and brimstone upon the cities of Sodom and Gomorrah in Genesis? Before that judgment fell, God sent two angels to warn Lot and his family that they needed to get out before it was too late.

The only family members willing to leave with Lot, and to separate themselves from those cities, were his wife and two unmarried daughters. But for Lot's wife, her heart was still in that place. So the angel had to take her by the hand and pull her out of the city. Even then, in spite of the angel's explicit command not to look back as judgment fell, Lot's wife lingered, looked back, and lost her life.

We know that the church is already in heaven with the Lord at this point in Revelation and that many unsaved people who are left behind will come to saving faith in these dark and demonic days.

So it is to those people the voice from heaven says, "Come out of her, My people, lest you share in her sins, and lest you receive her plagues." On the one hand, since believers have not taken the mark of the beast, they can't buy, sell, or do business. So this warning is saying, "Get away from her; otherwise, you'll get swept up in God's judgment against her." But the warning is also saying not to "share in her sins." Therefore, there must be some temptation or opportunity for compromise and for some of these tribulation believers to find a way to work with the system. But God's warning is clear, as it was to Lot: get out and get away.

Sandwiched between Lot and these tribulation believers, we find ourselves facing the same temptations for compromise. Paul exhorts us in Ephesians 5:11, "Have no fellowship with the unfruitful works of darkness, but rather expose them." When it comes to this world system, and the way the unsaved world thinks, we must not participate or compromise. Are you the same person at the communion table that you are at the business table? In the words of John, "Do not love the world or the things in the world. If anyone loves the world, the love of the Father is not in him. For all that is in the world—the lust of the flesh, the lust of the eyes, and the pride of life—is not of the Father but is of the world. And the world is passing away, and the lust of it; but he who does the will of God abides forever" (1 John 2:15–17).

Where we draw the line concerning many things in life is not always an easy discussion. There are issues of both legalism and liberty. As one commentator said, "Each of us must examine our own lives."[1] The basic question is this: we live in the world, but does the world live in us? Augustine said, "Let the world pass, lest you pass away with the world."[2]

Now let me also say, for the sake of biblical balance, that separation does not mean isolation. Jesus has called us to be both "the salt of the earth" and "the light of the world" (Matt. 5:13–14). So while we do not want to become entangled with the things of this world, neither do we want to isolate ourselves to the point of not bringing the light of the gospel to the people around us. Vance Havner put it this way: "We are not to be isolated but rather, insulated—moving in the midst of evil, but untouched by it."[3]

Another reason for this urgent warning for believers to separate themselves from the world system, here in verse 5, is that "her sins have reached up to heaven." In the ancient days of Babylon, people were attempting to build a tower that would reach up to heaven. But in the end, the only thing in Babylon that reaches heaven is her sins. God knows everything. God keeps track of everything. So we read that "God has remembered her iniquities." The good news for believers, who place their faith in God through Christ, is that God has cast away our sins and He remembers them no more. The bad news for the unsaved is that God remembers every sin, and there will be a reckoning.

In verses 6 and 7, we find the angel calling out to God for divine vengeance and vindication. On the surface, the angel seems to be saying, "Punish her double for her sins." But in God's justice and righteousness, the unsaved will receive exactly what they deserve: judgment and punishment. God will not give the unsaved a double punishment for their sins. Otherwise, God Himself would be unjust.

So the words "repay her double according to her works" is better translated "give her double punishment for her double sins." The angel is in fact calling for God to give Babylon exactly what she deserves—no more and no less. The angels in heaven know the holy character of God as well as anyone, and this angel would not be asking God to do something that was not within His divine character. This is born out in verse 7, where the angel goes on to say, "In the measure she has glorified herself and lived luxuriously, in the same measure give her torment and sorrow." It's critical for us to interpret and understand Scripture in light of God's character.

In these two verses, we get a picture of Babylon's specific sins, which have piled up to heaven. They include pleasure and possessions, as she "lived luxuriously." They also include pride, whereby she "glorified herself" and "sits as a queen." Again, quoting John, "All that is in the world—the lust of the flesh, the lust of the eyes, and the pride of life—is not of the Father but is of the world" (1 John 2:16).

Not only does Babylon sit in pride like a queen, but she also boasts that "she is no widow, and will never see sorrow." This is a demonic thread of pride that runs throughout the pages of Scripture. We read that when Satan was created as a holy angel named Lucifer, he became filled with pride. Lucifer made five pride-filled statements, beginning with the phrase "I will," in Isaiah 14:13–14.

237

Because Babylon says, "I am no widow, and will not see sorrow," God will punish her with that very fate. "Her plagues will come in one day"—plagues of "death, mourning, and famine." Like Sodom and Gomorrah, and like Babylon of old—both of which God destroyed in a single day—so will last-days Babylon be destroyed. Verse 8 records that "she will be utterly burned with fire," and that phrase literally means "burned to the ground and utterly consumed." We are not told the nature of this fire, other than it is the Lord who judges her. I would imagine it will be similar to when God rained down fire and brimstone on Sodom and Gomorrah.

The kings of the earth who committed fornication and lived luxuriously with her will weep and lament for her, when they see the smoke of her burning, standing at a distance for fear of her torment, saying, "Alas, alas, that great city Babylon, that mighty city! For in one hour your judgment has come." And the merchants of the earth will weep and mourn over her, for no one buys their merchandise anymore: merchandise of gold and silver, precious stones and pearls, fine linen and purple, silk and scarlet, every kind of citron wood, every kind of object of ivory, every kind of object of most precious wood, bronze, iron, and marble; and cinnamon and incense, fragrant oil and frankincense, wine and oil, fine flour and wheat, cattle and sheep, horses and chariots, and bodies and souls of men. The fruit that your soul longed for has gone from you, and all the things which are rich and splendid have gone from you, and you shall find them no more at all. The merchants of these things, who became rich by her, will stand at a distance for fear of her torment, weeping and wailing, and saying, "Alas, alas, that great city that was clothed in fine linen, purple, and scarlet, and adorned with gold and precious stones and pearls! For in one hour such great riches came to nothing." Every shipmaster, all who travel by ship, sailors, and as many as trade on the sea, stood at a distance and cried out when they saw the smoke of her burning, saying, "What is like this great city?" They threw dust on their heads and cried out, weeping and wailing, and saying, "Alas, alas, that great city, in which all who had ships on the sea became rich by her wealth! For in one hour she is made desolate."

Revelation 18:9–19

In this section, we see that the destruction of Babylon will affect all inhabitants of the earth in one way or another. In verse 9, we read

238

the reaction of the kings, who represent the political system, then in verse 11, the merchants, who represent the business system, and then in verse 17, the shipmasters, who represent the commercial system.

In verses 9 and 10, the kings and the rulers are mourning because the political empire of the Antichrist has fallen. Jay Leno points out that the word *politics* comes from a combination of two words: *poli*, which means "many," and *tics*, which means "bloodsuckers."[4] I truly feel sorry for those people who place their hope and trust in politics or political solutions. The words being used for "weep" and "lament" both refer to uncontrollable sobbing and crying.

In verse 11, the merchants are also weeping and mourning, but why? Is it because they have realized their sin? Is it over the death of the people living in Babylon? Is it because they have finally recognized that they were fighting against a holy God? Incredibly, the answer is none of the above. In verse 11, the entire world system is disintegrating before their very eyes, and all they can think about is their business losses. "I hate it when all that fire and brimstone comes falling down from the sky; it really cuts down on car sales!"

In verses 12 and 13, twenty-eight commodities are listed, and I won't take the time to comment on each one, as they are fairly self-explanatory. For the most part, they are luxury items, such as gold, silver, silk, and oil.

Now, two items on this list should certainly grab our attention: "the bodies and souls of men." In John's day, it has been estimated that there were around six million slaves throughout the Roman Empire, or roughly one-third of the population. Does this mean there will be a return to slavery in the last days? Absolutely—but in different and wicked ways. At the end of chapter 9, we read that the four main sins that will be prevalent in these last days include sexual immorality and drug use. Therefore, it's quite probable that the reference here to "the bodies and souls of men" has to do with international prostitution and drug trafficking.

Over a thousand people were killed in Mexico in the first two months of 2009 as a result of drug trafficking and drug wars. Imagine how that will escalate in the final days. At the same time, this reference to "the bodies and souls of men" undoubtedly includes selling babies and children on the black market. When the rapture takes place, all children, infants, and babies will be taken up into heaven, since they are below the age of accountability. So with an absence of babies and children, I have no doubt that there will be a global black market for buying babies and children who are conceived and born during the tribulation.

In verse 17, we find that the shipmasters, like the merchants, are weeping and wailing over the destruction of Babylon. We're reminded of the foolish rich man in Luke 12, who was consumed with building bigger barns as storehouses for his riches. Just when he thought he had arrived at the pinnacle of his financial dreams, the Lord said to him, "You fool! You will die this very night. Then who will get it all?" (Luke 12:20 NLT). We also think of the words of Jesus in Matthew 16, when He asked, "For what profit is it to a man, if he gains the whole world, and loses his own soul?"

> "Rejoice over her, O heaven, and you holy apostles and prophets, for God has avenged you on her!" Then a mighty angel took up a stone like a great millstone and threw it into the sea, saying, "Thus with violence the great city Babylon shall be thrown down, and shall not be found anymore. The sound of harpists, musicians, flutists, and trumpeters shall not be heard in you anymore. No craftsman of any craft shall be found in you anymore, and the sound of a millstone shall not be heard in you anymore. The light of a lamp shall not shine in you anymore, and the voice of bridegroom and bride shall not be heard in you anymore. For your merchants were the great men of the earth, for by your sorcery all the nations were deceived. And in her was found the blood of prophets and saints, and of all who were slain on the earth."
>
> Revelation 18:20–24

Babylon—both the city and the system—will disappear from the face of the earth. And in verse 20, while the unsaved world is mourning, the saints in heaven are rejoicing. It's oftentimes true that what makes the world rejoice makes heaven mourn, and what makes the world mourn makes heaven rejoice.

Now we don't want to get the wrong idea and think that heaven rejoices over the death and destruction of unsaved people. Quite the opposite is true, and as John MacArthur wrote, "Heaven rejoices, not over the damnation of sinners, but because of the triumph of righteousness, the exaltation of Jesus Christ . . . and the arrival of

His kingdom on the earth."[5] God's prophets and apostles particularly will rejoice, since they were routinely persecuted and killed for their faithfulness to God and to God's message.

In verse 21, God presents a picture of Babylon's sudden destruction when one of His holy angels casts a large millstone into the sea. It is with that same suddenness and decisiveness that Babylon will disappear in a single day. In verses 22–23, we read about the end of many familiar activities. The point of these verses is to say that any semblance of a so-called normal life will come to an end. Six times in these verses, we find the word *anymore*, as in, none of these activities will take place anymore.

No more music means no more joy or singing. No more craftsmen means no more working. No more sound of the millstone means no one preparing any food, as in grinding wheat and grain. No more light from a lamp means loss of light to live. No more sound of the bride and the bridegroom means no more wedding ceremonies. Now we might wonder why John would mention weddings. But we remember the words of Jesus in Matthew 24 concerning these last days, when He said, "But as the days of Noah were, so also will the coming of the Son of Man be. For as in the days before the flood, they were eating and drinking, marrying and giving in marriage, until the day that Noah entered the ark, and did not know until the flood came and took them all away, so also will the coming of the Son of Man be" (Matt. 24:37–39).

As it was with the first global judgment in Genesis, so it will be with the second global judgment in Revelation. The unsaved world will reject the warning signs and the gospel, and they will be preoccupied with the everyday events of life when judgment suddenly falls. Now look at verse 24 with me once again and notice the wording: "And in her was found the blood of prophets and saints, and of all who were slain on the earth." It almost sounds like an autopsy has been performed on Babylon's dead system. This autopsy of Babylon reveals "the blood of the prophets and saints."

The best piece of application to take with us now, as we continue being salt and light to a lost and dying world, is to make sure that we keep ourselves from being defiled by this godless world system. Or as Paul put it in Romans 12:2, "Do not be conformed to this world, but be transformed by the renewing of your mind, that you may prove what is that good and acceptable and perfect will of God."

24

A Marriage Made in Heaven

Revelation 19:1–10

In chapter 19, the scene shifts from earth back to heaven. People oftentimes wonder whether certain things that we enjoy on earth today will still be enjoyed in heaven. I'm a simple person with simple needs, so I'm simply hoping that, along with all our spiritual blessings, we still get to drink coffee in heaven. Over the years, I've been told that I drink too much coffee . . . but is that even possible? I asked my doctor about it, and he told me that my metabolism is so slow that I don't need to worry about it. So I've got that going for me!

If you're concerned about drinking too much coffee, I have a list of telltale signs. You know you're drinking too much coffee when:

- Your birthday is a national holiday in Brazil.
- You answer the door before people knock.
- You're the employee of the month at the local coffeehouse and you don't even work there.
- All your kids are named "Joe."

- You think being called a "drip" is a compliment.
- You don't sweat, you percolate.
- You name your cats Cream and Sugar.
- You help your dog to chase its tail.
- You chew on other people's fingernails.
- You grind your coffee beans in your mouth.
- You sleep with your eyes open.
- You haven't blinked since the last lunar eclipse![1]

What we do know that for sure will take place in heaven is the exaltation and adoration of God, as well as the marriage supper of the Lamb. Let's consider both topics as we study the first ten verses in this chapter.

After these things I heard a loud voice of a great multitude in heaven, saying, "Alleluia! Salvation and glory and honor and power belong to the Lord our God! For true and righteous are His judgments, because He has judged the great harlot who corrupted the earth with her fornication; and He has avenged on her the blood of His servants shed by her." Again they said, "Alleluia! Her smoke rises up forever and ever!" And the twenty-four elders and the four living creatures fell down and worshiped God who sat on the throne, saying, "Amen! Alleluia!" Then a voice came from the throne, saying, "Praise our God, all you His servants and those who fear Him, both small and great!" And I heard, as it were, the voice of a great multitude, as the sound of many waters and as the sound of mighty thunderings, saying, "Alleluia! For the Lord God Omnipotent reigns! Let us be glad and rejoice and give Him glory, for the marriage of the Lamb has come, and His wife has made herself ready." And to her it was granted to be arrayed in fine linen, clean and bright, for the fine linen is the righteous acts of the saints. Then he said to me, "Write: 'Blessed are those who are called to the marriage supper of the Lamb!'" And he said to me, "These are the true sayings of God." And I fell at his feet to worship him. But he said to me, "See that you do not do that! I am your fellow servant, and of your brethren who have the testimony of Jesus. Worship God! For the testimony of Jesus is the spirit of prophecy."

Revelation 19:1–10

After several chapters of discussing the details of God's judgment, it's nice for us to focus our attention on heavenly worship and a heavenly wedding. We begin, in verses 1–5, with *heavenly worship*. Once again, John begins this section with the familiar words, "After these things." So we want to understand the time frame. In the previous two chapters, John described his vision of God's judgment and destruction of religious and commercial Babylon. In chapter 19, just before the second coming of Jesus to the earth, we read about significant events taking place in heaven.

In verse 20 of the last chapter, in the midst of God's judgment of Babylon, we read about a voice in heaven exhorting God's people to rejoice. Now in these first few verses, we read more about that heavenly rejoicing. Revelation 19 opens with four "alleluias" in verses 1, 3, 4, and 6. *Alleluia* is the Greek form of the Hebrew word *hallelujah*. In Hebrew, *hallelujah* comes from two words: *hallel*, which means "praise," and *Yah*, which is short for Jehovah. Therefore, it simply means, "praise the Lord."

The Hebrew word *hallelujah* is used twenty-two times in the book of Psalms, where it is translated as "praise the Lord." After all the hallelujahs recorded in the Old Testament, you will probably be surprised to learn that this is the only place where it's found in the New Testament—in Revelation 19. *Alleluia* is a universal word, which is the same in all languages. So if you were to spend time with believers in a foreign culture, you might not speak their language, but at some point you would probably hear them say, "Alleluia."

It was from these verses that George Frideric Handel wrote his musical composition called *Messiah*, which includes the "Hallelujah" chorus. Handel wrote that wonderful piece in the summer of 1741, and it premiered the following April, in conjunction with the Easter season. After Handel's death, the "Hallelujah" chorus became connected to the Christmas season and the birth of the Messiah. But Handel took his inspiration from this passage, so the next time you hear the "Hallelujah" chorus, remember that it is about God's righteous triumph over evil, the exalting of Christ, and anticipation of His millennial kingdom.

Not only do I not have a good singing voice, but when I try to sing, people oftentimes don't even recognize the song! I'm quite sure that when I get to heaven, my singing voice will be greatly improved. I will be part of the "Hallelujah" choir—and so will you. God is not only our salvation, He is our song!

Now let's take a closer look at the four occurrences of this word *alleluia*. In verse 1, it is *the alleluia of salvation*. There are three aspects to our salvation. We *have been* saved (past tense), and that took place at our conversion. In the moment of our conversion, we were saved from the penalty and punishment of our sins and given the promise of heaven (John 5:24). We *are being* saved (present tense), and He who began a good work in us will complete it until the day when Christ returns (Phil. 1:6). Finally, we *will be* saved (future tense) when we are united with Christ in heaven and in His kingdom (Eph. 1:14). It is that third aspect of salvation, and our union with Christ, that is being emphasized here.

In verses 2 and 3, we have the second alleluia, and it is *the alleluia of judgment*. Heaven is praising God for His righteous judgments, because the Lord has judged the false religious and commercial system of the world. It is the same demonic system that has opposed God and shed the blood of God's people. Notice the first few words in verse 2: "For true and righteous are His judgments." From time to time, we hear people say that God is not fair or that God is unjust. However, heaven boldly declares, "True and righteous are His judgments." No one in heaven is accusing God or questioning God; everyone is praising and honoring God.

In verse 3, they proclaim that "her smoke rises up forever." Something else people say is that they do not believe in hell or eternal punishment. But the Bible is explicit about the eternal punishment of the wicked, and this is just one more example: "her smoke rises up forever and ever." The Bible is also clear that God is "not willing that any should perish, but that all would come to repentance" (2 Peter 3:9), and God takes no delight in the death of the wicked (Ezek. 33:11). That is why God sent His only begotten Son, that we might receive God's forgiveness through faith in Christ.

The judgment and destruction we've been reading about have come against those who persist in sin, rebellion, wickedness, and false religion—those who have rejected salvation in Christ. Another reason for this rejoicing in heaven over God's judgment is that this judgment against the demonic world system is final and complete. This is not a temporary judgment but a completed judgment, in which "her smoke rises up forever and ever." On the cross, Jesus said, "It is finished," in regard to His sacrifice for our sins and our salvation. Here, we finally see the end of Satan's demonic influence in the world. So it's no wonder that heaven breaks out in rejoicing.

In verses 4 and 5, we have the third alleluia, and it is *the alleluia of agreement*. From our study in chapter 4, we understand that the twenty-four elders represent God's people, while the four living creatures are the cherubim angels around the throne of God. So first, heaven rejoices in God's salvation, and then the saints rejoice in God's judgment. Now, they join this heavenly chorus in agreement with God, as they shout out, "Amen! Alleluia!" The word *amen* means "so be it." Therefore, they are proclaiming, "So be it! Praise the Lord!" You cannot say alleluia until you first say amen!

In verses 6 and 7, we find our fourth alleluia, and it is *the alleluia of communion*. But before we talk about that, notice in verse 6 just how loud this heavenly praise is. It's like the sound of many waters and the sound of thunder. I've stood next to Niagara Falls, and I've stood out in a Midwest thunderstorm, and both were definitely loud. Normally, I don't like loud noises, more so as I get older. But I do appreciate loud volume in the right circumstances, such as next to a waterfall or in a thunderstorm. The same will be true in heaven, where we'll appreciate the full volume of this praise and worship with the great multitude. As God's final victory is coming to pass, it's as if all those in heaven have jumped to their feet in a thunderous standing ovation.

This fourth alleluia is heaven rejoicing over God's power, and the marriage between Christ the Lamb and His bride, the church. In verse 6, the saints proclaim, "Alleluia, for the Lord God Omnipotent [or all-powerful] reigns." In verse 7, they rejoice and are glad because the time for the marriage of Christ and His bride has come. We read in the previous chapter that when Babylon is judged, "the voice of the bridegroom and of the bride will not be heard any longer." That will be true on earth but definitely not in heaven.

This brings us to the second main theme in these verses. Having briefly considered the heavenly worship, we come now to *the heavenly wedding* in verses 6–10. Before we break down these verses, it would be helpful for us to consider the Jewish wedding of that day, which was far different from how we think of weddings today. There were basically three phases leading up to, and completing, the Jewish wedding. The first phase was called the betrothal, or what we would call the engagement. However, an engagement in that culture was different from how we know it today.

When two people became betrothed, they were legally bound together, like husband and wife, except that they would not live together or sleep together until after the wedding ceremony. The betrothal, called the Kiddushin in the Jewish culture, could not be terminated except by divorce, just like a marriage. We remember these details in the story of Joseph and Mary, when Joseph learned that Mary was pregnant and he was going to divorce her privately, so as not to shame her (Matt. 1:18–19).

In more ancient days, the betrothal would oftentimes take place when the couple were children, and it was arranged by the parents. In today's culture, we would recoil at such an idea, but there is a biblical picture and perspective here of our marriage to Christ as believers. The Bible informs us that we were chosen by God for salvation, and as His bride, before the foundation of the world (Eph. 1:4). So while we must exercise faith to receive Christ, God has always known who would believe in Him by faith, and He has betrothed us to Himself.

As the Jewish children got older and closer to the day of their wedding, the bride-to-be would make her wedding dress, while the groom-to-be would prepare the place where they would live. Since a Jewish teenage boy would not have the means to buy a house, he and his father would build a room off his parents' house. This corresponds with John 14, when Jesus told His disciples, "In My Father's house are many mansions. . . . I go to prepare a place for you. And if I go and prepare a place for you, I will come again and receive you to Myself; that where I am, there you may be also." So as the church, we are betrothed to Christ, who is preparing that place for us in His Father's house.

The second phase of the Jewish wedding was the ceremony. As the day drew near, the bride would ready herself, along with her bridesmaids. And while they knew that the time was drawing near, they would not know the exact hour in which the groom would arrive to take her away from her parents' house. Once again, we see the biblical picture in the rapture of the church. We all recognize that the time for Jesus Christ to come and take us away is drawing near, but we don't know the exact day or hour. Therefore, we must be ready and watching. As J. Hudson Taylor said, "Since He may come any day, it is well to be ready every day."[2]

When it came time for the ceremony, the groom would go to the bride's house, where she was waiting with her bridesmaids, and claim her for himself. That's the background for the parable of the ten bridesmaids in Matthew 25. The groom would be accompanied by his friends, as well as musicians and singers. He would then take his bride and her bridesmaids from her parents' home and make a great procession to his father's house—to the place he had prepared for his bride.

As they made the great procession to his home, other family and friends would join them for the celebration. Once they arrived at the house, the celebration and festivities would begin, and oftentimes they would last for seven days—a biblical picture of the church being in heaven with Christ during the seven years of tribulation on the earth. This period would include the wedding ceremony itself and the marriage supper, which was the third phase of the Jewish wedding. This was the background of the wedding feast in Cana that was attended by Jesus and His disciples in John 2.

At our church, we have the joy of hosting many wedding ceremonies. When the ceremony starts, most eyes are on the bride and her wedding dress. I conducted a wedding in which the bride had made her own dress, and she did a beautiful job. Most ladies would never want to tackle such a project—making one's own wedding dress. But the fact of the matter is, spiritually speaking, that all of us are in the process of preparing the garments for our wedding in heaven. Look at verse 8 with me once again: "And to her it was granted to be arrayed in fine linen, clean and bright, for the fine linen is the righteous acts of the saints."

Our wedding garments will be made up of our "righteous acts" as saints. Let me explain what this means. When you and I came to faith in Christ—at that moment—the righteousness of Christ was imparted and imputed to each one of us, and we were saved by faith. There were no works, and there were no deeds that any of us could have done that could have saved us. As Isaiah the prophet plainly declared, "All of our righteousness is as filthy rags." That speaks of our attempts and efforts at achieving salvation apart from Christ (Isa. 64:6).

However, once we have come to Christ and have become new creations, the Holy Spirit empowers us to do works that are pleasing to God. These are not works to be saved but works that come as a result of having been saved. Paul writes in Ephesians 2:8–9, "For by grace have you been saved through faith, and that not of yourselves, it is the gift of God, not of works, lest anyone should boast." Our salvation is indeed the gracious gift of God that we receive by faith, and not by any works on our part. But then we need to read the next verse (v. 10), where Paul says, "For we are His workmanship, created in Christ Jesus for good works, which God prepared beforehand that we should walk in them."

As Christians living on earth and awaiting our union with Christ in heaven, we have been given a stewardship that includes responsibility and opportunity for good works of service and witnessing. As the Epistle of James so strongly teaches, those good works are the fruit and the evidence of our genuine faith. And John is now telling us, here in verse 8, that those very same good works as believers will make up our wedding garments. That's a pretty amazing statement. As the old saying goes, "Only one life, 'twill soon be past; only what's done for Christ will last."

You see, according to 1 Corinthians 3, there is a judgment ahead for every believer, and all of us will one day stand before the judgment seat of Christ. We will not be judged for our sins, because Jesus took the judgment for our sins upon Himself on the cross at Calvary. It is the unsaved who will stand before the great white throne judgment, and they will be judged for their sins and their rejection of God's salvation. We'll cover that topic in much greater detail when we get to chapter 20.

But in regard to the separate judgment for believers, Paul put it this way: "For we must all appear before the judgment seat of Christ, that each one may receive the things done in the body, according to what he has done" (2 Cor. 5:10). Paul also said this regarding our works and deeds: "Each one's work will become clear; for the Day will declare it, because it will be revealed by fire; and the fire will test each one's work, of what sort it is. If anyone's work . . . endures, he will receive a reward. If anyone's work is burned [up], he will suffer loss; but he himself will be saved" (1 Cor. 3:13–15).

This begins to answer a question commonly asked by believers: what will the church be doing in heaven, after the rapture and during the seven-year tribulation, while God is judging the world? The answer is that believers will be standing at the judgment seat of Christ, where He will be evaluating our lives as believers on earth. There will be simultaneous judgments taking place during the tribulation: one on earth for the unsaved, and one in heaven for the saints.

God will evaluate our actions and attitudes as believers on earth, as well as what we did with our spiritual opportunities. Every remaining spot and stain will be cleansed. Amazingly, for every act of faithfulness, God will reward us. In 1 Corinthians 3:14, we are not told what that reward will be. Many Bible students assume that it is in reference to the various crowns mentioned in the New Testament. While that's probably true, our reward may refer to the wedding garment spoken of here in Revelation 19:8.

Even so, we must always recognize that any good that comes from our lives is the result of God's grace. The righteousness of Jesus Christ makes our righteousness possible. And the faithfulness of Jesus Christ makes our faithfulness possible. There are two Scripture verses that I constantly put together in my life. The first is, in the words of Jesus, "without Me, you can do nothing" (John 15:5). The second is, "with God all things are possible" (Matt. 19:26).

In verse 9, we read, "Blessed are those who are called to the marriage supper of the Lamb!" *Blessed* means "happy and joyful," and that certainly describes this wedding ceremony and the marriage supper of the Lamb.

Now look with me once again at verse 9, and notice upon whom this blessing is bestowed: "Blessed are those who are *called* to the marriage supper of the Lamb!" So who are the ones called, or invited, to the marriage supper of the Lamb? It's not the church that Jesus brings up in the rapture, because the New Testament church is the bride of Christ. A wedding invitation is not sent to the bride for her own wedding. The guests are the Old Testament saints—all the believers of God who lived before Christ's death and resurrection. The actual marriage is between Christ the Bridegroom and the church, His bride. All other believers, such as Old Testament saints

250

and tribulation saints, will be the guests. John the Baptist, one of the last of the Old Testament saints, referred to himself as being the friend of the Bridegroom, speaking of Jesus (John 3:29).

Now you might be thinking, why are the New Testament saints the bride of Christ but not the Old Testament saints? That doesn't seem fair. But the same question oftentimes is asked about why God adopted Israel as His chosen people in the Old Testament and not the Gentiles. God had a special plan and purpose for Israel in the Old Testament, and He has a special plan and purpose for the church in the New Testament. And once the wedding ceremony and marriage supper are complete, all saints from all history will have the same heavenly standing with God.

Chances are, you have been to a wedding, so you can picture what a wedding is like. Now try to imagine this heavenly wedding for just a moment: the Groom is Jesus, and the bride is all the New Testament saints from the church age. God the Father is presiding, and in the audience are people such as Abraham, Isaac, and Jacob . . . Moses, David, and Elijah . . . Sarah, Ruth, and Hannah. What an amazing wedding this will be. And best of all, we are the bride of Christ!

Think back to Revelation 3 and our studies of the seven churches. To the church of Laodicea, the Lord says, "Behold, I stand at the door and knock. If anyone hears My voice and opens the door, I will come in to him and dine with him, and he with Me." The promise of Jesus dining with believers is the promise of intimate fellowship.

And here, we see the ultimate fulfillment of the promise of Christ to dine with us—at the marriage supper of the Lamb. When we receive Christ, we certainly experience many intimate moments with Him—in prayer, in His Word, in worship, and in times of communion. But it won't be until the moment that we see Jesus face-to-face and experience the marriage supper that we'll truly appreciate His magnificent invitation to dine with Him.

Now let's go back to verse 10: "And I fell at his feet to worship him. But he said to me, 'See that you do not do that! I am your fellow servant, and of your brethren who have the testimony of Jesus. Worship God! For the testimony of Jesus is the spirit of prophecy.'" John was so overwhelmed by the vision of what awaits us as believers in heaven that he lost sight of where he was, and whom he was speaking to, as he fell down to worship the angel showing him the vision. I don't believe John made the conscious decision to worship this angel but rather that he lost himself in the moment, and I think we can appreciate that.

One Jewish commentator made the suggestion that in the awe and wonder of the moment, John perhaps mistook the voice of the angel for the voice of Jesus and was good enough to correct the embarrassment of his mistake by recording it here.[3] Either way, the angel was right to rebuke John, for only God is to be worshiped. Angels are servants of God, just as believers are. In the book of Acts, Peter had to correct Cornelius, who fell down to worship Peter when he arrived at his house (Acts 10:25–26). In the same way, Paul and Barnabas had to rebuke the people of Lycaonia when they were worshiping the apostles as Greek gods (Acts 14:11–14).

The final statement of the angel, here in verse 10, is, "The testimony of Jesus is the spirit of prophecy." In other words, the main theme of Old Testament prophecy, as well as New Testament preaching, is Jesus the Messiah and Savior. Prophecy is intended to glorify Christ. In his book *He Is Not Silent*, R. Albert Mohler Jr. writes this: "Every single text of Scripture points to Jesus Christ. He is the Lord of all, and therefore He is the Lord of the Scriptures too. From Moses to the prophets, He is the focus of every single word of the Bible. Every verse of Scripture finds its fulfillment in Him, and every story in the Bible ends with Him."[4]

25

Return of the King

Revelation 19:11-21

I enjoy a good mystery. In addition to the Christian books I read, I also make time to read a few mysteries along the way. When it comes to movies, mysteries are my favorite category as well. Another outlet for my mystery addiction is the occasional theater play. The last time I went to a local play, it was with some friends to see an Agatha Christie whodunit. At the intermission, we all stepped outside for some coffee and were discussing our theories on the plot. My friends offered their theories as to who had done it and why. Then I gave them my detailed solution to the mystery. At the end of the play, it turned out that my conclusion was correct in every aspect, and this really impressed my friends. They said to me, "How in the world did you figure everything out like that?" My answer was quite simple. I told them, with a big smile on my face, "I've read the book."

Many people have questions about the last days and wonder how it's all going to end. But you and I already know the answer to that question, because we have read the book—and, of course, I'm talking about the Bible. Here in Revelation 19, we have come to that monumental event known as the second coming of Jesus Christ. Jesus came the first time to redeem, and He's coming the second time to rule and reign.

> Now I saw heaven opened, and behold, a white horse. And He who sat on him was called Faithful and True, and in righteousness He judges and makes war. His eyes were like a flame of fire, and on His head were many crowns. He had a name written that no one knew except Himself. He was clothed with a robe dipped in blood, and His name is called The Word of God. And the armies in heaven, clothed in fine linen, white and clean, followed Him on white horses. Now out of His mouth goes a sharp sword, that with it He should strike the nations. And He Himself will rule them with a rod of iron. He Himself treads the winepress of the fierceness and wrath of Almighty God. And He has on His robe and on His thigh a name written: KING OF KINGS AND LORD OF LORDS. Then I saw an angel standing in the sun; and he cried with a loud voice, saying to all the birds that fly in the midst of heaven, "Come and gather together for the supper of the great God, that you may eat the flesh of kings, the flesh of captains, the flesh of mighty men, the flesh of horses and of those who sit on them, and the flesh of all people, free and slave, both small and great." And I saw the beast, the kings of the earth, and their armies, gathered together to make war against Him who sat on the horse and against His army. Then the beast was captured, and with him the false prophet who worked signs in his presence, by which he deceived those who received the mark of the beast and those who worshiped his image. These two were cast alive into the lake of fire burning with brimstone. And the rest were killed with the sword which proceeded from the mouth of Him who sat on the horse. And all the birds were filled with their flesh.

Revelation 19:11–21

The first time we saw heaven open up in Revelation was in chapter 4, when John was called up into God's presence and was given this vision of future events. Now here in chapter 19, heaven opens up once again, and this time the Lord is returning with His saints. So first heaven opens up and John goes in (a picture of the rapture of the church), and now heaven opens up as Jesus comes out (a vision of the second coming).

As we discuss the details of these verses, I would like to look at them from the perspective of this question: "What happens when Christ returns?" One of the first things that happens when Christ returns is *prophecy is fulfilled*. The greater part of Bible prophecy has been preparing us and pointing us to the second coming of Christ at the end of the age.

The second coming of Christ is a major theme in Scripture, being mentioned over eighteen hundred times in the Old Testament and over three hundred times in the New Testament. It is referred to in twenty-seven Old Testament books and in twenty-three New Testament books. In the New Testament, one out of every twenty-five verses refers to the second coming. For every prophecy on the first coming of Christ, there are eight prophecies on the second coming.[1] When Christ returns, the saints will be glorified, the creation will be liberated, the devil will be defeated, and Jesus will personally rule and reign. It's no wonder that Spurgeon said, "The sound of His approach should be as music to our hearts!"[2]

As heaven opens up, here in verse 11, the first thing John sees is a white horse with a rider called Faithful and True. Just so there's no misunderstanding here, this is not the Lone Ranger riding his white horse, Silver! This is the Lord of lords. Some commentators believe this white horse is symbolic, while some believe it is literal. It has been pointed out that Elijah was taken up to heaven with a chariot and horses in 2 Kings 2, and therefore we shouldn't think it strange that there are horses in heaven. But it was specifically a "chariot and horses *of fire*" that carried Elijah to heaven in a whirlwind.

It appears that this horse is symbolic, just as the sword that comes from the mouth of Jesus in verse 15 is symbolic. Jesus came the first time as the suffering Savior. He's coming back the second time as a conquering King, and the white horse symbolizes that. When Jesus made His triumphal entry into Jerusalem, Jesus rode on the back of a donkey, in complete humility and in fulfillment of the prophecy recorded in Zechariah 9:9. But now Jesus is pictured as the conquering King. We also remember that, back in chapter 6 when the first seal was opened, we saw a picture of the Antichrist on a white horse, carrying a bow in his hand. But he had no arrows, symbolizing how he will subdue the world with false peace.

Jesus is called Faithful and True. This is in contrast with Satan, the liar and deceiver. Back in John 8:44, Jesus said of the devil, "He was a murderer from the beginning, and does not stand in the truth, because there is no truth in him. When he speaks a lie, he speaks from his own resources, for he is a liar and the father of it." Jesus is also Faithful and True in regard to keeping His promise that He would return and establish His kingdom on earth. We read in verse 11 that as Jesus judges and makes war with the unsaved, He does so in righteousness. There is nothing arbitrary or unjust about this judgment—and it comes only after God has saturated the world with the gospel message of salvation in the final days. He will do this through His 144,000 Jewish missionaries, His two bold witnesses, and an angel flying throughout the skies above the earth, proclaiming the everlasting gospel.

A few years ago, my wife and I were traveling through Montana on our way to Canada. We had the opportunity to travel through Glacier National Park in northern Montana, which is quite beautiful. About halfway through the park, we turned off the road into a small parking area to take some pictures of the panoramic view. In that parking area, I noticed a mountain goat licking up some antifreeze that had spilled from another car. I was saddened to see this mountain goat ingesting antifreeze that was going to kill him, especially as we were surrounded by freshwater streams and melting snow waters. Similarly, during the tribulation, unrepentant sinners will reject the rivers of living water and will choose to worship the Antichrist and take his mark, which lead to their physical and spiritual death.

In verse 12, Jesus has eyes like a flame of fire, which symbolize His discernment and His ability to see everything for what it really is. At the same time, John sees many crowns, or diadems, on His head. Crowns symbolize authority. Christ is the ultimate authority and ruler over the earth. These descriptions also remind us of Christ's divine attributes. He is omniscient (or all-knowing), symbolized by His eyes of fire; and He is omnipotent (or all-powerful) in His sovereign authority, symbolized by the many royal diadems. The One who rode into Jerusalem on a donkey now appears on a white horse, and the One who wore the crown of thorns now wears many royal diadems.

In verse 12, we read that when Jesus returns, He will bear a new name that no one except Christ Himself knows. Back in chapter 3, in His words to the faithful church of Philadelphia, Jesus promised that all faithful believers would receive His new name (Rev. 3:12). We are not told what that new name will be, but that is part of the blessing and anticipation of seeing Jesus face-to-face. As Vance Havner put it, "The early believers were not looking for something to happen, they were looking for someone to come. Looking for the train to arrive is one thing, but looking for someone we love to come on that train is another matter."[3]

We know that His name is Faithful and True, and now in verse 13, Jesus is also called the Word of God. The apostle John is the only writer in Scripture who calls Jesus the Word of God. In the first verse of his Gospel, we read, "In the beginning was the Word, and the Word was with God, and the Word was God." Before time even began, in eternity past, Jesus was with God, and at the same time, Jesus was and is God.

As John continues in his Gospel, he says, "And the Word became flesh and dwelt among us, and we beheld His glory, the glory as of the only begotten of the Father, full of grace and truth" (John 1:14). John was speaking of the incarnation, when God the Son became flesh—while still retaining His full deity. Jesus became flesh so that He could experience the full suffering and death of the cross, as the sacrifice and atonement for our sins. Here in Revelation 19:13, the Word of God appears at the end of the age, ready to establish His kingdom.

His robe is dipped in blood, and the meaning of this is explained to us in Isaiah 63. Speaking of the second coming of the Messiah, it says, "Who is this who comes from Edom [*Edom* means red], with dyed garments . . . this One who is glorious in His apparel, traveling in the greatness of His strength? . . . Why is Your apparel red, and Your garments like one who treads in the winepress? . . . 'I have trodden them in My anger, and trampled them in My fury; their blood is sprinkled upon My garments, and I have stained all of My robes. For the day of vengeance is in My heart, and the year of My redeemed has come'" (vv. 1–4). So the blood represents the blood from His judgment.

In verse 14, we find that when Jesus the King returns, He will not be coming alone. The armies of heaven will be coming to earth with Him. But who is included in the armies of heaven? Well, there's no real guesswork here, seeing that they're described as being "clothed in fine linen, white and clean." We just read about them in verse 8. They are the New Testament church—the saints who were raptured up to heaven by the Lord.

This would include the tribulation saints, as well as the Old Testament saints. They will also come with Christ and reign with Him in His kingdom. But we can't forget the holy angels either, and as Jesus said in Matthew 25:31, "When the Son of Man comes in His glory, and all the holy angels with Him, then He will sit on the throne of His glory." So all the saints and all the holy angels will be with Jesus at His second coming.

But there's another important piece of information we must recognize in verse 15, where it says, "Now out of His mouth goes a sharp sword, that with it *He* should strike the nations." When we return with Christ at His second coming, we will not be coming back to fight alongside Christ but simply to follow along with Him. *He* shall strike the nations with His sword, but none of us will. Notice that this army has no weapons, which is obviously abnormal. And when was the last time you saw an army dressed in white linen? Armies going to battle are dressed in military fatigues, not bed sheets. And, normally, the army commander does not engage in battle himself but stays back and gives direction to his troops as they fight the battle. But here, it's the opposite—our King will fight, and we, His army, will simply follow along and watch.

The sword that comes out of His mouth, with which He will strike the nations, makes complete sense when we connect it to Jesus being the Word of God. In Hebrews 4:12, we're told that the Word of God is like a two-edged sword. So the sword that is spoken of here symbolizes God's Word. In the beginning, God spoke the world and the universe into existence. "God said, 'Let there be light'; and there was light" (Gen. 1:3). Job said, "The breath of the Almighty gives me life" (Job 33:4). Jesus spoke to a violent storm on the Sea of Galilee, and the storm immediately stopped (Luke 8:24). In Gethsemane, Jesus told Peter that He could call to the Father, and He would instantly send twelve legions of angels to protect Him (Matt. 26:53). Here at the return of Christ, He will destroy His enemies not by fighting against them but by merely speaking the words of judgment against them.

In the middle of verse 15, we have reference to Jesus establishing His kingdom, which He will rule with a rod of iron. So in answer to the question "What happens when Christ returns?" the second thing we see is *His kingdom is established*. We'll get into more specifics about the millennial kingdom of Jesus in the next chapter, but one of the features of that coming kingdom on earth is that Jesus will personally rule and reign—and He'll do so with a rod of iron. So what does that mean, exactly?

Today, although God is sovereign, He has allowed people to exercise their free will. For the majority, that free will has been used to live in opposition to the teachings and truth of God. Those of us who belong to Christ have chosen to respond to the Holy Spirit in our lives by acknowledging our sin and by trusting Christ as our Savior. When Jesus returns and initiates His kingdom, people will no longer have this so-called freedom to rebel against Christ or His authority. Jesus will establish a theocracy, not a democracy. Everyone will be in submission to the Lord, whether they want to or not.

Now, you may be scratching your head, wondering who in the millennial kingdom would want to rebel against Christ. Let's leave that for when we discuss the millennial kingdom in detail. But let me just say that there will be unsaved people living on the earth during the millennial reign of Christ, and I'll explain how that all works in the next chapter.

The end of verse 15 reminds us that the judgment of Christ against the unsaved people on earth will resemble a giant winepress. As you remember, grapes were thrown in a large upper vat, where they were trampled underfoot. This process was called "treading out the winepress." The juice from those trampled grapes would then flow down to a lower vat. All Israel will become like a giant winepress, with the Valley of Megiddo becoming the main upper vat and the blood flowing down through the land. Jesus Himself will tread the winepress, or crush the grapes, as we read here—but they won't be grapes; they will be hard-hearted, unrepentant sinners.

For the third time in this passage, we read of a name for Jesus: "King of kings and Lord of lords." And under our question, "What happens when Christ returns?" the third thing we see is *Jesus is vindicated*. In answer to every earthly king who ever required people to worship and revere him as God, and for every false god to whom people have ever bowed down, Jesus Christ returns to set up His kingdom. On His robe and thigh are written, "King of kings, and Lord of lords." While the Antichrist will call for the whole world to worship his image, and many people will comply with this order, the very fact that every person will submit to Christ in the millennial kingdom demonstrates that He truly is King of kings and Lord of lords.

Now we come to verse 17, where an angel is in the sky, standing in front of the sun. He is essentially ringing the dinner bell and telling all the birds of the air, "Come and get it!" We've already looked at the first of two great suppers in this chapter. It was the marriage supper of the Lamb, where the people of God will dine with Christ in celebration of the wedding ceremony between Christ and His bride, the church. Now we read of the second great supper in Revelation 19—the judgment supper of God.

So here are the two choices that people in the last days will have: Would you rather be the main guest or the main course? Would you rather eat dinner or be eaten as the dinner? I would add that you cannot come to the marriage supper of the Lamb without a reservation.

In verse 17, the invitation is going out for supper, but it's going out to all the birds of the air to prepare to gorge themselves on the bodies of those who will be destroyed when Christ returns. In verse 18, this judgment is no respecter of persons; it includes the flesh of kings, of captains, of mighty men, and of all people—both free and slave, small and great. In Ezekiel 39:12, we're told that it will take seven months to bury all the bodies from this slaughter. What the birds can't eat will take that long to dispose of.

This is truly an incredible sight to imagine: the armies of the world look toward the sun and see an angel calling out to the birds of the air, inviting them to come and feast on their flesh. This will not be a battle but a slaughter. I'm just wondering, at what point does everyone suddenly realize that their bodies are about to become bird food? If I saw an angel standing in the sun, calling in the birds, and then I looked over my shoulder and saw a trillion crows flying toward me like some out-of-control Hitchcock movie, I think I'd say, "Okay, I give up; I repent!"

What we read instead is that the assembled armies gather to make war with Christ as He is returning to the earth. Initially, these armies have been drawn into the Valley of Megiddo and into Israel either to wipe out Israel or to fight against one another. But when they look up and see Christ coming, they will band together in a foolish attempt to fight against the Lord. But this whole thing will be over before it ever gets started.

In verse 20, we find the fourth thing that will happen when Christ returns: *the Antichrist and the False Prophet are judged.* The Antichrist, who required the world to worship him and to receive his demonic mark, as well as the False Prophet, who deceived the people with demonic signs and wonders are captured and sent directly to the lake of fire. We'll talk more about the lake of fire in chapter 20, but this is the final, eternal place of suffering for all unsaved people and the demons. Right now, all the unsaved who have died in their sins apart from Christ are in the place called Hades, awaiting judgment before God. But as we'll see in the next chapter, all those people will be brought out of Hades to stand before the Lord in final judgment. Then they will be cast into the eternal place of torment, the lake of fire.

But unlike all those unsaved people, we read here that the Antichrist and the False Prophet immediately are cast alive into the lake of fire. So wicked was their influence over the world in the last days that (to paraphrase the Monopoly game), "They go directly to jail—they do not pass Go, and they do not collect two hundred dollars!" This is the first reference in Scripture to the lake of fire, and these two wicked leaders are the first to arrive there. They will be there, just the two of them, for the next thousand years, and then they will be joined by all the others.

When the two leaders are snatched away, what will all the other assembled armies be thinking? Probably before they can even process what's happening, the Lord will destroy them with the Word of His mouth, and the battle of Armageddon will be over before it begins. So the fifth and final thing we see happening when Christ returns is *the unsaved are killed.* When Jesus returns, He will put an end to all rebellion against the King! And on all the tombstones of these rebels, we find their epitaph in the final sentence of verse 21: "All the birds were filled with their flesh."

26

The Millennial Kingdom

Revelation 20:1–6

Recently, we had some family over, including my three-year-old grandson Nathan—aka Nitro! He was dragging out different toys, which held his interest for five minutes, and then it was on to something new. At one point, he had gotten into the hall closet, where we have some jigsaw puzzles. He found a sixty-three-piece puzzle of Pinocchio and immediately started hounding me with chants of "Papa, this puzzle! Papa, this puzzle!" Before I could respond, he dumped the puzzle box out on the living room carpet. So I had to explain to my "little man" that it would be much easier if we put the puzzle together on the kitchen floor.

So there we were, sprawled out together on the kitchen floor, tackling the puzzle. Immediately, he tried to force two pieces together that didn't fit. So I explained to him about matching the pieces together. Well, that wasn't so much fun, so a minute later, he was off looking for another toy. In the meantime, I'm lying on the kitchen floor, putting together the sixty-three-piece Pinocchio puzzle, because now I'm hooked and want to finish it. A minute later, the phone rang, and it was one of my fellow pastors, calling for me. My wife, Lorraine, told him that I was lying on the kitchen floor, putting together a Pinocchio jigsaw puzzle, to which he replied, "I don't want to interrupt him when he's so busy!"

The thing about a jigsaw puzzle, when you're just getting started, is that it looks like a hopeless mess. But as you get about halfway through, it begins to take shape. Closer to the end, it really starts coming together and you can almost see the picture. Then the payoff comes when you are down to the final pieces. When we started this book about Revelation, it was like taking a giant prophetic jigsaw puzzle out of the box and dumping the pieces out on the table. Chapter by chapter, and piece by piece, we've been putting this prophetic puzzle together. Now we're beginning to put the final pieces in place.

Here in chapter 20, we've come to a very significant piece of the puzzle: the millennial kingdom. Before we look at specifics of the millennium, there's another important prophetic puzzle piece that fits right between the second coming of Christ, and the start of His millennial reign on earth. It's called the judgment of nations, an event Jesus spoke about in Matthew 25.

Jesus said that when He returns, He will sit on His throne of glory with all nations gathered before Him as He separates the sheep from the goats. The people of these nations are the survivors of the tribulation period. They include Jews and Gentiles who have trusted Christ as their Savior, as well as people who are not saved but somehow survived. A popular television show called *Survivor* has new locations for the series each season. Well, the ultimate *Survivor* series will take place on planet earth during the seven-year tribulation. The saved people, whether Jew or Gentile, are the "sheep" Jesus speaks of in Matthew 25, while all the unsaved survivors are the "goats."

In Matthew 25:34, Jesus says of the sheep, "Then the king will say to those on His right hand, 'Come, you blessed of My Father, inherit the kingdom prepared for you from the foundation of the world.'" So the saved survivors will immediately join Christ and the saints who have come with Him from heaven and enter the millennial kingdom. But to the goats at His left hand, Jesus will say, "Depart from Me, you cursed, into the everlasting fire" (Matt. 25:41). So the unsaved survivors will go into hell to wait for their final judgment at the great white throne, which we'll discuss in more detail at the end of Revelation 20.

Those saved survivors—people who received Christ during the tribulation and were not killed by the Antichrist—will join Jesus and the saints in the millennial kingdom. However, there is a big difference between the saints already in heaven who come back with Christ and these newer survivors. Those with Jesus at His second coming will be in their glorified bodies, while the earthly survivors are still in their physical bodies. So as Jesus commences His millennial reign, it will begin with these two groups of saved people.

This brings us to the description of the millennial kingdom here in Revelation 20:

> Then I saw an angel coming down from heaven, having the key to the bottomless pit and a great chain in his hand. He laid hold of the dragon, that serpent of old, who is the Devil and Satan, and bound him for a thousand years; and he cast him into the bottomless pit, and shut him up, and set a seal on him, so that he should deceive the nations no more till the thousand years were finished. But after these things he must be released for a little while. And I saw thrones, and they sat on them, and judgment was committed to them. Then I saw the souls of those who had been beheaded for their witness to Jesus and for the word of God, who had not worshiped the beast or his image, and had not received his mark on their foreheads or on their hands. And they lived and reigned with Christ for a thousand years. But the rest of the dead did not live again until the thousand years were finished. This is the first resurrection. Blessed and holy is he who has part in the first resurrection. Over such the second death has no power, but they shall be priests of God and of Christ, and shall reign with Him a thousand years.
>
> Revelation 20:1–6

The next thing John sees in this vision of the future—after Christ casts the Antichrist and the False Prophet into the lake of fire, and after Jesus swiftly defeats and destroys their armies—is an angel coming down from heaven. This angel has the key to the bottomless pit and a great chain in his hand. Having disposed of the Antichrist, the False Prophet, and the unsaved rebels of the earth, the final rebel to be dealt with is Satan himself. But unlike the Antichrist and the False Prophet, Satan is not cast into the lake of fire at this time (although he will be later).

God has one final purpose for Satan's demonic influence, so the devil is incarcerated in the bottomless pit. There are four names used here for him: he is the dragon and the devil; he is the serpent and Satan. The reference to him being "the serpent of old" takes us back to the Garden of Eden and the fall of mankind. Finally, after thousands of years of sin, deceit, and wickedness, Satan is bound.

In verse 1, we're not given the name of this angel, but there is little doubt in my mind that this is Michael the archangel. I say this because it was Michael and the holy angels that Satan and his demons fought against at the midpoint of the tribulation. We remember that war broke out in heaven in chapter 12 and that Michael and the holy angels prevailed; Satan and his demons were cast out of heaven once and for all. In Revelation 12, Satan is cast down to earth. Here, he is cast down into the bottomless pit, and in verse 10, he will be cast into the lake of fire.

This reminds us that Satan is not God's equal. Satan was created by God as an angel, but he chose to rebel against God's divine authority. Satan is a fallen angel—albeit the most powerful of fallen angels—and as such, his true equal or rival would be an archangel such as Michael. Here in verse 1, there is no need for God to bind Satan; one of His mighty angels is more than able to carry this out.

Of the demons in existence today, some are free and assisting Satan in his demonic influence over the world, while the worst of them are confined in this bottomless pit. This, then, is where Satan himself—the chief of the demons—will be confined for a thousand years during the time of the millennial kingdom on earth. Satan is "the prince of the power of the air" (Eph. 2:2), but when the Prince of Peace returns, the world will be radically altered. At the end of verse 3, we read that Satan will be released from the bottomless pit after the millennium, and the obvious question is why? The answer will be given later in this chapter, and we'll discuss the details then.

After Satan has been confined, we begin to read, in verse 4, about the aspects of Christ's earthly reign: "And I saw thrones, and they sat on them, and judgment was committed to them. Then I saw the souls of those who had been beheaded for their witness to Jesus and for the word of God, who had not worshiped the beast or his image, and had not received his mark on their foreheads or on their hands. And they lived and reigned with Christ for a thousand years." We call this thousand-year period the millennium. The end of verse 4 gives us the most simple and straightforward explanation of the millennium: God's people will "live and reign with Christ for a thousand years." But as straightforward as that would sound to most of us, this is a much-debated subject among believers.

Within the church, there are three primary positions on the millennium. They are premillennialism, postmillennialism, and amillennialism. Before I explain each position briefly, let me share something for us to keep in mind. While the millennium is an important biblical subject, it's not what we would consider an essential doctrine. I bring that up because in the area of essential doctrines, such as the Trinity, the deity of Christ, His virgin birth and resurrection, there is no room for disagreement. Those essential doctrines are the bedrock and basis of our faith, and we won't budge an inch.

But on a subject such as the millennium, there is room for discussion and disagreement without undermining the Christian faith. The bottom line is that all Christians believe Christ is coming back again to rule and reign, but how we interpret the details continues to be debated. I believe we should interpret the Bible literally, unless the text dictates otherwise, and therefore I believe in the doctrinal view of premillennialism. This simply means that Jesus Christ will return just before the millennium begins. In Revelation 19, the Lord returns at His second coming, and in the next chapter the millennium begins. Some would argue that these two events—the second coming and the millennium—are not necessarily in chronological order, but after describing the Lord's return in chapter 19, John begins chapter 20 with the words, "Then I saw . . ." In the Greek, John's wording definitely shows chronological progression. He essentially says, "I saw the Lord returning, and then I saw the millennial kingdom."

We must interpret Revelation just like we interpret the other sixty-five books of the Bible: take the literal meaning unless something is clearly symbolic and intended to have a figurative meaning. Therefore, I believe the Bible is teaching us that Christ will literally return to the earth at the end of the tribulation, that He will literally rule and reign on earth, and that His reign will literally last for a thousand years.

One of the differing positions is called postmillennialism. This is the belief that Christ will not return until after the millennium. Postmillennialism teaches that the kingdom of Christ will be ushered in by the church through preaching and, some would even say, through avenues such as Christian leadership in politics. Postmillennialism teaches that much of the world will be saved through the gospel, making the earth primarily a Christian world—and only then Jesus will return to rule and reign. Postmillennialism also states that this period might not be a literal thousand years and that this number could simply represent a long period of time.

The glaring problem with postmillennialism, besides rejecting the literal wording of Revelation 20, is the belief that the church will overcome evil in the world and that we as believers will usher in Christ's kingdom. Those who hold to a postmillennial position believe the world will get progressively better until Jesus returns. But our studies in Revelation have clearly shown us that the world will get much worse in every possible way—morally, politically, economically, and spiritually.

Another major problem with the postmillennial position is the belief that Satan is already bound. Postmillennialists believe Satan was bound by Christ's victory at the cross two thousand years ago. Let me ask you: do you believe that Satan has already been bound and that he's no longer influencing or impacting the world today? Several years after Calvary, the apostle Paul wrote to the church at Thessalonica and told them, "We wanted to come to you—even I, Paul, time and again—but Satan hindered us" (1 Thess. 2:18). And to the church at Corinth, Paul wrote and warned of Satan's tactics, saying, "We are not ignorant of his devices" (2 Cor. 2:11). Paul exhorted the Ephesian believers to take up the armor of God, so they would be able to "stand against the wiles of the devil" (Eph. 6:11). Joining Paul in his strong belief that Satan was not bound at Calvary, Peter warned fellow believers to "be sober, be vigilant; because your adversary the devil walks about like a roaring lion, seeking whom he may devour" (1 Peter 5:8). As someone has well said, "If Satan has already been bound, it must really be a long chain!"[1]

The other primary position on this subject is called amillennialism. This teaching denies a literal thousand-year reign of Christ on the earth. The prefix "a" means "no," so amillennialism means "no thousand years." Amillennialists believe in a symbolic millennium, not a literal thousand-year earthly kingdom with Christ ruling and reigning in person. They believe that it symbolically represents the church age here and now on earth and that Christ is ruling this earthly millennial kingdom right now, from His throne in heaven. But if this is the millennium, I want a refund!

Like postmillennialists, amillennialists believe Satan has already been bound by Christ's work on the cross. But there is no mention of the cross in this passage of Revelation. In fact, you'll notice here that it isn't even Christ on the cross who binds Satan in this text; it's an angel from heaven with a great chain. So how does that symbolically represent Christ on the cross? It just doesn't make any sense.

So, then, returning to verse 4 and John's vision of the millennial kingdom, there will be no devil, no demons, no Antichrist, no False Prophet, and no unsaved people. It's just Father, Son, Holy Spirit, believers, and angels. In the millennial kingdom, John sees thrones, and those who sit on those thrones are given authority to judge, or to rule. In Matthew 19:28, Jesus told the disciples that they would sit on twelve thrones in the kingdom and help to judge (or rule) the twelve tribes of Israel. In 1 Corinthians 6:2, Paul told the believers in Corinth that they would help judge the world. The New Testament saints, the Old Testament saints, and the tribulation saints who were martyred are all here, ruling and reigning with Christ in His kingdom.

In verse 5, we read that the rest of the dead did not live again until the thousand years were ended and that this is the first resurrection. Let's talk about what this means. The Bible teaches that there will be two resurrections: one for the saved and one for the unsaved. In John 5:28–29, Jesus says, "Do not marvel at this; for the hour is coming in which all who are in the graves will hear His voice and come forth— those who have done good, to the resurrection of life, and those who have done evil, to the resurrection of condemnation." So there is the first resurrection of the saved that leads to eternal blessing, and then a second resurrection of the unsaved that leads to eternal judgment. The first resurrection of the saved takes place in stages, while the second resurrection of the unsaved basically happens all at once.

The first resurrection actually began when Christ rose from the dead. Paul described the resurrection of Jesus Christ as being the firstfruits of all believers who have died (1 Cor. 15:20). Jesus was the first to rise from the dead and receive a glorified body. The next stage of this resurrection will take place at the rapture, when Jesus comes in the air to receive His church, and the dead in Christ shall be caught up first (1 Thess. 4:16).

The bodies of all deceased believers will be raised and transformed into new, glorified bodies. When believers pass away, their spirits immediately go to be with the Lord, while their bodies remain here on earth (2 Cor. 5:8). It's that body that Jesus will raise. Then the third phase of the first resurrection takes place at the end of the tribulation period, when the bodies of the Old Testament saints will be raised from the dead, as well as those of the tribulation martyrs (Rev. 20:4). Daniel 12:1–2 states how the Old Testament saints will be resurrected at the end of the tribulation.

So the first resurrection includes all of God's people, but it comes in three phases: Christ was raised first; then all believers from the church age will be raised at the rapture of the church; and finally, at the end of the seven-year tribulation, the Old Testament saints and tribulation martyrs will be raised as well. That completes the first resurrection. Then there will be a period of one thousand years before the second resurrection—that of the unsaved—takes place at the great white throne judgment, which is described at the end of Revelation 20.

Before leaving the topic of the millennium kingdom, I want to spend a bit more time on the characteristics and conditions of the millennium, as described in Scripture. As you may know, this isn't the only passage on the subject. There is quite a bit of information in the Old Testament as well. Let me share six of those characteristics with you, from Scripture.

1. *Christ will personally rule* (Luke 1:32–33; Rev. 19:15). In Luke 1, we read these words about Jesus, spoken by the angel Gabriel: "He will be great, and will be called the Son of the Highest; and the Lord God will give Him the throne of His father David" (v. 32). That speaks of an earthly throne and an earthly kingdom, like David's. Then Gabriel continues, "And He will reign over the house of Jacob forever, and of His kingdom there will be no end" (v. 33). Just as King David ruled and reigned, so will King Jesus rule and reign. After Christ's earthly reign of a thousand years has ended, His kingdom and His reign will continue forever in eternity.

2. *A period of peace* (Micah 4:2–4; Isa. 66:12–13). Ever since the beginning of time, mankind has been seeking peace in the world, but true and lasting peace will come only when the Prince of Peace returns and rules (Isa. 9:6). In Micah 4:3,

we read this about the millennial kingdom: "They shall beat their swords into plowshares, and their spears into pruning hooks; nation shall not lift up sword against nation, neither shall they learn war anymore." Because Jesus Himself will be ruling, there will be no wars, and therefore no weapons. Peace will rule the day when Christ rules the world!

3. *Long human life* (Isa. 65:20). Just as it was in the early days of mankind, and as we saw in the early chapters of Genesis, the human life span will be greatly extended—perhaps upwards of seven hundred, eight hundred, or nine hundred years. In describing the millennium, Isaiah writes, "No more shall an infant from there live but a few days, nor an old man who has not fulfilled his days; for the child shall die one hundred years old, but the sinner being one hundred years old shall be accursed." Now please understand that this does not describe those of us who are already saved. We'll be in our glorified bodies at this point. So the return to an extended life span is for those who come to Christ during the tribulation and enter the millennial kingdom in their physical bodies.

4. *Harmony with mankind and animals* (Isa. 11:6–8). Not only will mankind live in harmony, but so will the animal kingdom. Isaiah 11:6–8 says, "The wolf shall dwell with the lamb, the leopard shall lie down with the young goat; the calf and the young lion and the fatling together; and a little child shall lead them. The cow and the bear shall graze; their young ones shall lie down together; and the lion shall eat straw like the ox. The nursing child shall play by the cobra's hole, and the weaned child shall put his hand in the viper's den."

In the millennium, the curse of sin will not be fully removed, but it will be firmly restrained. This includes all of nature. Animals that were "natural" enemies will exist together, side by side, and in harmony. In the millennium, eHarmony will not be a dating service; it will refer to elephants, eagles, and elk all hanging out together. This also means no more *National Geographic* programs that show lions chasing down gazelles and killing them for dinner. Animals will return to being vegetarians rather than carnivores. Any animal would make a great pet for children.

5. *Holiness will prevail* (Isa. 35:8). In the millennial kingdom, we'll live in an age and atmosphere of holiness. Isaiah 35:8 tells us, "A highway shall be there, and a road, and it shall be called the Highway of Holiness. The unclean shall not pass over it, but it shall be for others." As believers, something we all grow weary of is the constant bombardment of profanity, godlessness, and immorality that is pushed at us daily. But when Christ rules and reigns, the world will be saturated with holiness and righteousness.

6. *Everyone will worship Jesus* (Isa. 66:23). Isaiah 66:23 says, "'And it shall come to pass that from one New Moon to another and from one Sabbath to another, all flesh shall come to worship before Me,' says the Lord." No longer will we hear people say, "You worship your God, and I'll worship my god." We will all worship the true and living God, in person! No longer will we hear God's people making excuses for not making time to worship Him. The number one priority and purpose for our lives in the millennium will be to worship Him.

The question could be asked: why will there even need to be a millennial kingdom on earth? Why don't we just go to heaven and call it a day? For several reasons. In the beginning, God created the world, mankind, and the environment to be perfect in holiness and harmony. But when mankind chose to sin, it brought about a curse that ruined everything. Having achieved the most important work of salvation, God will restore the earth to what it once was—to what it was created to be.

At the same time, Christ will be fulfilling His promise to return and reign. In Luke 1, Gabriel spoke of how Christ would personally rule in His kingdom. This was also a promise to Israel in the Old Testament (Isa. 65:17–25). In addition to this, Christ's kingdom on earth is the answer to the prayers of the saints for centuries: "Your kingdom come. Your will be done on earth as it is in heaven" (Luke 11:2). The millennial kingdom will also display the rightful glory of Christ, who was rejected and crucified at His first coming. Our prophetic puzzle of the last days is really coming together now, and the picture of our future is quite spectacular!

27

The Great
White Throne Judgment

Revelation 20:7–15

There was an elderly Christian woman who lived in an apartment next to a man who was an atheist. The elderly woman was barely able to make ends meet, but her faith was strong and she trusted the Lord daily. Oftentimes, when she was praying and thanking God for His faithfulness, or when she was worshiping God, her atheist neighbor could hear her, and it drove him crazy. The old woman had tried to share the gospel with him and invite him to church, but he wanted none of it.

One afternoon, the atheist overheard the old woman praying, "Dear Lord, You know that I don't have enough food to even make dinner tonight, but I'm trusting You." The atheist rubbed his hands together and thought to himself, "I know how to knock her off her spiritual wagon." So he drove down to the local supermarket, bought some groceries, and set the bags at the woman's door. Then he rang the bell and hid in some bushes.

When the old woman answered the door, there were the bags of groceries, with no one in sight. She was so excited that she looked up and said, "Thank you, Jesus!" Just then, the man jumped out of the bushes and said to the old woman, "Hey, lady—God didn't give you those groceries, I did! Do you see how stupid it is to believe in a God who doesn't even exist?" The old woman paused for a moment; then she looked upward and said, "Oh God, You're so amazing! Not only did You provide me with food, but You sent the devil to deliver my groceries!"

Speaking of the devil, here in Revelation 20, we read that God will get rid of him once and for all. Before that happens, God will have one final purpose for Satan at the end of the millennium. You will recall that after Jesus returns at His second coming and just before He commences His millennial kingdom, Satan will be captured and confined in the bottomless pit. So during that thousand-year period, we will see the best of both worlds: Jesus will rule, and Satan will be removed.

You will also remember that all the saints will be there with Christ, and they'll all be in their glorified bodies. At the same time, every person who comes to faith and survives the tribulation will remain on earth and join us in the millennial kingdom. However, all those believers will still be in their physical bodies. So the millennium will begin with Jesus ruling, Satan removed, and only believers residing in the kingdom, along with the holy angels. But then we find these unexpected words, as we resume our reading:

> Now when the thousand years have expired, Satan will be released from his prison and will go out to deceive the nations which are in the four corners of the earth, Gog and Magog, to gather them together to battle, whose number is as the sand of the sea. They went up on the breadth of the earth and surrounded the camp of the saints and the beloved city. And fire came down from God out of heaven and devoured them. The devil, who deceived them, was cast into the lake of fire and brimstone where the beast and the false prophet are. And they will be tormented day and night forever and ever.
>
> Revelation 20:7–10

In sports, there is an often-used phrase: "It isn't over until it's over." After being incarcerated for a thousand years, Satan is released one final time. The obvious question is why? And the other burning question would be: who is Satan being released to deceive, seeing that the millennium launches with saints and saved believers? Inquiring minds want to know! Let's answer the second question first. Who will Satan deceive, seeing that the millennium begins with no unsaved people?

As I've said, some of those believers who reign with Christ in the millennial kingdom are the saved survivors of the tribulation period, who walk right into the millennium in their physical bodies. In our last study, we talked about how the earth will be returned to an Eden-like environment during the millennium. Those thousand years will be marked by tremendous peace, as Christ is ruling and reigning while Satan is bound. We also talked about how those believers who are still in their physical bodies will experience an extended life span, just as it was in the days of Genesis (Isa. 65:17–25).

But what we have not yet discussed is how those saved survivors from the tribulation, who are still in their physical bodies, will produce children. People will get married, have children, and raise families. With the death rate greatly reduced and the birthrate greatly increased, the population of the world during the millennium will rise speedily and steadily. But in spite of those idyllic conditions, there's still a little problem called the sin nature. So while the saved survivors from the tribulation are born-again believers, every person born after the millennium begins will need to find salvation by placing faith in Jesus Christ. No one is born a Christian; everyone must be born again. Those offspring who are born during the millennium are unsaved unless and until they trust Christ as their Savior by faith.

So while we can assume that many of those offspring will receive Christ, especially under such godly conditions, not everyone will. Jesus will be ruling, and Satan will be bound, so there will be no open rebellion during that time. But while many will come to saving faith, many will choose not to. It is like the unsaved teenager in the strong Christian family. They're living in a Christian home, and they cooperate with their parents—even going to church weekly—but in their hearts, they've never made a personal commitment to Christ. Outwardly they conform, but inwardly there's no conversion. That's precisely how it will be for some during the millennium—outward conformity without inward conversion.

Now this might sound strange to us, when these offspring will have the decided advantage of Christ being there personally and of not having Satan around to tempt them. While that will indeed be the case, each of them will still be born with a sin nature and a depraved heart. One thing we've definitely learned from Bible history is that a perfect home does not produce a perfect heart. Think of all those angels that were created to be holy and were residing in the very presence of God in heaven. In spite of that perfect and holy environment, one-third of those angels, led by Lucifer, decided to rebel against God and were cast out of heaven.

Another example is Adam and Eve in the Garden of Eden. There they were in a perfect environment and in perfect fellowship with God. But after Lucifer fell from heaven and became Satan, he invaded that garden and tempted Eve into disobeying the Lord. The fact that Adam and Eve were in the perfect environment didn't prevent them from exercising their free will to disobey God. In the millennium, the same type of thing will happen. As Jeremiah wrote, "The heart is deceitful above all things, and desperately wicked" (Jer. 17:9).

So while peaceful conditions will be maintained by the Lord as He rules and reigns in the millennium, many of the offspring born during that time will cooperate outwardly but remain unconverted inwardly. If we understand this, we can begin to understand why God will release Satan one final time at the end of the millennium. Knowing the hearts of mankind, God will release Satan from the bottomless pit and allow him to deceive the unsaved people of the world one final time. God gives us a free will and the ability to decide for ourselves whether we accept Christ or reject Him. I'd like to tell you that only a few people would be so foolish, having experienced the blessings of Christ personally. But the end of verse 8 reveals that the rebels will be in number as the sand of the sea.

Like the hardened criminal who spends several years in prison and then is released, only to commit more of the same terrible crimes, Satan will be released from the bottomless pit and will pick up where he left off—deceiving the nations.

For those unsaved offspring born during the millennium, the Lord will release Satan one final time to lead them in their foolish attempt to rebel and fight against God. Because they have chosen not to follow God, they will choose, of their own free will, to follow Satan in this final rebellion. These unsaved people, like all unsaved people today, are the enemies of God. They are called Gog and Magog in verse 8, names in Scripture synonymous with the enemies of God.

After Satan's release, he will gather together all the unsaved people from the four corners of the earth. They will surround the beloved city of Jerusalem, which Jesus has made the capital of His millennial kingdom. Like the battle of Armageddon that we read about back in chapter 19, this will be a complete slaughter and nothing resembling a battle. As God has often done in His judgment throughout history, fire will fall from heaven to devour and destroy these rebels. God will deal swiftly with this final rebellion. Then God will cast Satan into the lake of fire—to everlasting punishment.

Notice that the lake of fire is described in verse 10 as "where the beast and false prophet are." The Antichrist and the False Prophet will have been sent there a thousand years earlier, at the start of the millennium. Satan joins them at the end of the millennium, and we read that "they will be tormented day and night forever and ever." The great tormentor will now spend eternity in torment. Let me also point out the wonderful news that there is no mention of Satan in the remaining two chapters of the Bible. God is going to vanquish Satan once and for all!

This brings us to the great white throne judgment. This final judgment resembles a courtroom setting, but as Warren Wiersbe points out, "There will be a Judge but no jury, a prosecution but no defense, a sentence but no appeal."[1]

Then I saw a great white throne and Him who sat on it, from whose face the earth and the heaven fled away. And there was found no place for them. And I saw the dead, small and great, standing before God, and books were opened. And another book was opened, which is the Book of Life. And the dead were judged according to their works, by the things which were written in the books. The sea gave up the dead who were in it, and Death and Hades delivered up the dead who were in them. And they were judged, each one according to his works. Then Death and Hades were cast into the lake of fire. This is the second death. And anyone not found written in the Book of Life was cast into the lake of fire.

Revelation 20:11–15

The first thing we see, here in verse 11, is *the Judge.* We know for certain that this Judge is the Lord Jesus. In John 5:22, Jesus stated, "The Father judges no one, but has committed all judgment to the Son." Since Jesus is the One who provided salvation, He is the One who will judge those who have rejected that salvation. We can't help but think of how people sat in judgment of Jesus when He was on the earth. Caiaphas, Annas, Herod, the Sanhedrin, Pilate, the Romans, and the religious leaders all passed judgment on Jesus. Imagine how they'll feel at this moment when, one by one, they appear before Christ, whom they crucified and who still bears the marks of His crucifixion! They rejected Him as their Savior, and now they will face Him as their Judge.

The throne that Jesus the Judge will be sitting on is described as both "great" and "white." I would assume that it is great in size, but more importantly, it is great in that it represents the divine judgment of God. The fact that it is white in color symbolizes the holiness, purity, and righteousness of the One who sits in judgment.

As verse 11 continues and as this judgment begins, the earth and heavens have fled away. This refers to the destruction and dissolving of the universe. Peter spoke of this in the third chapter of his second Epistle, when he said, "The heavens will pass away with a great noise, and the elements will melt with fervent heat; both the earth and the works that are in it will be burned up . . . all these things will be dissolved" (2 Peter 3:10–11). John MacArthur states that the present heaven and earth "will be uncreated and go totally out of existence."[2]

Now some of us may wonder why the earth, and especially why heaven, must be destroyed and re-created? Both heaven and earth have been badly polluted with sin. There has been rebellion against God, both in heaven and on earth. So rather than cleansing or purifying them, God will dissolve them and then re-create them. Some Bible students believe that God will completely uncreate the universe and then re-create it. Others believe that God will take the elements that have been dissolved and use them to create the new heaven and earth. The latter group would compare that process to our glorified bodies, in which the Lord resurrects the elements of the old body and transforms them into a new glorified and eternal body. But the point is that the unsaved will have no place to hide from this final judgment. As the text says here, "And no place was found for them." There's an old saying, "You can run but you can't hide." In this case, no one is able either to run or hide.

In verse 12, John informs us that all the unsaved will stand before the Lord, individually, regardless of their status or stature on the earth. John says, "I saw the dead, small and great, standing before God." Death and judgment are great equalizers. Rulers and kings, paupers and peasants—there is no distinction when it comes to the Lord's judgment. At this point, everyone is simply an unsaved sinner. In Hebrews 9:27, we read, "It is appointed for men to die once, but after this the judgment."

I've wondered, from time to time, how long this final judgment will take—individually as well as corporately. How much time will Jesus spend with each person, showing them the sinfulness of their lives? God is so fair and just that I would assume He will spend considerable time with each one. So how long will it take for Jesus to finish judging every last unsaved sinner who has ever lived in the course of human history? Time will not be a factor, but even so, that's a lot of people who will have to appear before the Lord.

In verse 13, we read that all the unsaved dead—whether in graves, in the sea, or in Hades—will be resurrected to stand before the Lord. Hades is where the souls and spirits of unsaved people go today when they die, as they await this final judgment (Luke 16). The reference to the sea is perhaps meant as a reminder of all the people who perished in the global flood of Genesis and who will now finally stand before the Lord at this judgment. It would include unsaved sinners whose bodies ended up in the sea or whose ashes were spread at sea after their cremation. The point is that it doesn't matter how, when, or where they died—the bodies of all unsaved sinners will be resurrected.

We've talked about the first resurrection, which is for believers only (Rev. 20:6). Here, we're reading about the second resurrection—one thousand years later—and it's for nonbelievers only. Just as believers will be resurrected and fitted with a glorified body that is suited for eternity in heaven, the unsaved will be resurrected and fitted with a body that is suited for eternal punishment. This body will allow them to experience all the pain and torment of the lake of fire forever, without being annihilated.

As these unsaved people stand before the Lord, verse 12 tells us that books (plural) are opened, and then a book (singular) is opened. All the unsaved are being judged by what is recorded in these books. The multiple books apparently contain a record of every sinful word, thought, and deed that each unsaved person has ever committed. Recently, I had the opportunity to share the gospel with a stranger for over an hour. He was a nice, sincere person, and he asked many good, typical questions that unsaved people ask in those conversations. But ultimately, his statement to me was, "I don't want to go to heaven, and I don't want to live forever with God." If nothing changes in his life spiritually, he will one day stand before this throne of judgment, and Jesus will open the books and show him that statement.

In addition to all the deeds and thoughts of unsaved people, these books would certainly contain a record of every instance in which that person has heard the gospel or anything related to God's plan of salvation, including His warnings of judgment. Jesus is a meticulous bookkeeper, and when the time comes, the books will be opened and unsaved people will give an accounting of their lives. Our second point in this passage is *the judgment*. The Judge is commencing judgment on all unsaved people based on their lives, as recorded in those books.

A question that is often asked is, "What about people who have never heard the gospel; how will God judge them?" The answer is this: God will judge them very much like everyone else. First, every person at this judgment is there because he or she is an unsaved sinner. Second, every person will be at this judgment because he or she rejected Christ and the gospel or he or she rejected God. The gospel is the good news that Jesus took the penalty for our sins on Himself. When I was speaking with that unsaved man the other day, I was very clear about what God had done for him through Christ on the cross. So when a person rejects the gospel, he has rejected the only remedy for the sins that condemn him in this divine courtroom of judgment.

When unsaved persons have not heard the gospel, the Bible tells us in Romans 1–2 that they have their own conscience, as well as the witness of God's creation, to testify to them of God's existence. That is more than enough light to point them to the Lord, and God

279

is faithful to give them more light. We are reminded in 2 Peter 3:9 that God is "not willing that any should perish, but that all should come to repentance." The road that leads to salvation may be narrow, but it's well marked! In America today, for every person who believes he's going to hell, there are 120 who believe they're going to heaven.[3] Those numbers don't line up with the words of Jesus about the broad and narrow roads (Matt. 7:13–14). When has there been a time like this—with so many people claiming to believe in God but living like atheists?

All of us travel along the main road of life, which leads to destruction, and we encounter two signs. One sign reads, "Dead End Ahead," while the other sign reads, "Make U-turn for Christ." Most people choose to keep going straight ahead toward that dead end of destruction, in spite of the warnings. Fortunately, others have heeded the sign to change direction in life and have chosen to make that U-turn and follow Jesus on the road that leads to life.

In addition to the books that record every sinful deed and thought, there is a singular and separate book found at this final judgment. This is the Book of Life, which records the names of every saved person. So the final step that is taken at this judgment, after Jesus reviews their lifelong works and gospel opportunities, is to search for people's names in the Book of Life. Jesus will perhaps turn to the angels who are assisting Him and ask them, "Does this person's name appear in My Book of Life?" Unfortunately, since that person is already at the great white throne judgment, the response will always be the same: "No, Lord, their name is not here."

At that point, Jesus will prepare to sentence the person to eternal punishment. Our third point is *the justice*. Some will try to defend or justify themselves, saying, "Lord, Lord, have we not prophesied in Your name, and cast out demons in Your name, and done many wonders in Your name?" But Jesus will say, "I never knew you, depart from Me" (see Matt. 7:22–23). As I was sharing with that unsaved person the other day, he said to me, "I know that I've done bad things in my life, but it's not like I've murdered anyone or done anything really terrible like that." I was able to explain to him that while it's true that some people sin more than others, nevertheless, the Bible states that we're all sinners in need of a Savior. Then I told him, "God doesn't grade on the curve; he grades on the cross!"

Another reason the Lord will judge these unsaved sinners according to their specific sins, recorded in those books, is that the Bible teaches us there will be varying degrees of pain and punishment in hell. In Matthew 11, Jesus referred to this when He said, "Woe to you Chorazin! Woe to you Bethsaida! . . . It will be more tolerable for Tyre and Sidon in the day of judgment than for you. And you Capernaum . . . it shall be more tolerable for the land of Sodom in the day of judgment than for you" (vv. 21–24).

We often think of the Old Testament cities of Sodom and Gomorrah as symbolizing the worst-case scenario when it comes to sin. And as vile as the people in those cities were, Jesus said that the people of Capernaum were guilty of worse sin. The reason is that Jesus Himself walked among the people of Capernaum—they saw God come in the flesh, they witnessed His miracles and healings, and they heard His teachings. Therefore, since the light and revelation were greater for them, they're guiltier in their sin than the people of Sodom and Gomorrah who did not have the same light.

So then, the purpose for judging these unsaved people according to their works includes determining the amount of light they've received during their life from the gospel and from God. It's a truly frightening thought that some unsaved people will have gone to church for most of their lives but were never converted. All that light will come crashing down on them at this sentencing, making their eternal punishment far worse.

Years ago, there was a massive pileup of nearly a hundred cars in England, because of thick fog on one of the busy roadways. Visibility was very limited, and ten people died before the police arrived. When the first two officers did arrive, they attempted to slow down traffic heading for the accident scene, but commuters were in such a hurry that they continued to whiz by the officers in the fog. The sound of cars crashing into the pileup continued to echo in the fog. Finally, in desperation, the officers began throwing orange cones at the windshields of oncoming cars in an attempt to save lives. Every time the gospel is shared, it's like a barrage of orange cones being thrown at somebody's windshield on the road of life. But people are bent on speeding down that broad road of destruction.

After Jesus finishes judging the unsaved, they will be condemned to this place called the lake of fire. They will remain there for all eternity. Their pain and torment will never cease. They will never have the opportunity for release. And each of these chilling details is part of what is called the second death. The first death is physical, and we all experience it unless we are raptured. The second death is spiritual, and it is never-ending suffering in eternity. Those who belong to God will never experience the second death; the lake of fire will be inhabited only by fallen angels and unsaved people. Verse 14 also states that "death and Hades are cast into the Lake of Fire." After this judgment, there will be no more death and no need for that place called Hades, where the souls of unsaved people go today.

Another question that emerges from the text is this: where is the lake of fire? The Bible does not tell us specifically, but we can glean pieces of information from Scripture. As I mentioned, the universe as we know it will be dissolved, so it's not there. And the new heaven and earth will remain undefiled by anything sinful or wicked, according to the next chapter (Rev. 21:27).

Hell is also described in Scripture as being "a place of outer darkness" as well as "the blackness of darkness forever." So when we put this information together, it seems quite possible that hell, or the lake of fire, is located in some far-removed galaxy. That would certainly fit the Bible's description of outer darkness and eternal separation. It may even be located on some distant star of enormous proportions, which would account for the fact that it's a place of continual burning. Wherever and whatever it is, let us give heartfelt thanks to the Lord that it does not involve us.

This sobering chapter ends with the statement that those who end up in the lake of fire are those whose names are not written in the Lamb's Book of Life. God is continuing to invite people to leave the broad road that leads to destruction, make a U-turn, and join Him on the narrow road that leads to life. At the great white throne judgment, many will say to Jesus, after it's too late, "Lord, Lord, have we not prophesied in Your name, and cast out demons in Your name?" But Jesus will say, "I never knew you, depart from Me" (Matt. 7:22–23).

28

The Best Is Yet to Come

Revelation 21:1-8

People who have a passion for eating often really enjoy buffet-style meals. For some, it's the variety and choices that a buffet offers, while for others, it's simply a matter of massive amounts of food. Whenever I get into buffet lines, I watch the people in front of me loading up on the first part of the buffet—the salads, veggies, fruit, and other assorted rabbit foods. I think to myself, "These poor people; they just don't get it! All the best food items—the chicken, fish, and steak, as well as the desserts—are at the other end of the buffet line, and you have to hold out. Otherwise, your plate is filled up with rabbit food."

Now I know you are probably thinking, "Silly Jeff, all you have to do is go back, grab another plate, and get more food." Well, yes, but (silly reader) you've filled up on rabbit food, and now you're not as hungry for all the really good stuff. The trick to buffets is being patient and holding out for the best stuff—trust me on this, I am a trained professional! In most buffet lines, the best is yet to come!

283

You go ahead and load up on the carrot sticks and the carrot salad; I'll wait for the carrot cake!

As we come to the final two chapters of Revelation, we're going to see that, in terms of our spiritual lives, the best is yet to come, which is the title of this chapter. If the title sounds familiar, you might be old enough to remember that Frank Sinatra had a hit song with that title back in 1964. In fact, it was the last song Sinatra sang publicly, in 1995. I'm not sure, in Sinatra's case, that the best was yet to come, but I guess we'll find out some day. The opening lines of a Robert Browning poem also have a similar theme: "Grow old along with me! The best is yet to be."[1] That's a very nice sentiment. However, the later years of life can oftentimes be the most difficult, so the only sure way to say, "The best is yet to come," is by being ready for eternity in heaven. As we come to the end of Revelation—and for that matter, the end of the Bible—we quickly realize that God has saved the best for last. The best is yet to come!

It's significant that God ends both this book and the Bible with two chapters on the subject of our eternal home in heaven. In fact, chapter 21 is the longest chapter in Revelation. So while there is much about heaven that we don't know, the Bible does tell us a lot. These last two chapters are filled with wonderful descriptions. As Christians, we know that "our citizenship is in heaven," as Paul wrote in Philippians 3:20. Like Abraham, we look for a city "whose builder and maker is God" (Heb. 11:10).

> Now I saw a new heaven and a new earth, for the first heaven and the first earth had passed away. Also there was no more sea. Then I, John, saw the holy city, New Jerusalem, coming down out of heaven from God, prepared as a bride adorned for her husband. And I heard a loud voice from heaven saying, "Behold, the tabernacle of God is with men, and He will dwell with them, and they shall be His people. God Himself will be with them and be their God. And God will wipe away every tear from their eyes; there shall be no more death, nor sorrow, nor crying. There shall be no more pain, for the former things have passed away." Then He who sat on the throne said, "Behold, I make all things new." And He said to me, "Write, for these words are true and faithful." And He said to me, "It is done! I am the Alpha and the Omega, the Beginning and the End. I will give of the fountain of the water of life freely to him who thirsts. He who

overcomes shall inherit all things, and I will be his God and he shall be My son. But the cowardly, unbelieving, abominable, murderers, sexually immoral, sorcerers, idolaters, and all liars shall have their part in the lake which burns with fire and brimstone, which is the second death."

Revelation 21:1–8

There are several hundred references to heaven in the Bible, and fifty of them are here in Revelation. In verse 1, we quickly learn that there are going to be some significant changes in eternity. God is going to "make all things new." The first new things we see are "a new heaven and a new earth, for the first heaven and the first earth had passed away."

We looked at this passing away in our last chapter. We learned that the old heaven and earth are going to pass away with a great noise and a fervent heat (2 Peter 3:10). In Isaiah 65, we read words similar to those here in Revelation 21. God said, "Behold, I create new heavens and a new earth; and the former shall not be remembered, or come to mind. But be glad and rejoice forever in what I create; for behold, I create Jerusalem as a rejoicing, and her people a joy" (vv. 17–18). God is both the Creator and the Re-creator.

Something that rarely seems to be mentioned, but is clearly stated here and in other Scripture passages, is that God is creating a new earth. We tend to focus on heaven, which is a good thing to focus on, but eternity includes a new earth. And from what we can tell, in many ways it will be like the present earth—only better. John is not referring to some spiritualized earth-like eternal place but to another literal earth. From the Greek word *ge*, used here for "earth," we get our English word *geology*. It refers to soil and to solid earth. So there will be a new earth—something like the one we have now but new and perfect.

One of the differences, however, is that there will be "no more sea." We remember that John was on a small island called Patmos, surrounded by water, when he received this revelation, so I'm sure this vision startled him. Today, nearly three-quarters of the earth's surface is covered with water, but that is going to change. Now, if you love the ocean and activities related to the sea, you may be disappointed to read this verse. But I think that we should not assume the worst here. "No more sea" does not necessarily mean no more large bodies of water.

Perhaps God will do away with the seas and salt waters and replace them with large bodies of freshwater, which we can enjoy in the same way. The amount of oceans today, and the way that they cover so much of the earth's surface, may have something to do with the global flood of Genesis. If so, then the new earth will potentially have large bodies of freshwater that we can enjoy in some of the same ways that we enjoy the ocean today. The bottom line is that whatever God has waiting for us, it will be absolutely, positively better than what we have today.

In verse 2, John begins to describe the capital city of the new heaven: the New Jerusalem. This holy city that John sees is coming down from heaven. In the Old Testament, there was the city of Jerusalem, which David made the capital of his kingdom. The Old Testament also describes the renewed city of Jerusalem as the capital and headquarters where Christ will reign in the millennium (Zech. 14:16).

Notice that this holy city has been "prepared." We should immediately connect that word to a well-known statement made by Jesus, when He told His disciples, "I go to prepare a place for you. And if I go and prepare a place for you, I will come again and receive you to Myself, that where I am, there you may be also" (John 14:2–3). "Prepared" here in verse 2 is the same Greek word used by Jesus in John 14:2. It's also the same word used by Paul in 1 Corinthians 2:9 when he said, "Eye has not seen, nor ear heard, nor have entered into the heart of man the things which God has *prepared* for those who love Him."

It's no coincidence that when Jesus worked with His adoptive father Joseph, prior to His ministry, He worked as a carpenter. After all, being God, Jesus created all things, and all things are held together by Him (Col. 1:16–17). This same Jesus has gone to prepare a place for us. The holy city of New Jerusalem is described as a beautiful "bride adorned for her husband." We should take that description in two ways. First, just like a bride at her wedding ceremony, so is this new city in its appearance—radiant and beautiful. Having done many dozens of weddings, I always enjoy that moment when the bride appears and all eyes turn toward her.

But in another sense, we should remember that the bride of Christ is the New Testament church, and by this point in eternity, it's all of God's people. It is the holy city because of our holy God and because of all the holy people.

In verse 3, the best part will be that God personally dwells with us. It's the presence of God that makes heaven, heaven. Ever since Adam and Eve sinned in the Garden of Eden, that personal fellowship and closeness with God has been broken. But here in heaven, it will be completely restored. Without God, the streets of gold would be worthless and the angels' voices would be empty.

We've read that this New Jerusalem will come down from heaven—a fact that is repeated in verse 10. So where is this city coming down to? Since John tells us that he sees a new heaven and a new earth, the sequence here strongly suggests that this heavenly city, where God's people reside, is coming down to the new earth. Just as Jesus became flesh and dwelt with mankind on the old earth, God will dwell among His people on the new earth. So we'll have a new heaven and a new earth that are joined by this New Jerusalem. In the next chapter, we'll read about the measurements and the materials associated with this holy city.

In verse 4, we find one of the greatest promises in all of Scripture: no more tears, no more death, no more sorrow, no more crying, and no more pain. Talk about "the best is yet to come!" This verse is one that we pastors love sharing at the funeral services of believers. One of the pastors I work with (who shall remain nameless in order to protect the embarrassed) went to quote this verse at a believer's funeral service. But he accidentally read from Revelation 20 instead of Revelation 21. So as he read, he said, "Then I saw an angel coming down from heaven, having the key to the bottomless pit and a great chain in his hand. He laid hold of that dragon, that serpent of old, who is the Devil and Satan." Right about there he stopped and said, "Excuse me, I'm reading from the wrong chapter." Yeah, no kidding! Perhaps verse 4 should read that "God will wipe away every blooper from their lips." I'm sure He will anyway.

But truly, verse 4 is a phenomenal verse and promise. Think about this: no more sickness, or medical tests, or doctor's reports, or medications, or hospitals, or cemeteries, or obituaries, or funeral homes . . . and no more death! The reality is that heaven is the land of the living, while this world is the land of the dying. As Thomas Boston said, "Believers will swim forever in an ocean of joy."[2]

A common question regarding verse 4 has to do with how we won't experience any more tears or sorrow in heaven, despite the fact that some of our loved ones didn't make it to heaven. If we return to the words of Isaiah 65:17, we read, "Behold, I create new heavens and a new earth; and the former shall not be remembered or come to mind." In heaven, we won't have any memory of those who aren't there.

This also begins to answer another common question, which is whether we'll still be capable of sinning in heaven. Let's remember that Satan and his demons will be banished to the lake of fire for all eternity, so there won't be that temptation. Better yet, God Himself will be there with us personally. In addition, we'll be in our new, glorified bodies, not those old bodies of flesh that were controlled by our sin nature (Rom. 7). Also, we remember that Romans 6:23 says, "The wages of sin is death." Since there is no more death, then there is no more sin. Sin is what causes death. The final words in verse 4 tell us, "For the former things have passed away." All past things, such as sin, death, and sorrow, are permanently removed.

Verse 4 includes the promise of no more pain. That would include both physical and emotional pain. No more pain from a broken body or from a broken heart. No more broken bones, broken marriages, or broken dreams. No more pain from the regrets and failures of the past. John Blanchard described it by saying, "There are no regrets in heaven, no remorseful tears, no second thoughts, no lost causes."[3] It's no wonder then, in verse 5, that God declares, "Behold, I make all things new."

Now when it comes to bad things—sin, sickness, suffering, and sorrow—we're very relieved to hear God say, "Behold, I make all things new." But what about things that weren't necessarily so bad? Christians often ask whether we'll still eat and drink in the heavenly eternity. I believe that the answer is yes—a very strong yes for that matter. When Jesus made His postresurrection appearances (there were ten of them that we know about), He was oftentimes eating with His disciples.

Even before His death and resurrection, Jesus told His disciples in the upper room, as they were partaking of communion, "I say to you, I will not drink of the fruit of the vine until the kingdom of God comes" (Luke 22:18). Back in Revelation 19:9, we talked about the marriage supper of the Lamb and the great wedding banquet that we'll all share together with Jesus. Now that will be the buffet to end all buffets! Since I'm thinking that we can eat whatever we want, whenever we want, I won't have to use my super-duper buffet line strategy.

Another common question in regard to eternity involves the age we will appear to be in heaven. This question is asked in light of the fact that people have died at various ages in life—from the very young to the very old. If a child dies at the age of one year, or an elderly person dies at the age of 101 years, what will their appearance be like in heaven?

The Scriptures seem to imply that we will live throughout eternity in glorified bodies that may reflect the prime age of our earthly bodies—perhaps around the age of thirty years. When Adam and Eve were created, they were not created as babies or children but rather as full-grown adults, capable of producing children. Since aging and death are direct consequences of sin, we know that Adam and Eve would never have aged had they not sinned. They would have lived forever in their created bodies. We don't know how old they were in physical terms, but it seems that we can make a case for an age of about thirty.

According to the Old Testament, priests had to be thirty years old before they could minister before the Lord in the temple (Num. 4:3). Since we're told that we will be priests and rulers with Christ in the millennium, it seems reasonable to think that we might be the same "age" in our heavenly bodies. Joseph was thirty years old when he began to rule in Egypt (Gen. 41:46), as was David when he became king over Israel (2 Sam. 5:4). Jesus was thirty when He began His public ministry (Luke 3:23). This same apostle John tells us in his first Epistle, "It has not yet been revealed what we shall be, but we know that when [Jesus] is revealed, we shall be like Him" (1 John 3:2).

This much we do know: our new bodies will be perfect and will last forever. There won't be any handicaps or deformities. I will have a full head of hair! Or will I? What if baldness is actually part of the perfect new body? Then I've already got that going for me!

One other question I would like to touch on now is whether we will see our pets in heaven. Let's remember that God created the animals, as well as mankind. Remarkably, Genesis states that God gave them both "the breath of life," using the same Hebrew word (Gen. 1:30; 2:7). Obviously, God gave the animals different bodies. More importantly, God did not create the animals in His image, as He did with mankind. But it is significant that God created the animals with the same "breath of life" and that they were part of the original creation. Later on, the global flood of God's judgment came, and God saved Noah's family, as well as the types of animals. After the flood, God told Noah, "I establish My covenant with you and your descendants after you, and with every living creature that is with you . . . every beast of the earth" (Gen. 9:9–10).

When God gave His laws to Moses and the people, many of those laws had to do with animals and how they were to be treated (Lev. 22). In Romans 8, Paul talks about both mankind and the creation groaning to be released from the curse and bondage of sin. In our recent discussion of the millennial kingdom, we saw that the animal kingdom will thrive and that the curse that affects the animal kingdom will be removed. This will bring complete harmony to the animals themselves, as well as harmony between mankind and animals.

Now in Revelation 21, we've been reading how God will create both a new heaven and a new earth. What biblical or logical reason is there for not assuming that animals will be with us again in heaven? Since God is going to create a new earth and make "all things new," why would animals not be a part of that? "All things" would include the earth and everything in it that God originally created for us. That would include the animal kingdom as well as nature.

We understand that when Jesus died on the cross, it was to atone for the sins of mankind and to provide salvation for every person who believes by faith. Jesus did not die on the cross for fallen angels, as we read in Hebrews 2:16, nor did He die for the animals. But here's something to consider: the death of Christ on the cross did provide for future removal of the curse of sin. When that curse is done away with, it will include liberating the animal kingdom from bondage in that curse.

So indirectly, the cross of Christ benefits and blesses the animal kingdom. But in no way does it affect the angels. I think the key that unlocks the whole question is found in the Garden of Eden. When God created the world, He created mankind, the animals, and nature. All of that creation is connected, and I firmly believe that all of it will be restored in the new earth when God makes all things new.

More specifically, what about our beloved pets—Fido and Fluffy? Will Rogers once said, "If there are no dogs in heaven, then when I die, I want to go where they went."[4] Mark Twain put it this way: "Heaven goes by favor—if it went by merit, you would stay out and your dog would go in!"[5] And not to neglect any of our cat-loving friends, some anonymous person wrote, "Thousands of years ago, cats were worshiped as gods, and apparently they have never forgotten this!"[6]

Whether or not we'll have our beloved pets in heaven remains to be seen. But I'm in complete agreement with people such as C. S. Lewis, Joni Eareckson Tada, and Hank Hanegraaff, who all ask the simple question in regard to our pets being in heaven: why not? Why wouldn't God restore those pets who have brought us so much joy and love? As Hank Hanegraaff puts it, "If God resurrected our pets, it would be in total keeping with His overwhelming grace and goodness."[7]

Returning our thoughts to verse 5, what we have seen is a new eternity. Not only does God say, "Behold, I make all things new," but he also says to John, "Write, for these words are faithful and true." We read these verses, and just when we start wondering whether all this is too good to be true, God says, "These words are faithful and true." Is it really true? No more death, no more sorrow, and no more pain? Will all things really become new? God says, "Yes, it's absolutely true!" We never want to place a question mark where God has placed an exclamation point.

In verse 6, God continues His emphatic promises of making everything new, and He says, "It is done!" On the cross at Calvary, Jesus cried out, "It is finished!" Having promised us that He was going to heaven to prepare a place for us, we now hear the words, "It is done!" God always finishes what He has started. He is "the Alpha and the Omega, the beginning and the end."

At the end of verse 6, when He says, "I will give of the fountain of the water of life freely to him who thirsts," He speaks of how heaven will quench that spiritual thirst that every person has. In

Psalm 42, the writer says, "As the deer pants for the water brooks, so pants my soul for You, O God. My soul thirsts for God, for the living God. When shall I come and appear before God?" (vv. 1–2). To the Samaritan woman at the well in John 4, Jesus offered living water—the same water described here in verse 6.

In verse 7, we read about more wonderful promises that almost seem too good to be true, including the promise to inherit all things, as well as being a child of God. But the greatest promise to the genuine believer is when He says, "And I will be His God."

A family in our church fellowship recently adopted a son from Ethiopia. As the process was under way, all the paperwork and procedures were completed. Ultimately, it was just a matter of time before that little guy arrived here in America. Sure enough, after months of waiting, the family flew to Ethiopia and picked up their new child. Having arrived here in the United States, he is officially part of their family; he is their son. That day is coming for us as well—when we'll arrive safely in heaven, our adoption by God will be complete, and He will call us His son or His daughter.

In verse 8, John closes out his vision of the new heaven and new earth with a witness and a warning. The witness is that nothing sinful or vile will ever be found in God's new creation. Heaven will be inhabited only by believers, and hell will be inhabited only by the unsaved. At the same time, John's words are a warning to the reader. For those who read these words, the warning is there, and there is still time before it is too late.

We can essentially divide the people listed in verse 8 into three groups, although ultimately they're all unsaved sinners. We have the first group, who are *the cowardly*. These are the people who are too afraid or too ashamed to confess Jesus Christ as their Lord. The second group is *the unbelievers*. These people are simply unwilling to believe that they are sinners going to hell or that they need Christ as their Savior. They're unconvinced, and therefore, they're unconverted unbelievers. The third group is *the abominable*; they are further identified as "murderers, sexually immoral, sorcerers, idolaters, and habitual liars." These are the people who love the darkness much more than the light and therefore refuse to repent (John 3:19). These types of sins are all fairly self-explanatory, although I would again point out that "sorcerers" comes from the Greek word *pharmakeia*, from which we get our English words *pharmacy* and *pharmaceutical*. So it includes both the occult and drug use. The good news is, none of these groups or sins will be anywhere near the new heaven and new earth. The bad news, for those people who practice such things and refuse to come to Christ, is that they will end up in the lake of fire and will suffer God's eternal punishment.

In the meantime, our longing for heaven has a very positive and helpful impact on our current lives and circumstances:

1. It keeps us strong in our trials. Knowing that our trials are only temporary and light, in comparison with our future hope and glory in heaven, gives us strength (Rom. 8:18).
2. It helps us to remember that this world is not our home and that we are citizens of heaven (1 John 2:15–17; Phil. 3:20).
3. It helps to keep us holy and desirous to live lives that are pleasing to God (2 Peter 3:11).
4. It gives us a sense of purpose, knowing that God has called us to share the gospel, because it is the power of God to salvation for everyone who believes (Rom. 1:17).

29

Home Sweet Home

Revelation 21:9–27

A very elderly couple, having been married for over sixty-five years, passed away at the same time, and they both went to heaven. They had been in exceptionally good health in their latter years because of the wife's insistence on eating healthy. When they reached the pearly gates, Peter greeted them and took them to their mansions, which had beautiful views of the universe. As they "oohed" and "aahed," the old man asked Peter how much everything was going to cost. "It's free," Peter replied. "This is heaven."

Next they saw a lavish buffet with every desirable food laid out. "How much does it cost to eat?" asked the old man. "Don't you understand?" Peter replied. "This is heaven; it's all free!" "Well, where are the low-fat and high-fiber foods?" the old man asked timidly. "That's the best part," Peter said. "You can eat as much as you like, of whatever you like, and you'll never gain weight or get sick. Remember, this is heaven." The old man looked at his wife and said, "You and your stupid bran muffins—we could have been here ten years ago!"

There are many misconceptions about heaven, as well as some surprising realities. Over the years, harps, pearly gates, and streets of gold have all been associated with heaven, and, biblically speaking, that's completely accurate. However, misconceptions such as Peter being at the pearly gates or people in heaven becoming angels and floating around on clouds are not biblical.

When we arrive safely in heaven, it will be "home sweet home." Even though we've never been there until that moment, I strongly believe that it will feel as if we're coming home. Solomon wrote that God "has made everything beautiful in its time. Also He has put eternity in [our] hearts" (Eccl. 3:11). That is to say, God has created us to feel at home in our eternal destination. It was C. S. Lewis who said, "If nothing in this world satisfies me, perhaps it is because I was made for another world."[1]

Then one of the seven angels who had the seven bowls filled with the seven last plagues came to me and talked with me, saying, "Come, I will show you the bride, the Lamb's wife." And he carried me away in the Spirit to a great and high mountain, and showed me the great city, the holy Jerusalem, descending out of heaven from God, having the glory of God. Her light was like a most precious stone, like a jasper stone, clear as crystal. Also she had a great and high wall with twelve gates, and twelve angels at the gates, and names written on them, which are the names of the twelve tribes of the children of Israel: three gates on the east, three gates on the north, three gates on the south, and three gates on the west. Now the wall of the city had twelve foundations, and on them were the names of the twelve apostles of the Lamb.

Revelation 21:9–14

Interestingly, John's tour guide for this vision of the New Jerusalem is one of the seven angels who had poured out the final bowl judgments of the tribulation period, more than a thousand years earlier. One of the wonderful things about angels is that they are both witnesses and workers who carry out everything that the Lord directs them to do. As John Calvin put it, "Angels are the ministers of God's wrath, as well as His grace."[2]

This angel takes John to a high mountain to get a nice panoramic view of the holy city. John's being taken up in this vision from the rocky remote island of Patmos to a mountaintop view of the heavenly city is a picture of our departure from the harsh realities of life on earth to the eternal blessings that are awaiting us in heaven.

In these final two chapters of Revelation, John uses the term *city* eleven times in referring to our new home in heaven. Notice in verse 9 that the angel's description of the great city is "the bride, the Lamb's wife." As mentioned before, the New Jerusalem is a holy city because it belongs to our holy God, and it is filled with God's holy people. Today, there are the buildings that we call the church, but the real church is God's people. In the same way, what makes heaven, heaven isn't the many mansions; it is Jesus Himself and God's people united together.

In verse 11, as John is attempting to describe the indescribable to us, he sums up this eternal city as "having the glory of God." When Moses finished the first tabernacle, and Solomon completed the first temple, both structures were described as "the glory of God filled . . ." (Exod. 40:35; 1 Kings 8:11). Here, our new eternal home in heaven is also described as "having the glory of God." God's glory is the radiance of His deity and His divine nature. In attempting to describe that radiance, John likens it to a precious stone—"a jasper stone, clear as crystal." Several commentators believe that this is referring to a diamond. The New Jerusalem will be the crown jewel of the heavens.

When I got the chance to visit the Smithsonian Institute in Washington DC, one of the many great things I got to see, besides the ruby slippers from *The Wizard of Oz*, was the Hope Diamond. It weighs 45.5 carats and has an estimated value of $350 million. In the past hundred years, there have been numerous reports of a curse attached to the Hope Diamond that has allegedly affected many of the people who either owned or handled it. The heavenly city of New Jerusalem, as it descends from heaven, will look very much like a colossal diamond that reflects the radiant glory of God. And the curse from our sin will have been removed, so there's no curse associated with *this* diamond.

Beginning in verse 12, we are given some specific descriptions of the heavenly city, and they are literal descriptions. Jesus told His disciples, "In My Father's house are many mansions," and, "I am going to prepare a place for you" (John 14:2). Jesus was speaking literally of a place, a house, and many mansions. Here in Revelation 21, we read about that place Jesus went to prepare. Heaven is not some symbolic spiritual fantasyland; it is a real place that is being prepared for us. And here on earth, God is preparing us for heaven.

In verse 12, we begin to read about the high wall and the twelve gates of the New Jerusalem. Later, in verse 21, we will read that these twelve gates are made from individual pearls. But let me point out that Peter is not standing at the pearly gates of heaven. Instead, we read that there are twelve angels—one for each gate. The twelve gates have names written on them: the names of the twelve tribes of Israel. Jacob's sons will have their names eternally inscribed on the gates of heaven, and they represent God's people, Israel.

The fact that Israel is eternally remembered in this way reminds us of God's Old Testament covenant and relationship with His chosen people. As New Testament Christians, we're grateful to the Jewish people for the truth and knowledge that have been passed on to us. Israel was certainly not perfect, just as the New Testament church is not perfect—but this is about God's faithfulness and His covenant with His people.

In verse 13, these gates are laid out with three on each side of the New Jerusalem—east, west, north, and south. Going back to the book of Numbers, we read that the tabernacle was set up in the wilderness with three tribes stationed on each of the four sides of the structure. We now see a similar layout here, with the twelve gates being equally divided among the four sides of the city and bearing the names of the twelve tribes.

The question might be asked: is there any need for these gates, since gates of ancient cities were built for protection and security? In those ancient cities, the gates were closed at sunset and reopened at sunrise, with watchmen guarding them at night. But in verse 25, these heavenly gates will never be closed, and one reason is that there will be no night in the eternal city. Since there is nothing evil or sinful, there is no need to guard these gates. So those angels are not there to protect but to serve as attendants.

The fact that the gates will always be open speaks to us of how we'll be going in and out of the New Jerusalem. As we will see, the city itself is going to be plenty big for all of us, but we'll also be going out into the expanse of the new heaven and earth. This is just the capital city. Jesus said, "I am the gate; whoever enters through Me will be saved. He will come in and go out, and find pasture" (John 10:9 NIV).

Verse 14 brings to mind the fact that the New Testament church has been "built on the foundation of the apostles" (Eph. 2:20). The wall of the heavenly city will sit on twelve foundations, and the names of the twelve apostles will be inscribed on those twelve foundations. Oftentimes, people will write their names in fresh cement, and it may last for many years. I doubt that these foundations are made of cement, but they are inscribed with the names of the apostles, and those names will last for all eternity. Unlike structures that have a single foundation, this eternal city sits on twelve foundations.

A question that some people have (myself included) is the identity of the twelfth apostle. We know that Judas the betrayer was replaced in Acts 1 with Matthias; however, we never hear of him after that. I'm of the personal opinion that Paul will be that twelfth apostle. Like the other original apostles, Paul met the same requirements as Matthias, and Paul described himself as "one born out of due time" (1 Cor. 15:8).

As we read about these twelve gates and foundations, it reminds us that our knowledge of God originally came through the Old Testament gates of the Jewish people, while our faith is built upon the New Testament foundation of the gospel message and the apostles' doctrine. Having read these verses, let me quote what the writer of Hebrews says, and it should have fresh meaning: "By faith Abraham obeyed when he was called to go out to the place which he would receive as an inheritance. . . . By faith he dwelt in the land of promise as in a foreign country, dwelling in tents . . . for he waited for the city which has *foundations*, whose builder and maker is God" (Heb. 11:8–10).

And he who talked with me had a gold reed to measure the city, its gates, and its wall. The city is laid out as a square; its length is as great as its breadth. And he measured the city with the reed: twelve thousand furlongs. Its length, breadth, and height are equal. Then he measured its wall: one hundred and forty-four cubits, according to the measure of a man, that is, of an angel.

Revelation 21:15–17

In the words of commentator Henry Morris, "The New Jerusalem is composed of such beautiful materials, such unique construction, and such amazing dimensions as to be almost beyond human comprehension."[3] The angel showing John this vision has with him a gold reed to measure the city, as well as its gates and wall. The length, width, and height of the city are all equal measurements, making it a perfect cube. Interestingly, we read in 1 Kings that the Holy of Holies in Solomon's temple was a twenty-cubit, cube-shaped room (1 Kings 6:16). Just as the Holy of Holies was the place where God dwells, so this cube-shaped heavenly city will be the place where God dwells with His people.

The twenty cubits of that holy place in Solomon's temple is equal to thirty feet in height, and width, and length. The New Jerusalem, however, will be a cube shape of twelve thousand furlongs (one furlong is 660 feet), which equates to about fifteen hundred miles in length, in width, and in height. I have no doubt that these are literal dimensions, as the end of verse 17 states that these measurements are "according to the measure of a man, that is, of an angel." In other words, while this angel is providing the measurements, they are the same measurements used by a man.

So our eternal home city of New Jerusalem will be fifteen hundred miles long, fifteen hundred miles wide, and fifteen hundred miles high. If we laid these dimensions over the United States, it would cover an area from Canada to Mexico and from Los Angeles to St. Louis—about three-quarters of the United States. Some Christians have wondered whether that will be enough space for all the people who belong to God. Here is the response of Randy Alcorn, from his book titled *Heaven*: "We don't need to worry that heaven will be crowded. The ground level of the city will be nearly two million square miles. This is forty times bigger than England, and fifteen thousand times bigger than London. It's ten times as big as France or Germany and far larger than India. But remember, that's just the ground level."[4]

Alcorn goes on to describe the fact that this heavenly city will be fifteen hundred miles high, and if this eternal city contains levels or stories, the New Jerusalem could be over six hundred thousand stories. That means that billions of people could occupy the city with many square miles per person. And let's not lose sight of the fact that this is only describing the capital city in eternity. This does not include the vast expanse of the new heaven and the new earth.

Since there are billions of galaxies in the present heavens, why would there be less in the new heaven? Why would there not, perhaps, even be more? I'm convinced that there will be lots of room to roam and to stretch our legs—lots of places to explore and to enjoy. Not to mention that there won't be any crime, traffic, pollution, long trains, leaf blowers, stinky garbage cans, or obnoxious neighbors.

The wall around this city will be 144 cubits high, and a cubit is eighteen inches—a measurement based on the distance between the tip of a man's middle finger and the elbow. So this wall will be 216 feet high. Our immediate reaction might be that this is a really high wall, but when we remember that the city itself is 1,500 miles high, this is really just a tiny retaining wall.

You've undoubtedly noticed the repetition of the number twelve in these verses. In his book *Number in Scripture*, E. W. Bullinger describes twelve in biblical numerology: "The number twelve is a perfect number, symbolizing perfection of government, or of governmental perfection. It is found as a multiple in the Bible with all that has to do with ruling."[5]

We've read about twelve gates, twelve angels, the twelve tribes of Israel, twelve foundations, and twelve apostles' names; the city is 12,000 furlongs in every direction, and the wall is measured at 144 cubits (which is twelve times twelve). So the repetition of the number 12 serves to remind us that this great heavenly city is constructed in such a way as to represent God's perfect and divine governmental rule. Isaiah 9:6, the familiar verse we like to quote at Christmastime, says, "Unto us a Child is born, unto us a Son is given; and the *government* will be upon His shoulder."

> The construction of its wall was of jasper; and the city was pure gold, like clear glass. The foundations of the wall of the city were adorned with all kinds of precious stones: the first foundation was jasper, the second sapphire, the third chalcedony, the fourth emerald, the fifth sardonyx, the sixth sardius, the seventh chrysolite, the eighth beryl, the ninth topaz, the tenth chrysoprase, the eleventh jacinth, and the twelfth amethyst. The twelve gates were twelve pearls: each

individual gate was of one pearl. And the street of the city was pure gold, like transparent glass.

Revelation 21:18–21

The wall of the city has the appearance of jasper—or potentially a diamond—while the city itself is described as pure gold. Who needs the emerald city of Oz when we can have the golden city of heaven! The twelve foundations we've been reading about, inscribed with the names of the twelve apostles, are also decorated with twelve precious stones. So the foundations of this city are visible and beautifully decorated.

We don't really know the significance of these precious stones, although several of them match up with the stones in the breastplate worn by the high priest in the Old Testament. We know that they do have significance, because they've been listed here for us; we're simply uncertain of that significance. I would connect this to the words of Paul in 1 Corinthians 2:9: "Eye has not seen, nor ear heard . . . the things which God has prepared for those who love Him."

In verse 21, each of the twelve gates is made of a single pearl. I'd hate to see the size of those oysters! There are actual pearly gates in heaven. There is also a street of pure gold that looks like transparent glass. Now think about this: here we have things that the unsaved world craves and lusts after—pearls, diamonds, gold, and other precious stones. But what so many people lust after on earth is nothing more than building material in heaven. Gold is like asphalt and pearls are like lumber.

In Matthew 13:45–46, we read, "The kingdom of heaven is like a merchant seeking beautiful pearls, who, when he had found one pearl of great price, went and sold all that he had and bought it." That parable can be taken two ways, and both are very biblical. On the one hand, it describes a lost sinner, searching for meaning and purpose in life, who hears the gospel and, having believed it, gives up everything in his life to possess that pearl of truth and salvation. But it can also be taken to describe Jesus as that merchant; He gives up everything to purchase us on the cross at Calvary. Jesus certainly laid aside many of His divine prerogatives and humbled Himself in becoming a man in order to suffer and die for us. Perhaps as we go into the city through those pearly gates, we'll remember what Christ did for us, and when we go out, we'll be reminded of how happy we are to have traded in the marbles of earth for the diamonds of heaven.

> But I saw no temple in it, for the Lord God Almighty and the Lamb are its temple. The city had no need of the sun or of the moon to shine in it, for the glory of God illuminated it. The Lamb is its light. And the nations of those who are saved shall walk in its light, and the kings of the earth bring their glory and honor into it. Its gates shall not be shut at all by day (there shall be no night there). And they shall bring the glory and the honor of the nations into it. But there shall by no means enter it anything that defiles, or causes an abomination or a lie, but only those who are written in the Lamb's Book of Life.
>
> Revelation 21:22–27

According to verse 22, there will be no temple in heaven, since God Himself will be that temple. We have churches and temples as places where we can worship God. But with God always there in the New Jerusalem, there's no need for a temple in which to worship Him.

Verse 23 says, "The city has no need of the sun or of the moon to shine in it, for the glory of God illuminates it, and the Lamb is its light." The text does not say that the sun or the moon no longer exists, but rather that there will be no need for the light that they produce, seeing that God will provide us light through His radiant glory. If I walk out to my mailbox at noon to pick up my mail, I don't need to bring a flashlight; I have the sunlight. In this case, our eternal city has no need of the light from the sun or the moon; God's glory is the greater light.

Just recently, I was out walking and was blessed by a beautiful sunset. When some believers read verse 23, they instantly assume that there will be no more sunsets or sunrises. I don't necessarily agree with that. As I mentioned before, I believe the universe of the new heaven will be greater and better than before, including billions and trillions of galaxies, planets, and stars like the sun. In Psalm 148, the psalmist exhorts the creation to praise the Lord, including the sun, moon, and stars. Then the psalmist says, "He [has] established them forever and ever" (v. 6). "Forever and ever" means eternally. So while God will re-create the universe, His Word declares that the sun, moon, and stars are established forever.

302

However, the light that shines forth from the sun, moon, and stars of the new universe will pale in comparison with the light of God's glory. We'll constantly walk in the greater light of God. Now, someone might point out that verse 25 states that there shall be no night there. So how can we still have sunsets, sunrises, and moonlight if there is no night there? Please read it again, with an added emphasis on the last word: "There is no night *there*." *There* is referring to the city of New Jerusalem and not to the rest of the new heaven and new earth.

There, in that huge city, measuring 1,500 miles in every direction, there is no night. But the New Jerusalem is only one small part of the new heaven and new earth. As God re-creates the heavens and an expanded universe, I believe it will include suns and moons that continue to produce sunsets and moonlight. This much I'm certain of: in our dwelling places within the new city, we won't have to plug anything in. I can never find enough electrical outlets at home or in my office. So I use those power strips that have several outlets. I plug several things into one strip, but it looks like a deranged octopus underneath my desk. No more electrical strips, blown fuses, or light bulbs burning out—God is the unending source of light in our eternal home.

Verses 24 and 26 make reference to "nations" and "kings" bringing their glory and honor to the eternal city. This has generated some confusion, since it sounds as if we'll continue to have various nationalities and segments of people. But remember back to Revelation 7:9, when John was describing the people he saw in heaven; John said, "I looked and behold, a great multitude which no one could number, of all nations, tribes, peoples and tongues, standing before the throne and before the Lamb." The word used here for "nations" is also translated "peoples."

So those people who are in heaven will have come from all the various nations, tribes, and tongues on earth, as well as from a variety of social and economic positions. This brings us to another question about heaven: will we all speak the same language? Or will there continue to be numerous languages? There are approximately sixty-five hundred spoken languages in the world today.[6]

I believe we'll all speak one language. That's how God originally created it to be. Genesis 11:1 states, "The whole earth had one language and one speech." It was after the fall, in the area that would become Babylon, that the people were attempting to live independently—apart from God's authority. They attempted to build a tower that would reach into the heavens. Therefore, God confused the language so that they could not understand each other, and it caused the people to scatter in different directions. Without that shared language, they could no longer unite in their rebellion against God.

Genesis 11:9 says, "Therefore its name is called Babel, because there the LORD confused the language of all the earth; and from there the LORD scattered them abroad over the face of all the earth." The Hebrew word *Babel* means "to confuse."[7] With everyone in heaven wholly committed to God, I believe there will be no need for various languages. We will be united once again, as it was in the beginning, with one language. The Lord's words in Zephaniah 3:9 may be referring to this: "I will restore to the peoples a pure language, that they all may call on the name of the LORD, to serve Him with one accord."

So the next question would logically be: which language will be spoken in heaven? Each person would undoubtedly like to think that it's the language that he already speaks. Today, English is the second most widely spoken language in the world, with over five hundred million people using it. The number one most widely spoken language is Mandarin Chinese, with more than one billion people speaking it. What language will be spoken in heaven? Is it even a language that exists today? We don't know.

The final delight of our eternal home, recorded at the end of this chapter, is the absence of anything evil, wicked, or untruthful. Only those citizens who belong to God and whose names are written in the Lamb's Book of Life will be there. No sin and no sinners—just the saints and their Savior. Psalm 16:11 says, "In Your presence is fullness of joy; at Your right hand are pleasures forevermore."

30

Great Expectations

Revelation 22:1–5

An Iowa farmer by the name of Dick Kleis decided that for his wife's sixty-seventh birthday, flowers and a box of chocolates just wouldn't cut it. So using his mowed-down Iowa cornfield, he wrote out a massive message that read, "HAPPY BIRTHDAY, LUV U"—and used nearly 124,000 pounds of manure to write out his words. Kleis was quoted as saying, "I was going to put a heart there after 'HAPPY BIRTHDAY,' but I ran out of manure."[1] I would give Mr. Kleis an A for effort but a D for using 124,000 pounds of manure! I'm not convinced that Mrs. Kleis wouldn't have preferred the chocolates and the flowers, which definitely would have smelled better!

As Christians, we often wonder what the Lord has prepared for us upon our arrival in heaven. And while we all agree that there is much about heaven that we don't know, there is quite a bit of information given to us in Scripture. We certainly understand that it will far exceed flowers and chocolates! As one person wrote, "Heaven will be a world of sanctified excitement."[2] As we study the first five verses of Revelation 22, we will discover that we do have very much to be excited about. I'm borrowing the title of this chapter from Charles Dickens's novel *Great Expectations*, because that is exactly what we as Christians have.

> And he showed me a pure river of water of life, clear as crystal, proceeding from the throne of God and of the Lamb. In the middle of its street, and on either side of the river, was the tree of life, which bore twelve fruits, each tree yielding its fruit every month. The leaves of the tree were for the healing of the nations. And there shall be no more curse, but the throne of God and of the Lamb shall be in it, and His servants shall serve Him. They shall see His face, and His name shall be on their foreheads. There shall be no night there: They need no lamp nor light of the sun, for the Lord God gives them light. And they shall reign forever and ever.
>
> Revelation 22:1–5

When we looked at chapter 21, we were given a glimpse of the New Jerusalem primarily from an outward perspective, which included the walls, the gates, and the foundations. Here in chapter 22, we are given more of an inward perspective, beginning with the river of life. We should note that these first five verses in chapter 22 are a continuation of what we were reading in chapter 21, as it begins with the word *and*. The same angel who had been showing John the wall and the gates now shows him the river of life and the tree of life. Scripture's description of heaven keeps getting more intimate; it was first described as a kingdom, then a city, and now a garden.

One of my favorite words in Scripture to describe heaven is *paradise*. There are three instances of the word *paradise* in the New Testament. The first is when Jesus told the thief on the cross, "Today you will be with Me in paradise" (Luke 23:43). Some believers have asked how that thief could be with Jesus in heaven on Good Friday, seeing that Jesus was not resurrected until that Sunday and did not ascend to heaven until forty days later.

Before the ascension of Jesus into heaven, paradise for believers was in the section of Hades called "Abraham's bosom" (Luke 16:22). In Luke 16, we read about two men who died, one saved and one unsaved, who both went into Hades. That story that Jesus shared has been called the parable of the rich man and Lazarus, but I believe Jesus was sharing an actual story and not a parable. If it were a parable, it would be the only parable in which Jesus gave someone an actual name.

The saved man named Lazarus went to the section of Hades called Abraham's bosom, while the unsaved man went into the section of torment. So Jesus was speaking of Abraham's bosom to that converted thief on the cross when He said, "Today you will be with Me in paradise" (Luke 23:43). Since His death, resurrection, and ascension into heaven, Jesus has given New Testament believers direct access to heaven at the moment of death (2 Cor. 5:8). Ephesians 4 makes reference to Jesus ascending on high and leading "captivity captive." In other words, believers who were once unsaved sinners held captive by Satan and by sin now belong to Christ, and He has led them up into heaven.

The second use of the word *paradise* is in 2 Corinthians 12:4, when Paul describes being caught up into paradise, which he also describes as the "third heaven" (2 Cor. 12:2). Paul was referring to the presence of God. The third use of this word in the New Testament comes from Revelation 2:7, where faithful believers at the church in Ephesus are promised to "eat from the tree of life, which is in the midst of the paradise of God." Once again, this is a reference to heaven and to what we're reading about here in Revelation 22.

Paradise comes from an old Persian word that means "an enclosed park or garden." Therefore, in the Old Testament, the word *paradise* was associated with the Garden of Eden, and it now refers to the garden-like paradise of heaven. In the first book of the Bible we see paradise lost, but here in the last book we see paradise restored. The first two chapters of the Bible describe the paradise that God created for us on earth, while these final two chapters of the Bible describe the paradise God has created in heaven.

It seems to me that no two people will be more appreciative to be in the paradise of heaven than Adam and Eve. First of all, I believe Scripture indicates that Adam and Eve were saved. In Genesis 3:21, we read that, after their fall and banishment from Eden, they received from the Lord animal skins to cover up their nakedness. Prior to that, they had sewn fig leaves together as the means for covering up their nakedness.

Those animal skins are the first reference to an animal sacrifice in Scripture. This foreshadowed the Old Testament sacrificial system, which required the shedding of blood to atone for sin. More importantly, the sacrifice pointed toward Jesus on the cross and His shed blood for our sins. This information indicates that Adam and Eve received the forgiveness offered to them by God when they received those animal skins. The skins replaced the fig leaves, which are symbolic of human efforts to cover up their sin and shame.

So who would appreciate this Eden-like paradise of heaven more than Adam and Eve? Besides being the only two people who have experienced Eden and God's daily fellowship firsthand, they were also the ones directly responsible for losing paradise for the rest of mankind. Talk about finally getting the monkey off your back! The two most ecstatic people in heaven might very well be Adam and Eve!

In this garden-like environment, John is shown an exceptional river. The uniqueness of this river is that its source is the throne of God. Back in Eden, there was also a river that flowed from the garden, and then it split off into four (Gen. 2:10). This river in the heavenly city is described as being "clear as crystal," which means that it is transparent. Everything we've been reading about in the New Jerusalem will radiate and reflect God's glory.

While this is a literal river of water, it also symbolizes eternal life. Back in John's Gospel, Jesus said, "If anyone thirsts, let him come to Me and drink. He who believes in Me . . . out of his heart will flow rivers of living water" (John 7:37–38). That statement was a gospel invitation for salvation and eternal life. Jesus used similar wording with the woman at the well, when He told her, "Whoever drinks of the water that I shall give him . . . [it] will become in him a fountain of water springing up into everlasting life" (John 4:14).

In verse 2, we find that not only is the river of life restored to paradise, but so too is the tree of life. Back in Eden, God told Adam and Eve that while they could eat of the fruit from any of the other trees, they were not to eat the fruit from the tree of the knowledge of good and evil. But as we know, that's exactly what they did. As a result, sin entered the human race, and so did physical death.

Therefore, God, in His mercy, drove Adam and Eve out of the garden and banned them from the tree of life. God kept them away in order to protect them, for if they had eaten of that fruit, they would have remained in their fallen condition for all of eternity. But when we get to heaven, we will be in our glorified bodies, and we will be able to eat fruit from the tree of life.

I've already mentioned the words of Jesus in Revelation 2:7, when He said, "To him who overcomes I will give to eat from the tree of life" in paradise. That statement tells us a couple of things. For one, we will literally eat the fruit from the tree of life. This goes back to the earlier discussion about whether we will eat and drink in heaven.

Second, this tree is specifically called "the tree of life," so we know that it's the same tree of life that is spoken of in Genesis. Scripture only mentions the tree of life in reference to Eden and to heaven. In Scripture, there are three trees of particular importance: the tree of life, the tree of the knowledge of good and evil, and the tree on which Jesus was crucified. Because Adam and Eve ate the fruit from the tree of the knowledge of good and evil, in disobedience to the Lord, sin entered the human race. As a result, mankind was banished from the paradise of Eden and from the tree of life. But Jesus came and hung on a tree at Calvary to take away our sins and to restore us to the paradise of heaven, which includes that same tree of life.

According to the description in verse 2, there will be a great street of gold in the heavenly city, and running right down the middle of this street will be that river of life. Somehow, this tree of life will stand on both sides of that river, bearing its fruit. From this description of the tree of life, we learn something that we didn't know from Genesis: this tree bears twelve types of fruit. Back in the Garden of Eden, we know that Adam and Eve ate of the fruit of the tree of the knowledge of good and evil, but we don't know what kind of fruit it was. In some way, people through the years have assumed that it was an apple, but the Bible never states that it was an apple, or any specific fruit for that matter.

The only fruit that we know, for certain, to have been in the Garden of Eden was figs, because Adam and Eve sewed fig leaves together to cover up their nakedness. I would be extremely disappointed to think that Eve disobeyed God and plunged all of humanity into sin because she was tempted by a fig. I've been tempted by a package of Fig Newtons in the kitchen pantry but never by a fig hanging on a tree.

Some of these twelve fruits that will grow on the tree of life may be types of fruit we've never seen or heard of (1 Cor. 2:9). In addition to bearing a different fruit each month, the tree of life will bear leaves that will be for "the healing of the nations." I think we have a couple of things to talk about here, wouldn't you agree? Since we are dealing with eternity here, why are we still talking about time in terms of months? And since we will be free from death and disease, why are we still talking about healing?

In heaven, we will no longer be bound by time, but that doesn't mean that time will not exist. On the one hand, there will be no more wristwatches, alarm clocks, or cooking timers. But the Bible never says that time will cease to exist, as some people have assumed. Earlier in Revelation, we read that the saints in heaven "serve Him day and night" (Rev. 7:15). And here, we read about different types of fruit growing on the tree of life, one fruit for each month. The reference to each of the twelve months also indicates a continued perspective in terms of years.

When my dad was still alive and in retirement, I would visit with him and he would often ask me, "What day is today?" He didn't ask me that because he had lost his memory; he asked me that because, in his retirement years, he had lost track of the days. His retirement was not driven by whether it was Monday or Friday, the beginning of the week, or the end of the month. In his retirement, one day was pretty much the same as another.

In a much broader sense, that's how time will be viewed in eternity. In the busyness of our lives, we track most things by the hours, days, weeks, and months. We often wish there were more hours in the day. That view of time will cease in eternity. Scripture gives every indication that time will continue. But as in my dad's retirement years, our perspective of time will change. We'll have the same eternal time perspective as God: "One day is as a thousand years, and a thousand years as one day" (2 Peter 3:8).

The words of Moses in Psalm 90—"Lord, teach us to number our days"—will no longer apply. We won't lose time, gain time, or run out of time. As Randy Alcorn describes it, "We'll live with time, [but] no longer under its pressure." Alcorn also cites the hymn "Amazing Grace" by John Newton and the words that describe our new perspective on time: "When we've been there ten thousand years, bright shining as the sun; we've no less days to sing God's praise, than when we'd first begun."[3]

Now, this reference to "the healing of the nations" is somewhat puzzling, so we must interpret Scripture with Scripture. We have recently read, in Revelation 21:4, that in heaven there will be no more death or pain. The Greek word used in verse 2 for "healing" is *therapeia*, which gives us our English word *therapeutic*.[4] So rather than healing from sickness, these leaves will guarantee the continued health and vigorous living that we'll already be experiencing. In heaven, no one will be calling in sick or wearing masks to protect themselves from disease.

This brings us to a specific list of wonderful blessings in eternity. In verses 3–5, John makes seven statements using the word *shall* (or *will*), telling us more about what heaven will be like. As we read about these heavenly blessings, we can't help but smile. When Charles Spurgeon was training young students for the ministry, he used to tell them, "When you talk about heaven, let your face light up with a heavenly glow . . . and when you talk about hell, your everyday face will do just fine."[5]

The first blessing that John shares with us is that *there shall be no more curse.* This isn't referring to cursing in the sense of cussing, but I can confidently say that there will be no more of that either. Ever since Adam and Eve disobeyed God in Eden, the curse of sin has affected mankind. That curse, recorded in Genesis 3, includes the intense labor pains of childbearing for women and the painful efforts of making a living for men. It's worth noting that Adam's curse included the thorns and thistles of his labors. We remember how Jesus suffered and was mocked when a crown of thorns was thrust upon His head. So thorns were the curse of man, and they were the crown of Christ.

Genesis 3 also states that mankind will work hard to obtain daily bread, and it will be by "the sweat of his face." We remember that as Jesus was preparing for the cross, He was agonizing in Gethsemane. He sweat, as it were, "great drops of blood falling down to the ground" (Luke 22:44). But an even worse result from the curse of our sin is physical death. Around the world, three people die every second, 180 every minute, and almost 11,000 people every hour. On any given day, some 250,000 in the world are dying and entering eternity. So we also remember how Jesus suffered death on the cross in order to take that curse of sin away.

In heaven, there will be no more discussions about death. I heard about a little boy and his mother who were walking along the beach one day, and they came upon a dead seagull. "What happened to that bird, Mommy?" the little boy asked. The mom wanted to soften the harsh reality of death, so she said, "Well, honey, that little bird got real sick, so God allowed it to die and go to heaven." The little boy thought about that for a moment and said, "So why did God throw him back down here?"

Not only is mankind under this curse from sin, but so is the creation, including the animal kingdom and the environment. In our study of the millennial kingdom, we saw that while this curse will not be fully removed, it will be firmly restrained. But better yet, in the heavenly kingdom of God, the curse will be completely removed once and for all. I've had enough of my brain cells dying and my fat cells multiplying! No more curse will include no more dieting—hallelujah! There have never been as many popular diets as there are today, and yet more Americans are overweight than ever before! That definitely has to be connected to some sort of curse!

The next blessing we read about in verse 3 is how *the throne of God and of the Lamb shall be there*. In the previous chapter, we read that there will be no temple, but here we read that God's throne will be there. As believers today, we approach the throne of God in prayer, but one day soon, we will approach the throne of God in person. Back in chapter 4, when we first encountered the throne of God in heaven, we read about the host of heaven praising and worshiping God. That great privilege and joy will continue.

We've all had the frustrating experience of desiring to worship God in a church service but being distracted by the thoughts and cares of life. But at the same time, we've all had the satisfying experience of worshiping God and feeling lifted up—right into the presence of God—with no thought of anything else. Take the latter worship experience, multiply it ten thousand times, and it gives us some sense of what our worship experience in heaven will be like.

In verse 3, we find our third blessing: *His servants shall serve Him*. Sometimes we hear of believers asking the question: will heaven be boring? My first thought usually is: are you kidding me? And then my second thought is: your view of God is very feeble. It reminds me of a Far Side cartoon that shows a man sitting on a cloud in heaven, looking bored. The bubble above his head, revealing his thoughts, reads, "Bummer, I should have brought a magazine." There are two popular misconceptions today about eternity. One is that hell is a place where unbelievers will be partying with their friends, and the other is that heaven will be boring. Science fiction writer Isaac Asimov was quoted as saying, "For whatever the tortures of hell, I think the boredom of heaven would be worse."[6]

I once heard actress Kathleen Turner interviewed on a talk show. She shared the story of how she spray-painted the words, "Better to rule in hell than to serve in heaven," on the hallway walls of her all-girl dormitory at a religious school. She did so because she was tired of hearing about God. She laughed as she told her interviewer that she was expelled from that school the next morning, calling it "the happiest day of her life." She must have been studying the works of John Milton at that school, because her spray-painted words were a quote from his poem "Paradise Lost."

Apart from God's forgiveness, it will indeed be paradise lost for unsaved people such as Turner and Asimov. I believe, with all my heart, that one of the ways God will vindicate Himself, in light of all the false accusations and assumptions about heaven, is by blessing us with an eternity that will forever blow our minds and make our faces grin from ear to ear! As C. S. Lewis well said, "Joy is the serious business of heaven."[7] Missionary martyr Jim Elliot put it this way: "Eternity shall be at one and the same time, a great eye-opener and a great mouth-shutter."[8]

So we'll be serving God, and the natural question is: serving Him by doing what? Those of us who serve the Lord in some ministry capacity realize the joy of serving God by serving the church body. But I think the answer to this question is found by going back to the original paradise of Eden. There in Eden, God gave Adam and Eve dominion and stewardship over the creation. I believe that this will be one of the primary ways in which we serve God. I believe that when God re-creates the heaven and earth, they will include a universe that is not only vast beyond comprehension but perhaps even limitless. So every believer may be assigned to a portion of the universe as caretaker and steward. By the way, let me be clear that I'm not espousing Mormonism here. Their belief is that their members will attain various levels of the afterlife. For some, that will include receiving their own planets, along with several wives in which to populate their planets. That sounds just like something a guy would dream up!

In an issue of *National Geographic* magazine from several years ago, there was an article about the Hubble Space Telescope. The article stated that scientists had pointed the Hubble Telescope toward one of the "emptiest" regions of the universe. The telescope was focused on a region roughly the size of a grain of sand held out at arm's length. And what scientists saw was "layer upon layer of galaxies," each "one containing billions of stars."[9] Whatever the size of our universe, I believe that the new heavenly universe will far exceed it. It will be ours both to enjoy and care for.

Our fourth blessing, found in verse 4, is that *we shall see His face.* To see the face of God will be the true and ultimate joy of heaven. Seeing God face-to-face was the desire of God's people in Scripture. Moses asked God to allow him to see His glory. God allowed Moses to see His glory in a momentary and limited fashion, as God clearly stated to Moses, "You cannot see My face; for no man shall see Me, and live" (Exod. 33:20). John 1:18 tells us, "No one has seen God at any time." In our humanity, we are incapable of seeing God in His full essence and holiness; it would destroy us. But in heaven, with our glorified bodies, we'll be able to see God face-to-face. Better yet, we'll see Him for the rest of eternity!

This continues to remind us that the true glory of heaven is seeing God and being with Him. Vance Havner puts it this way: "The New Testament writers did not speak of going to heaven so much as going to be with the Lord. It is not the other shore that charms us so much as it is Jesus on the shore."[10]

A common question about relationships in heaven is whether we'll recognize one another. I say yes, because I immediately think of Jesus on the mount of transfiguration with His disciples Peter, James, and John. We read that on that mountaintop, Moses and Elijah appeared and were talking with God. Immediately, Peter asked the Lord if he should build three shelters, one each for Jesus, Moses, and Elijah. We do not read that any introductions were made, but as soon as Moses and Elijah appeared, Peter knew who they were (Matt. 17:1–8). Peter recognized Moses and Elijah without ever having met them before. That makes a strong case for our recognizing the people we *do* know. Dr. W. A. Criswell, who is with the Lord, was asked when he was pastoring, "Will we recognize one another in heaven?" I love his response: "We won't really know each other until we get to heaven."[11]

In addition to seeing God face-to-face and seeing fellow believers, I look forward to spending time with many heroes of the faith—people such as Abraham and Moses, Joshua and Caleb, Ruth and Esther, Elijah and Elisha, James and John, Martha and Mary, Peter and Paul, and many more. And of course, that would include Adam and Eve, if for no other reason than to ask them what fruit it was that they ate in the garden. I still hope it wasn't figs! I'm also eager to meet and talk with others, including Spurgeon, Moody, Luther, Tyndale, and Edwards. Plus, we'll be reunited with our loved ones.

In the last part of verse 4, we find the fifth blessing: *His name shall be on our foreheads*. Back in Revelation 3:12, Jesus promised faithful believers, "I will write on them My new Name." This will be a permanent mark and a divine seal of ownership, indicating that we eternally belong to God. We will be God's everlasting exhibit of His grace and glory.

The sixth blessing will be *no more night there*. There will be no need for lamps or sunlight. God's glory will be all the light we need. The New Testament teaches that God is love, God is life, and God is light. This same apostle John tells us in 1 John 1:5 that "God is light and in Him is no darkness at all." That light speaks of His holiness and purity. It's that same pure, divine glory that will be our light in heaven.

Finally, in verse 5, the seventh blessing is that *we shall reign forever and ever*. Not only will we serve forever, but we'll also reign forever. Like Adam, back in Eden, we'll have dominion over all the creation. I believe that this will include the angels. Because we're still in our physical bodies, we are considered to be "a little lower than the angels" (Heb. 2:7). But once we're in heaven and in our glorified, spiritual bodies, we will reign above and over the angels. The angels are not said to be created in the image of God, as we were. In fact, in the words of Paul, we will one day judge the angels (1 Cor. 6:3).

As we talk about heaven, do you have great or feeble expectations? And let me just say that your view of heaven has much to say about your view of God. One of the reasons Revelation was written is to increase our anticipation and appreciation for heaven. As the apostle Paul wrote, "Eye has not seen, nor ear heard, nor have entered into the heart of man, the things which God has prepared for those who love Him" (1 Cor. 2:9).

31

Responding to Revelation

Revelation 22:6–21

A doctor was at a social gathering when a woman walked over to him and asked whether he would mind giving her his opinion on a particular ailment she had. He patiently listened and then gave her his medical opinion for treatment. Afterward, that doctor walked over to a lawyer friend and said to him, "A lady just took up fifteen minutes of my time asking me for medical advice. It frustrates me that she would seek my medical advice at a social gathering like this. Do you think it would be out of line for me to send her a bill in the mail?" "Not at all," the lawyer responded, "I definitely think you should." Three days later, the doctor received a bill in the mail for seventy-five dollars from the lawyer, charging him for his legal advice!

It's usually easier to apply things to other people than to make personal application. We hear a good Bible study and we wish that a certain person were there, because "they really need to hear that message!" In the meantime, God is speaking directly to us. As we come now to our final passage in Revelation, we have a great opportunity for personal application. It was James, the brother of our Lord, who said, "Be doers of the word, and not hearers only" (James 1:22).

> Then he said to me, "These words are faithful and true." And the Lord God of the holy prophets sent His angel to show His servants the things which must shortly take place. "Behold, I am coming quickly! Blessed is he who keeps the words of the prophecy of this book."
>
> Revelation 22:6–7

We often think of heaven as being a destination—which it is—but as Warren Wiersbe states, "Heaven is more than a destination; it is a motivation."[1] If we're motivated by heaven, then we're going to keep moving forward for the kingdom of God. In these final verses, we find at least four ways in which we can press forward, in personal application, toward heaven. The first of these four ways is stated in verse 7: *keep His Word*. Obedience to the Word of God is, first and foremost, how we demonstrate our sincere love for Him (John 14:15). In the words of Martin Luther, "I would rather obey than work miracles."[2]

The word *keep*, in verse 7, means "to hold fast, preserve, and watch over." As you will recall, there was a special promise given to us back in verse 3 of chapter 1—a blessing to "everyone who reads, hears, and *keeps* the things that are written" in this book. This is the only book of the Bible that records this special blessing, although it is understood that there is a blessing that comes with obeying all of God's Word. As Vance Havner put it, "What our Lord said about cross-bearing and obedience is not in fine type. It is in bold print on the face of the contract."[3]

In verse 6, we're given four important reasons for our continued obedience to God's Word. For one, "these words are faithful and true." This is an ironclad guarantee from God Himself that everything we've been reading in this book is trustworthy and reliable. Don't let that truth pass you by too quickly; every detail and description in this book is going to take place. Second, the Old Testament prophecies received from God by the "holy prophets" all came true, and therefore so will the words of this last-days prophecy. Third, "God sent His angel to show" us these things. This angel showed

John the vision, and in turn, John has recorded these words for us, God's servants. These words are divinely sent and angelically delivered. Fourth, these things "must shortly take place." The time until the Lord returns and all these things are fulfilled is getting shorter and shorter. Therefore, our opportunity to keep and apply these truths by obedience is getting shorter and shorter. Once again, I quote Vance Havner, who said, "If we are ever going to be or do or say anything for our Lord, now is the time."[4]

> Now I, John, saw and heard these things. And when I heard and saw, I fell down to worship before the feet of the angel who showed me these things. Then he said to me, "See that you do not do that. For I am your fellow servant, and of your brethren the prophets, and of those who keep the words of this book. Worship God." And he said to me, "Do not seal the words of the prophecy of this book, for the time is at hand. He who is unjust, let him be unjust still; he who is filthy, let him be filthy still; he who is righteous, let him be righteous still; he who is holy, let him be holy still." "And behold, I am coming quickly, and My reward is with Me, to give to every one according to his work."
>
> Revelation 22:8–12

Back in Revelation 19:10, we read of John falling down at the feet of an angel and feeling so overwhelmed by what he was seeing and hearing that he worshiped the angel. That angel immediately rebuked John, and as I shared with you, I don't necessarily think that John made the conscious decision to worship that angel, as much as John lost himself in the moment and forgot that it was an angel speaking to him rather than God. Now, you might be wondering, how could John make the same mistake twice?

The unimaginable majesty and splendor of this vision would undoubtedly send each one of us face down on the ground. But perhaps we should consider the possibility that John didn't actually fall down in worship before this angel for a second time. Rather, he is referring back to that earlier incident in Revelation 19. Remember that these are the final words, the epilogue, and the summation of Revelation. Therefore, it's entirely possible that John was reminding us of his earlier response to the glory of this vision. Perhaps John was simply

318

encouraging us not to make the same mistake he had made earlier and reminding us that all of this amazing truth should drive us to worship God.

In verse 10, the angel instructs John not to seal the message of this book. In the Old Testament, Daniel was instructed by the Lord to "shut up the words, and [to] seal the book until the time of the end" (Dan. 12:4). This didn't mean that the book of Daniel was to be locked away somewhere, but rather that his prophecies were to be preserved and kept for the last days, when many of the things that Daniel recorded would be better understood in the light of end times. Many of Daniel's prophecies had to do with the second coming of Christ, who hadn't come yet the first time, so his words needed to be kept for these last days. What the book of Daniel predicted, the book of Revelation proclaims.

In the New Testament, when the apostle Paul was caught up into the third heaven—God's heavenly abode—he wrote that he heard things about which he was not permitted to speak (2 Cor. 12:4). Here in the final chapter of the Bible, John is instructed to do the opposite: to make sure that the words of this prophecy are shared with believers. In John's day, that was specifically referring to the seven churches. Today, this message is for all believers to read, hear, and keep.

The primary reason for not sealing up this book is that "the time is at hand." There are many references in these final sixteen verses that highlight the imminent nature of these events. Already, in verse 6, they are described as "the things which must shortly take place." In verse 7, Jesus declares, "Behold, I am coming quickly." And now in verse 10, we read that "the time is at hand."

Verse 11 is an interesting verse that is occasionally misunderstood or misinterpreted. A casual reading of this verse might make it sound as though sinners are encouraged to live as sinners, while saints are exhorted to continue living as saints. When I was a kid and had been acting up, my parents would frequently say to me, "Just keep it up, mister, and we'll see what happens!" Do you think my parents were actually encouraging me to continue acting up? In reality, they were warning me; that's the gist of what we read here in verse 11.

As we read the words of warning in this book and as we recognize the times in which we are living, we must make our decision for or against God now. This is both a challenge and a warning.

Verse 12 helps to explain the meaning of verse 11. It says, "And behold, I am coming quickly, and My reward is with Me, to give to everyone according to his work." At the moment when a person dies, or at the Lord's second coming, a person's eternal character will be firmly sealed. These verses destroy any unbiblical notions of purgatory, reincarnation, spiritual limbo, or second chances after death. Make no mistake—the time to decide your eternal destiny is right now.

The time is coming when it will be too late to change our eternal standing. At that point, the unjust and filthy sinner will remain in that state forever, while the forgiven saint will forever be righteous and holy. If you respond to the warnings recorded in this book by trusting Jesus Christ as your Lord and Savior by faith, then you will live with God in heaven forever.

Verse 12 is encouraging news for faithful believers: when Jesus returns, His reward will be with Him. Our next point of personal application is *keep working*. One of my favorite verses on this subject is 1 Corinthians 15:58, where Paul writes, "Therefore, my beloved brethren, be steadfast, immovable, always abounding in the work of the Lord, knowing that your labor is not in vain in the Lord."

I hope we all understand that salvation and forgiveness of sins only come by placing one's faith in Christ and in His sacrifice for our sins on the cross. There is no work that we can do to be saved, except the work of believing. In John 6, people in the crowd asked Jesus, "What shall we do, that we may work the works of God? Jesus answered and said to them, 'This is the work of God, that you believe in Him whom He sent'" (John 6:28–29).

But now having been saved, we serve the Lord with our lives, using every spiritual opportunity that He gives to us. Those are the works that we do today, and it will be for those works that Jesus will reward us. The reward for our faith is salvation and eternal life in heaven; the reward for our efforts as believers on earth will include greater opportunity and responsibility in heaven (Matt. 25:21).

"I am the Alpha and the Omega, the Beginning and the End, the First and the Last." Blessed are those who do His commandments, that they may have the right to the tree of life, and may enter through

320

the gates into the city. But outside are dogs and sorcerers and sexually immoral and murderers and idolaters, and whoever loves and practices a lie. "I, Jesus, have sent My angel to testify to you these things in the churches. I am the Root and the Offspring of David, the Bright and Morning Star." And the Spirit and the bride say, "Come!" And let him who hears say, "Come!" And let him who thirsts come. Whoever desires, let him take the water of life freely.

Revelation 22:13–17

In verse 13, we read familiar words from the Lord, that He is "the Alpha and the Omega, the beginning and the end, the first and the last." This is God's promise to us, based on His character, that everything He begins He will complete. He, who created paradise on earth, will create paradise in heaven. He, who came the first time, is coming again the second time. He, who is the Lamb of God, is also the Lion of Judah. He, who began a good work in us, will complete it until the day of Jesus. On Ruth Graham's gravestone is the inscription, "End of construction. Thank you for your patience."[5]

Those who exhibit lives of obedience are demonstrating their genuine faith and conversion. As a result, these genuine believers will walk through the gates of the New Jerusalem and will eat the fruit from the tree of life in the middle of the heavenly city. All of this reflects our eternal life in heaven. A common question that believers ask (especially new believers) is: how can I know for certain that I'm saved? One of the best places to find the answer is in 1 John, which was written by this same John to strengthen the faith of believers. Let me share the identity marks of a believer, as described in 1 John:

1. *We walk in the light* (1 John 1:6–7). To walk in darkness is to walk in sin and unbelief. But God is light—referring to His truth and holiness. So if we are genuinely saved, we're going to walk in the light of His truth and holiness . . . never perfectly, but certainly with consistency.
2. *We keep His commandments* (1 John 2:3). One of the most tangible evidences of genuine faith is ongoing obedience to the Word of God. There is no substitute for obedience—not even a

321

profession of love—because the way in which we demonstrate our genuine love for God is *by* our obedience (1 John 5:3).

3. *We love other people* (1 John 2:9–11). We cannot say that we love God and hate people at the same time. Those are incompatible claims—like an oxymoron. Many oxymorons are amusing, like jumbo shrimp, soft rock, acting natural, government intelligence, and nondairy creamer. However, "God-loving people-hater" is an oxymoron that is not amusing. That is why we talk in terms of hating the sin but loving the sinner. A genuine love for God will manifest itself in a genuine love for other people. Christian love is the distinguishing mark of a Christian life.

4. *We do not practice sin* (1 John 3:9–10). Please note that I did not say "commit sin" but rather "practice sin." There's a big difference. Every believer is a sinner saved by grace through faith. And on this side of heaven, while we remain in these bodies of flesh, we'll never be free from sin (Rom. 7:18–19). First John 1:10 clearly states, "If we say that we have not sinned, we make Him [God] a liar, and His word is not in us." So the intended meaning of this fourth identifying mark is that the genuinely saved person abides in God and does not habitually, continuously practice sin. The person who deliberately and habitually sins is clearly demonstrating that he or she is not saved.

5. *We put our faith into action* (1 John 3:16–19). This is the same theme of James's Epistle: a genuine faith will naturally produce good works. Anyone can profess to be a Christian, but if there is no fruit, how can a dead faith save him? A genuine faith will produce a genuine change that reflects conversion. Paul declares in 2 Corinthians 5:17 that salvation makes us new creations in Christ. Any person who claims to have trusted Christ as Savior but who thinks, behaves, and talks just as he did before is deceiving himself. The easiest person to deceive is oneself.

According to verse 15, while genuine believers will walk through the pearly gates of the eternal city and eat the fruit from the tree of life, the unsaved outside will practice the sinful things listed here. This is not an exhaustive list of the sins that will keep someone out of heaven but merely a representation of people who are characterized by the lowest moral standard. The term *dogs* refers to perverse sinners and not to our beloved canine companions.

Now don't get a picture in your mind that all of these unsaved people are walking right outside the wall of the holy city. The heavenly city is just one small part of the new heaven and earth. Outside the heavenly area, in the lake of fire, is where these people will be. Remember that hell is described as a place of outer darkness. Its location is outside the heavenly realm.

In verse 16, Jesus is speaking, and He reminds us that He has sent His angel to testify of these truths to the churches. In this context, "the churches" refer to those seven churches of Asia Minor that we looked at in chapters 2 and 3. But His statement includes all of God's churches that have existed since that time. Then Jesus refers to Himself as "the Root and the Offspring of David, the Bright and Morning Star." The titles of "Root and Offspring" refer to the fact that Jesus is both God and man. As God, Jesus was the Root or the source of David, in that He created him. As a man, Jesus was the Offspring or descendant of David. The lineage of Jesus traces back through the line of David. One interesting side note: David is the first and the last human name recorded in the New Testament (Matt. 1:1; Rev. 22:16).

Jesus is also the "Bright and Morning Star." If you rise up early enough in the morning—say, about ninety minutes before sunrise—you will see a bright star in the sky. That morning star signals the imminent arrival of a brand-new day. So this reference to Jesus reminds us that when things look dark—as they do right now in these last days—He is the Morning Star who is going to usher in a new day and a new era in eternity.

In verse 17, we come to our third point of personal application: *keep witnessing.* In context here, the Holy Spirit and the bride (which is the church) are inviting Jesus to come, in the sense of His imminent return. But in this same verse is the invitation for those who thirst to come and receive salvation. That invitation and the responsibility to proclaim the gospel belong to the Holy Spirit and the church. A. T. Pierson rightly said, "Witnessing is the whole work of the whole church for the whole age."[6]

One of the ministries of the Holy Spirit is calling people to salvation. The Holy Spirit is the One who convicts people of their sin and points them to Jesus (John 16:8). The church is the vehicle by which the gospel message is to be proclaimed. In Mark 16:15, the marching orders of Jesus to His disciples were, "Go into all the world and preach the gospel to every creature." Here we see that God's gracious offer of salvation is to anyone who hears and to anyone who thirsts. Anyone who so desires, let him or her come and receive the waters of eternal life freely; this is not limited to a select group.

Let us never lose sight of why Jesus has not yet returned. It's certainly not because the world isn't deserving of judgment, because it truly is. Over and over again, Jesus says, "Behold, I am coming quickly!" And we have just read of the Spirit and the church bidding Jesus to return as well. But He hasn't returned yet, and the reason is spelled out for us in 2 Peter 3:9: "The Lord is not slack [or tardy] concerning His promise, as some count slackness, but is longsuffering toward us, not willing that any should perish, but that all should come to repentance."

Not only are the long-suffering of Christ and the delay of His return for the purpose of more people being saved, it's also the reason the church remains on earth and is not already in heaven where it belongs. God is using His church to reach a lost world with the gospel. However, our citizenship is in heaven and this world is not our home (Phil. 3:20). It has been pointed out that everyone in the world today is out of place—saints belong in heaven, sinners belong in hell, and the devil belongs in the lake of fire.

Now we come to a very serious warning:

> For I testify to everyone who hears the words of the prophecy of this book: If anyone adds to these things, God will add to him the plagues that are written in this book; and if anyone takes away from the words of the book of this prophecy, God shall take away his part from the Book of Life, from the holy city, and from the things which are written in this book.
>
> Revelation 22:18–19

This book began with a special promise of blessing for the person who reads, hears, and applies the words written within. Now it ends with a somber and serious warning to any person who would presume to add to or take away from these words. God will not tolerate anyone who dares to tamper with this book. You can accept it, or

324

you can reject it, but you had better not change it. His warning is stern and the penalty is severe. The plagues described in this book will come upon the person who dares to add to these words. This is not a warning about Spirit-filled commentators or pastors who have differing viewpoints on the meaning of certain verses or passages. It's a warning against the person who intentionally adds to or takes away from the intended meaning.

This warning is in regard to the prophecy of this book of Revelation, but there are similar warnings in Scripture against tampering with the Bible. In Deuteronomy 4:2, we read, "You shall not add to the word which I command you, nor take from it, that you may keep the commandments of the LORD your God which I command you." Again, in Deuteronomy 12:32, it says, "Whatever I command you, be careful to observe it; you shall not add to it nor take away from it."

Proverbs 30:5–6 says, "Every word of God is pure . . . do not add unto His words, lest He rebuke you and you be found a liar." Also, in Galatians 1:8, Paul said, "If we, or an angel from heaven, preach any other gospel to you than what we have preached to you, let him be accursed." The word used there for accursed is *anathema*, and it means devoted to destruction. So this is a consistent theme throughout Scripture. As John Blanchard put it, "We have no more right to tamper with Scripture than a postman has to edit our mail."[7]

Now we come to the closing benediction and to the final two verses of the Bible:

> He who testifies to these things says, "Surely I am coming quickly." Amen. Even so, come, Lord Jesus! The grace of our Lord Jesus Christ be with you all. Amen.
>
> Revelation 22:20–21

It was Billy Graham who said, "I've read the last page of the Bible, and it's all going to turn out all right."[8] In these final two verses, we have encouragement from heaven and encouragement for earth. In verse 20, it's Jesus in heaven reminding us of His imminent return. In verse 21, it's the blessing of grace for us all here on earth.

In verse 20, we find the last recorded words of Jesus in the Bible: "Surely I am coming quickly." Sometimes we're told that the final words of Jesus were the Great Commission at the end of Matthew, or His words spoken to His disciples on the Mount of Olives just before His ascension into heaven, in Acts 1. Others state that His final words were those recorded to the seven churches in chapters 2 and 3 of this book. But here are the last words of Jesus: "Surely I am coming quickly." This is now the third time in this final section that Jesus has made that statement; do you think He might be trying to tell us something? Jesus is coming quickly in the sense that when He does come, it will happen swiftly, and the prophecies of this book will take place in very rapid succession.

The response of John is, "Amen. Even so, come, Lord Jesus!" Hopefully, this is our heart and desire as well: that we're watching and anticipating His return. Our fourth and final point of personal application is *keep watching*. Keep His Word, keep working, keep witnessing, and now, keep watching for His return. This does not mean it's wrong for us to have hopes and dreams here and now. It simply means that in the midst of our hopes and dreams, we recognize and we welcome the fact that Christ could come again at any moment and that would be better than any of our hopes and dreams here on earth.

A fun way to travel leisurely is by train, as my wife and I have done a couple times. If I'm at a train station and I'm there to leave on a trip, I'm simply waiting for the train. But if a loved one whom I haven't seen for a long time is arriving by train to visit me, then I'm not just waiting for the train; I'm watching for it! Some believers are merely waiting for the Lord's return, while other believers are eagerly watching for His return, as John was. "Amen. Even so, come, Lord Jesus!"

The New Testament closes with a blessing for the grace of Christ to be with us all. Interestingly, the Old Testament closes, in the fourth chapter of Malachi, with a warning of God coming and striking the earth with a curse. But it was Jesus, through His sacrifice on the cross at Calvary, who took away the penalty of that curse from those of us who have believed by faith. And ultimately, in heaven, that curse will be removed permanently. Therefore, since Jesus personally took that curse upon Himself, it's fitting that the New Testament would end with the blessing of His grace upon us.

Notes

Introduction

1. Vance Havner, origin of quotation unknown.

Chapter 1 Pulling Back the Curtain

1. Spiros Zodhiates, *The Complete Word Study Dictionary, New Testament* (Chattanooga: AMG Publishers, 1992), 225.
2. Cyrus Scofield, *Scofield Reference Bible* (Oxford: Oxford University Press, 1909), 1330.
3. John Foxe, *Foxe's Book of Martyrs* (John Day, 1563), 19–30.

Chapter 2 What Does Jesus Look Like?

1. John MacArthur, *Revelation 1–11, MacArthur New Testament Commentary* (Chicago: Moody, 1999), 21.
2. Warren Wiersbe, *The Bible Exposition Commentary,* vol. 2 (Colorado Springs: Victor, 1989), 566.
3. John Kaye, *Tertullian: Ecclesiastical History of the Second and Third Centuries* (Cambridge: J. Smith, 1829), 138.
4. Philip Schaff, *History of the Christian Church* (Peabody, MA: Hendrickson, 2006).
5. http://en.wikipedia.org/wiki/It_Is_Well_With_My_Soul. Accessed June 2009.

Chapter 3 What Christ Thinks of the Church—Part 1

1. David Noel Freeman, ed., *The Anchor Bible Dictionary* (New York: Doubleday, 1996).
2. Ronald Youngblood, *Nelson's New Illustrated Bible Dictionary* (Nashville: Thomas Nelson, 1995), 895.
3. John Blanchard, *The Complete Gathered Gold* (Darlington, England: Evangelical Press, 2006), 85.
4. Bob Kelly, *Worth Repeating: More than 5,000 Classic and Contemporary Quotes* (Grand Rapids: Kregel, 2003), 55.

Chapter 4 What Christ Thinks of the Church—Part 2

1. http://www.biblebb.com/files/mac/sg1439.htm. Accessed August 2010.

2. John Blanchard, *The Complete Gathered Gold* (Darlington, UK: Evangelical Press, 2006), 445 (quote attributed to Benjamin E. Fernando).

3. David Barrett and Todd Johnson, *International Bulletin of Missionary Research* (2000).

Chapter 5 What Christ Thinks of the Church—Part 3

1. C. H. Spurgeon, as quoted by Warren Wiersbe at the Billy Graham Training Center in Asheville, NC, May 19, 1993.

2. www.gallup.com/poll/103459/Questions-Answers-About-Americans-Religion.aspx. Accessed June 2009.

3. Vance Havner, origin of quotation unknown.

4. Kenneth Wuest, *The New Testament: An Expanded Translation* (Grand Rapids: Eerdmans, 1961), 160.

5. Warren Wiersbe, as quoted at the Billy Graham Training Center in Asheville, NC, October 3, 1996.

Chapter 6 What Christ Thinks of the Church—Part 4

1. John MacArthur, *Revelation 1–11, MacArthur New Testament Commentary* (Chicago: Moody, 1999), 124.

2. http://dictionary.reference.com/browse/laodicean. Accessed June 2009.

3. William Barclay, *Letters to the Seven Churches* (Louisville: Westminster John Knox, 2001), 98.

4. Vance Havner, *Repent Or Else!* (Grand Rapids: Revell, 1943), 81.

5. John R. Stott, *What Christ Thinks of the Church* (Grand Rapids: Eerdmans, 1980), 116.

6. G. Campbell Morgan, *A First Century Message to Twentieth Century Christians* (London: Revell, 1902), 154.

Chapter 7 Casting Crowns

1. John Blanchard, *The Complete Gathered Gold* (Darlington, UK: Evangelical Press, 2006), 290 (quote attributed to John Blanchard).

Chapter 8 The Lion and the Lamb

1. Unknown.
2. Unknown.

3. Donald Gray Barnhouse, quoted in John MacArthur, *Revelation 1–11, MacArthur New Testament Commentary* (Chicago: Moody, 1999), 170.

4. James Strong, *The Exhaustive Concordance of the Bible* (Peabody, MA: Hendrickson, 1988), Greek 88.

Chapter 9 The Four Horsemen of the Apocalypse

1. Billy Graham, *Approaching Hoofbeats* (Minneapolis: Grason, 1983), 9.

Chapter 10 Heavenly and Earthly Responses

1. Herman Melville, *Moby Dick* (Mineola, NY: Dover Publications, 2003), 100.
2. John Blanchard, *The Complete Gathered Gold* (Darlington, UK: Evangelical Press, 2006), 213.
3. Ibid., 256.
4. Ibid., 342.

Chapter 11 Who Is Able to Stand?

1. www.palmsprings.com/services/wind.html. Accessed June 2009.
2. James Strong, *The Exhaustive Concordance of the Bible* (Peabody, MA: Hendrickson, 1988), Greek 20.
3. Ibid., Greek 51.
4. Ibid., Greek 21.

Chapter 12 The Terrible Trumpets

1. M. R. DeHaan, *Studies in Revelation* (Grand Rapids: Kregel, 1998), 138.
2. Spiros Zodhiates, *The Complete Word Study Dictionary, New Testament* (Chattanooga: AMG Publishers, 1992), 125.

Chapter 13 Something Wicked This Way Comes

1. James Strong, *The Exhaustive Concordance of the Bible* (Peabody, MA: Hendrickson, 1988), Greek 1.
2. John MacArthur, *Revelation 1–11, MacArthur New Testament Commentary* (Chicago: Moody, 1999), 268–69.
3. http://en.wikipedia.org/wiki/World_War_I_casualties and http://en.wikipedia.org/wiki/World_War_II_casualties. Accessed June 2009.
4. Warren Wiersbe, *Be Victorious: In Christ You Are an Overcomer* (Colorado Springs: David C. Cook, 1985), 83.
5. Strong, *Exhaustive Concordance*, Greek 95.
6. Ibid., Greek 73.

Chapter 14 A Message from God

1. Jon Courson, *Tree of Life Bible Commentary: Revelation*, vol. 1 (Jacksonville, OR: Olive Press, 1998), 176.
2. Spiros Zodhiates, *The Complete Word Study Dictionary, New Testament* (Chattanooga: AMG Publishers, 1992), 337.
3. Ray Stedman, *God's Final Word: Understanding Revelation* (Grand Rapids: Discovery House Publications, 1991), 203.

Chapter 15 The Temple and the Two Witnesses

1. Associated Press, *Karma? Bug Eviction Ends with Blazing Temple*, September 4, 2008, www.msnbc.msn.com/id/26541899/. Accessed June 2009.

Chapter 16 A History of Hatred

1. Rev. 12:1, 3; 13:13, 14; 15:1; 16:14; 19:20.
2. Harry Ironside, *Revelation* (Grand Rapids: Kregel, 2004), 208 (paraphrased).
3. James Strong, *The Exhaustive Concordance of the Bible* (Peabody, MA: Hendrickson, 1988), Hebrew 153.
4. John Blanchard, *The Complete Gathered Gold* (Darlington, UK: Evangelical Press, 2006), 353.
5. C. H. Spurgeon, "That Memorable Night," www.wholesomewords.org/etexts/spurgeon/chsblood.html. Accessed June 2009.
6. Spiros Zodhiates, *The Complete Word Study Dictionary, New Testament* (Chattanooga: AMG Publishers, 1992), 473.
7. Strong, *Exhaustive Concordance*.

Chapter 17 The Blasphemous Beast

1. Spiros Zodhiates, *The Complete Word Study Dictionary, New Testament* (Chattanooga: AMG Publishers, 1992), 735.

Chapter 18 Satan's Worship Leader

1. www.uslaw.com/us_law_dictionary/g/Globalization. Accessed June 2009.
2. James Strong, *The Exhaustive Concordance of the Bible* (Peabody, MA: Hendrickson, 1988), Greek 98.
3. Warren Wiersbe, *The Bible Exposition Commentary*, vol. 2 (Colorado Springs: Victor, 1989), 606.

Chapter 19 The Certainties of God

1. www.sermoncentral.com/Illustrations/God/humor.
2. Jon Courson, *Tree of Life Bible Commentary: Revelation*, vol. 2 (Tree of Life Publications), 23.
3. John MacArthur, *Revelation 12–22, MacArthur New Testament Commentary* (Chicago: Moody, 2000), 84.
4. Unknown.
5. James Strong, *The Exhaustive Concordance of the Bible* (Peabody, MA: Hendrickson, 1988), Greek 61.

Chapter 20 The Beginning of the End

1. Randy Alcorn, *Heaven* (Carol Stream, IL: Tyndale, 2004), xx.
2. John Blanchard, *The Complete Gathered Gold* (Darlington, England: Evangelical Press, 2006), 446.
3. Evelyn Underhill, http://thinkpoint.wordpress.com/category/spiritual-disciplines/. Accessed June 2009.
4. Warren Wiersbe, *Real Worship: Playground, Battleground or Holy Ground?* (Grand Rapids: Baker, 2000), 26.
5. Blanchard, *Gathered Gold*, 255.

Chapter 21 God's Righteous Judgments

1. Lehman Strauss, *The Book of Revelation* (Winona Lake, IN: BMH Books, 2008), 286.
2. Napoleon Bonaparte, as quoted by Ray Stedman, www.pbc.org/files/messages/5752/4207.html. Accessed June 2009.

Chapter 22 Judgment of the Harlot

1. Jerry Seinfeld, www.seinfeld-online.com/quotes. Accessed June 2009.
2. Sigmund Freud, www.famousquotesandauthors.com/authors/sigmund_freud_quotes.html. Accessed June, 2009.
3. Robert G. Lee, www.famousquotesandauthors.com/authors/robert_g__lee_quotes.html. Accessed June 2009.
4. John Blanchard, *The Complete Gathered Gold* (Darlington, UK: Evangelical Press, 2006), 527.
5. Ibid., 82.
6. Ibid., 30.

Chapter 23 Babylon Is Fallen!

1. Gary Benfold, *Revelation Revealed* (Leominster, UK: DayOne Publications, 2005), 148.
2. John Blanchard, *The Complete Gathered Gold* (Darlington, UK: Evangelical Press, 2006), 680.
3. Dennis Hester, *The Vance Havner Quote Book* (Grand Rapids: Baker, 1986), 209.
4. Jay Leno, as quoted at www.campusnut.com/joke.cfm?id=138. Accessed June 2009.
5. John MacArthur, *Revelation 12–22, MacArthur New Testament Commentary* (Chicago: Moody, 2000), 190.

Chapter 24 A Marriage Made in Heaven

1. Aviv M. Ilan and David Ilan, *You Know You're Drinking Too Much Coffee When . . .* (Holbrook, MA: Adams Media Corporation, 1996), 5, 7, 10, 15, 18, 26, 29, 57, 62, 78, 116.
2. John Blanchard, *The Complete Gathered Gold* (Darlington, UK: Evangelical Press, 2006), 564.
3. David H. Stern, *The Jewish New Testament Commentary* (Clarksville, MD: Jewish New Testament Publications, 1992), 838.
4. R. Albert Mohler Jr., *He Is Not Silent: Preaching in a Postmodern World* (Chicago: Moody, 2008), 96.

Chapter 25 Return of the King

1. George Sweeting, *Who Said That?* (Chicago: Moody, 1995), 391.
2. John Blanchard, *The Complete Gathered Gold* (Darlington, UK: Evangelical Press, 2006), 565.
3. Dennis J. Hester, *The Vance Havner Quote Book* (Grand Rapids: Baker, 1986), 205.

Chapter 26 The Millennial Kingdom

1. Unknown.

Chapter 27 The Great White Throne Judgment

1. Warren Wiersbe, *Be Victorious: In Christ You Are an Overcomer* (Colorado Springs: David C. Cook, 1985), 144.

2. John MacArthur, *Revelation 12–22, MacArthur New Testament Commentary* (Chicago: Moody, 2000), 249.

3. Randy Alcorn, *Heaven* (Carol Stream, IL: Tyndale, 2004), 23.

Chapter 28 The Best Is Yet to Come

1. Robert Browning, http://thinkexist.com/quotation/grow_old_along_with_me-the_best_is_yet_to_be-the/150979.html. Accessed June 2009.

2. Thomas Boston, *Of Man's Chief End and Happiness,* www.the-highway.com/Boston_chiefend.html. Accessed June 2009.

3. John Blanchard, *The Complete Gathered Gold* (Darlington, UK: Evangelical Press, 2006), 291.

4. Will Rogers, www.goodreads.com/quotes/show/18943. Accessed June, 2009.

5. Mark Twain, www.goodreads.com/quotes/show/691. Accessed June 2009.

6. Unknown.

7. Hank Hanegraaff, *The Bible Answer Book* (Nashville: Thomas Nelson, 2004), 135.

Chapter 29 Home Sweet Home

1. C. S. Lewis, www.giga-usa.com/quotes/authors/c_s_lewis_a001.htm. Accessed June 2009.

2. John Blanchard, *The Complete Gathered Gold* (Darlington, UK: Evangelical Press, 2006), 18.

3. Henry M. Morris, *The Revelation Record* (Carol Stream, IL: Tyndale, 1983), 449.

4. Randy Alcorn, *Heaven* (Carol Stream, IL: Tyndale, 2004), 250.

5. E. W. Bullinger, *Number in Scripture* (Grand Rapids: Kregel, 1967), 253.

6. www.infoplease.com/askeds/many-spoken-languages.html. Accessed June 2009.

7. James Strong, *The Exhaustive Concordance of the Bible* (Peabody, MA: Hendrickson, 1988), Hebrew 16.

Chapter 30 Great Expectations

1. *Reader's Digest*, Sept. 2010, 90.

2. John Blanchard, *The Complete Gathered Gold* (Darlington, UK: Evangelical Press, 2006), 290 (quote attributed to Maurice Roberts).

3. Randy Alcorn, *Heaven* (Carol Stream, IL: Tyndale, 2004), 267, 269.

4. James Strong, *The Exhaustive Concordance of the Bible* (Peabody, MA: Hendrickson, 1988), Greek 41.

5. Charles H. Spurgeon, as quoted by Warren Wiersbe at the Billy Graham Training Center in Asheville, NC, March 22, 1995.

6. Isaac Asimov, en.wikiquote.org/wiki/Isaac_Asimov. Accessed June 2009.

7. Blanchard, *Gathered Gold*, 290.

8. Ibid., 173.

9. *National Geographic*, April 1997, 11–12.

10. Dennis J. Hester, *The Vance Havner Quote Book* (Grand Rapids: Baker, 1986), 109.

11. Source unknown.

Chapter 31 Responding to Revelation

1. Warren Wiersbe, *Wiersbe Bible Commentary NT* (Colorado Springs: David C. Cook, 2007), 1082.

2. John Blanchard, *The Complete Gathered Gold* (Darlington, UK: Evangelical Press, 2006), 435.

3. Ibid.

4. Dennis J. Hester, *The Vance Havner Quote Book* (Grand Rapids: Baker, 1986), 245.

5. blog.christianitytoday.com/ctliveblog/archives/2007/06/ruth_grahams_ep.html. Accessed June 2009.

6. Blanchard, *Gathered Gold*, 677.

7. Ibid., 55.

8. Billy Graham, quotationsbook.com/quote/16504/. Accessed June 2009.

Jeff Lasseigne has been the assistant pastor at Harvest Christian Fellowship in Riverside, California, serving under senior pastor Greg Laurie, since 1989. In addition to his administrative duties, Jeff teaches the midweek Bible study and helps to oversee leadership training. Jeff's previous book is *Highway 66*, an overview of the 66 books of the Bible. Jeff, a lifelong resident of Riverside, has three adult children and six grandchildren with his wife, Lorraine.

FINDING HOPE IN THE LAST WORDS OF JESUS

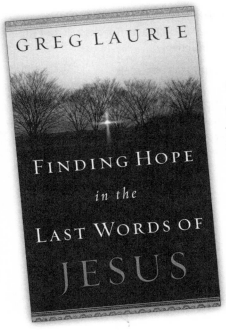

Finding Hope in the Last Words of Jesus

9780801071904 • 64 pp.

This booklet takes each of the last seven statements from the cross and presents insightful nuggets for devotional reading and outreach.

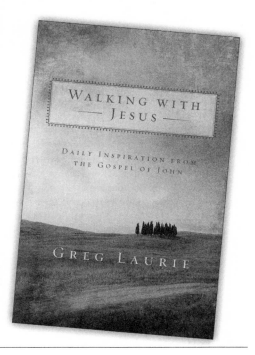

Walking with Jesus

9780801068157 • 320 pp.

In his accessible style, Greg Laurie takes readers through 90 days of walking with Jesus through stories and images of Jesus found in the Gospel of John.

BakerBooks
a division of Baker Publishing Group
www.BakerBooks.com

ENGAGING YOUR FAITH

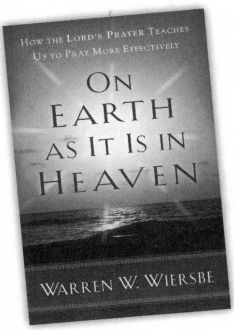

**On Earth as It Is in Heaven:
How the Lord's Prayer Teaches Us to Pray
More Effectively**

9780801072192 • 160 pp.

In *On Earth as It Is in Heaven*, beloved teacher and writer Warren W. Wiersbe explains and applies the elements of the Lord's Prayer to everyday prayer so readers get excited about maturing in their personal prayer ministries. Any reader wanting to experience a more satisfying and effective prayer life will cherish this thoughtful book.

On Being a Servant of God

9780801068195 • 144 pp.

Wiersbe helps readers realize that the key to growing and maintaining their spiritual effectiveness is to build their Christian character. In a warm and conversational style, he explains what to do and how readers can evaluate what they're doing when they pursue the service of God.

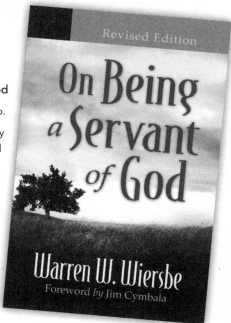

BakerBooks
a division of Baker Publishing Group
www.BakerBooks.com